'Vedic meditation is now part of my daily routine. It has been hugely beneficial in so many ways. Will is very supportive and nurturing and makes learning seem easy and fun. I feel extremely grateful this has come into my life.'

Cressida Bonas, actress

'Will's practical, non-woo-woo approach to meditation has enabled thousands of busy people to find a way to fit a regular practice into their lives.'

Lesley Thomas, *The Times*

'Will Williams did nothing less than open my eyes to meditation by teaching me how to close them. Of all the practices I tried, and I tried many, his was the most welcoming, the most inclusive and inspiring. And it works. We could all do with a little Will Williams in our lives.'

Nick Duerden, author of *Get Well Soon*

'Vedic meditation has been very transformative for me. I've noticed that I'm able to calm my nervous system down, I'm ten times more aware and my intellectual capability is increased. I've got more energy and I'm appreciating special moments with my two children.'

Sam Branson, documentary maker

THE
EFFORTLESS
MIND

Meditation for
the Modern World

WILL WILLIAMS

**SIMON &
SCHUSTER**

London · New York · Sydney · Toronto · New Delhi

A CBS COMPANY

First published in Great Britain by Simon & Schuster UK Ltd, 2018
A CBS COMPANY

1 3 5 7 9 10 8 6 4 2

Simon & Schuster UK Ltd
1st Floor
222 Gray's Inn Road
London WC1X 8HB

www.simonandschuster.co.uk
www.simonandschuster.com.au
www.simonandschuster.co.in

Simon & Schuster Australia, Sydney
Simon & Schuster India, New Delhi

A CIP catalogue record for this book
is available from the British Library

Hardback ISBN: 978-1-4711-6790-4
Trade Paperback ISBN: 978-1-4711-6791-1
eBook ISBN: 978-1-4711-6792-8

Typeset in Bembo by M Rules
Printed and bound by CPI Group (UK) Ltd, Croydon, CR0 4YY

Simon & Schuster UK Ltd are committed to sourcing paper
that is made from wood grown in sustainable forests and support the Forest
Stewardship Council, the leading international forest certification organisation.
Our books displaying the FSC logo are printed on FSC certified paper.

To my nephews Ryan, Lloyd and Owen,
and my godchildren Dexter and Charlie.
You are all so very precious.

CONTENTS

Preface

Why Are You Here?

Don't worry – that's not an existential question. What I mean is: why are you here, now, reading this book?

It might be because you've been curious about meditation or mindfulness for a while and have decided to see what it's all about. Or perhaps you've tried other forms of meditation in the past but for some reason or another they haven't been quite right for you. You might have a specific problem that you are desperate to resolve, maybe an illness, a difficult relationship, or issues at work. Equally, you may have no real problems to overcome; you're a generally happy individual, yet feel as if there might be more to life – that you could feel happier, more satisfied.

Whatever your reason, I'm really pleased you've decided to take the time to read this. And whatever it is you're looking for, I'm pretty sure I can help.

Before we get going, a bit about me. I'm Will, and I've been teaching meditation for six years, mostly in London, but also in many other places around the world. I've found that every country I've visited, just like every person I've taught, has its own unique characteristics, and yet, underneath it all, there are always the same themes concerning the human condition and the human story that transcend all cultural orientations.

My approach to teaching meditation is to do so in the most accessible and easily understandable way, so that literally anyone can do it. I've taught artists and academics, housewives and hipsters, judges and janitors, lawyers and labourers, psychologists and scientists, bankers and billionaires, athletes and addicts. I've even had the rare privilege of teaching royalty! In each case, everyone is ultimately looking for the same things. The key, I always say, lies in how they go about finding them.

A lot of people have preconceived notions of what a meditation teacher might look or sound like, and I don't quite fit that stereotype. I don't wear robes and I don't speak in flowery, cryptic language. I don't live in a cave, an ashram, or on a mountain top, and I don't do denial. I live in a flat in south London and I'm very much of the pleasures of this world.

But I do know my stuff. I've studied and come to comprehend all the fundamental principles behind the ancient practice I teach, and I understand the science – the physics, the neuroscience, the biology – that backs it all up. I can show you how and why meditation works, and that's what I want to do in this book.

I'll also explain why meditation is so relevant to the way we live now. We're a long way from the Indian Himalaya, where this technique was originally developed thousands of years ago, but it can and does make an enormous difference to modern, Western lives. And there's an incredible level of convergence between the ancient wisdom behind this form of meditation and current scientific understanding.

One of the most important lessons I learned on my journey to becoming a teacher was that the greatest and most powerful techniques are often the simplest. The form of meditation I teach is just that. It can be done by anyone, anywhere, at any time, and provides the perfect antidote to the enormous levels of stress and over-stimulation that we in the Western world experience every day. I know – and the research backs it up – that meditation helps: with mental health, physical health, relationships, work, creativity and spirituality.

For many people, a simple technique for enriching daily life with greater calm, clarity and capability is enough. Others have a desire to take a deeper dive into the ancient knowledge base. Both of these paths can be taken using the tools I teach, which have been handed down from master to student for thousands of years.

For me, the individual challenges we face, and indeed the wider global ones, always come back to the fundamental quality of consciousness. There's a quote from the genius that was Albert Einstein that, when I first read it, elicited the most profound 'Eureka!' moment of my life. He said: *'You cannot solve problems from the same state of consciousness that created them.'*

That very wise epithet confirmed my intuitive sense that teaching meditation was the most powerful way I could help bring about meaningful change in the world – by expanding people's states of consciousness (I'll talk more about exactly what that means later on) and thereby enabling them to see the challenges they face in life from a much more enlightened perspective. By helping people find a sense of purpose, peace, inspiration and fulfilment, expanding their empathy, compassion, co-operation and creativity, I give them the tools to engage with the world in a far more effective way.

This, above all, is why I believe meditation is so important. The power to effect momentous change – whether that be within our own lives or in the larger, more universal sense – is available to each and every one of us, and I'd like to show you how to find and harness it.

As I mentioned before, the wonderful thing about this form of meditation is how simple and easy it is. It takes only twenty minutes, twice a day, and you don't have to try to empty your mind or learn any complicated techniques to do it successfully. In the modern world, with its many pressures and demands, life can often become stressful, which makes everything seem more of a challenge. The type of meditation I teach, as you might have guessed from the title of this book, is effortless, yet it leads the people who practise it to a state whereby everything in life 'flows', where your mind can find peace and your body can heal itself – all of which means that you can really thrive (rather than just survive).

In this book I also want to share with you, in their own words, the stories of some of the people I've taught. Some of them simply needed a little boost in life, to be a bit happier, or to feel more inspired. Others had found themselves in very dark places and were struggling to find a way out. What these people have in common is that they *are* all now happier, and much more in control of their lives. I hope their stories inspire you.

I'll also be explaining exactly how my form of meditation works, on a physical, mental, emotional and spiritual level. And, as well as going into the science and philosophy behind it, I'll give you practical tips on how to integrate the practice into your everyday life.

A NOTE ON THE UNCONSCIOUS

I will sometimes refer to the term 'unconscious' when describing how some psychological phenomena interact with and are affected by meditation. 'Unconscious' has many different meanings, but for our purposes we will use the term to refer to thoughts, feelings, memories or beliefs that we are not aware of but (as some of these stories will show) have a massive effect on how we feel, think and behave.

What Form of Meditation Do I Teach?

My form of meditation is inspired by the Vedic tradition, which originates from the Himalayan region of northern India and is many thousands of years old. It is part of an ancient, holistic way of understanding and enhancing one's life experience, and sits alongside yoga and Ayurveda. Yoga is arguably the most famous example of this very rich knowledge base, but you may well have come across Ayurveda before too. The word Ayurveda means 'science of life' in Sanskrit, the sacred language of ancient India from which most Indo-European languages derive. From this ancient worldview, the key to the science of life is attained by putting yourself in a state of calm, balance and heightened brain function. I feel that's very relevant to our lives today, which is why I've adapted this particular form of meditation to suit the thoroughly modern world we find ourselves in. It's about living to your full potential, in each and every moment, and it's the most powerful technique that I've found – if I'd come across a better one, I'd be teaching that!

The Power of Sound

There are many different forms of meditation, and they all use different methods to achieve a state of greater balance and awareness, each having a unique effect on our physiological and neurological programming. The form of meditation that I teach is based on the power of sound.

When I introduce someone to meditation, I give them a sound, which comes from an ancient repository that I, as a teacher, have learned. I allocate them to each student using my understanding of which one I intuitively feel would resonate with them and optimally impact on their nervous system, which will thereby change the way their mind and body behave. You might have heard of these kinds of sounds (mantras) before, or even be familiar with them in other types of meditation, such as the Buddhist mantra '*Om mani padme hum*' or the yogic '*So hum*'. The key difference in this practice is that, since every individual (and nervous system) is unique, your personalised sound will thereby be able to carry you much more easily and effortlessly into a very calm, meditative state.

The student then repeats their sound very gently in their head, for about twenty minutes. It isn't chanted or even articulated in any way – you just allow it to come into your mind. If other thoughts appear, you simply repeat the sound whenever it occurs to you. Unlike some forms of meditation, which stem from monastic practices, there's no attempt to concentrate or control the mind. Your personal sound works as a vehicle to transport you beyond your cares and concerns, to a place of no thought.

There are no tricks, no special techniques. The beauty of this form of meditation lies in its simplicity.

Within minutes, you're physiologically more deeply relaxed than when you're in deep sleep – on average a good 30–40 per cent deeper – and neurologically in a much clearer and more coherent state. From this state of deep, restful and coherent awareness, the mind, body and nervous system can begin self-correcting and purge themselves of unnecessary pain, trauma, stress and emotion, which leaves you feeling fresh, clear and much more balanced.

THE DIFFERENCE BETWEEN
VEDIC MEDITATION AND TM®

Some of you will have heard of Transcendental Meditation® (TM®), or even tried it. Like the form of meditation that I teach, it's based on the power of sound. There are many similarities between the two techniques, but I just want to add a note on the differences.

TM® was popularised in the 1960s and '70s by Maharishi Mahesh Yogi, a great teacher and real sage. It was taken up by all sorts of cool people – most famously, perhaps, the Beatles. Like my own form of meditation, it originates from the Vedic technique of *nishkam karma yoga*, which involves sitting quietly with your eyes closed, effortlessly repeating a personalised sound in your mind for twenty minutes at a time. This sound helps you get into a physiologically restful and neurologically powerful state that the ancient sages of India called *turiya*, which is a state of transcendence that's very nourishing to body and mind. This is why the Maharishi called his movement Transcendental Meditation®.

The origins of the techniques, therefore, are the same, however I allocate the sounds slightly differently to TM®, and I weave in other knowledge from other traditions to make my approach as universal as possible. Whereas TM® is a large organisation, each Vedic-inspired teacher is fully independent, which means it's possible for them to really personalise what they teach, and tailor it to each individual. Our aftercare differs too, in that my team and I offer considerably more follow-up support to ensure that the people we work with always have access to someone who can answer their questions and support them in their meditative journey.

There are many great TM® teachers out there, and it's always worth trying out a few different techniques to see which works best for you.

Why Do We Need This So Much Now?
What Makes This Ancient Technique
So Relevant to Our Lives Today?

The answer to both questions is simple: stress.

Everywhere I look I see stressed people. The symptoms are fairly ubiquitous: anxiety, depression, insomnia, anger, eating disorders, chronic fatigue, digestive complaints, broken relationships, toxic workplaces – the list goes on and on.

An understanding of how we've evolved as a species is essential if we wish to know why we find ourselves in this desperate situation.

For most of the 2.5 million years we humans have been roaming the earth, our lives consisted of foraging for a few hours each day, while spending the rest of our time socialising, procreating and sleeping. Except, of course, when a predator or adversary entered the picture, in which case we had two choices: we could either run away to escape the danger or fight for our lives. In the face of a threat, our bodies instinctively prepared us for both scenarios, a reaction that has become well-known as our innate 'fight or flight' response. You may well have heard of it.

Now, imagine you're a human wandering the savannah 30,000 years ago. You see a predator padding towards you, triggering your 'fight or flight' response. What happens?

- A little part of your brain called the amygdala, which is geared solely towards survival, is immediately activated.
- Stress chemicals such as cortisol, adrenaline and noradrenaline are released, sending alarm signals racing throughout your body.
- Blood vessels become constricted so that blood can travel faster around your body, while your lungs start

hyperventilating in order to deliver oxygen to your muscles, which will be needed whether you fight or flee.

- Your blood fills with clotting agents in preparation for any wounds you may receive, so that you can continue fighting or fleeing even while injured.
- The part of your immune system that deals with bacteria spikes up in case you suddenly find yourself inundated with foreign bacteria, should you be wounded by your adversary.
- Your digestive system shuts down, since your body sees this as an unnecessary waste of energy – who needs to extract nutrients from food when you might be dead in twenty seconds?
- Fat cells immediately release all the fat and sugar in your bloodstream to break down into glucose, which will give you the energy to race across the savannah or deliver a knockout blow to your adversary.
- Your adrenal glands release steroid hormones called glucocorticoids, which help to accelerate all these biological changes. One of the ways they do this is to start inhibiting various centres within your brain that are now considered surplus to requirements. So, they race to the rear of your brain and limit your sensory perception, narrowing your vision to whatever threat you're currently facing. They travel to the mid-brain, where your memory centre sits, and start to suppress most of your memory functions. (After all, you don't need to remember what day of the week it is or what you had for lunch when something with big teeth is chasing after you.)
- Most significant of all, perhaps, are the changes that occur in the front of the brain, in the area called the prefrontal cortex. This is the most highly evolved part

of the human brain, and it plays a key role in our executive functions, like learning new skills, prioritising tasks, organising information and so on. Creativity, problem-solving, lateral thinking, the ability to feel love, compassion and empathy are all processed here too. These functions become inhibited, and fear, aggression and hypervigilance take over.

Your body is now prepared to fight to the death or run like crazy to escape your lethal foe.

So What Does All This Mean for Us Now, in the Twenty-First Century?

The principles of natural selection mean that those with the fastest and most effective fight or flight response are the ones who survive. The very fact that we're here today is because our ancestors were those with the most evolved responses to such threatening stimuli. To put it simply, we are the evolutionary masters of stress.

Ten thousand years ago, the most significant event in human history took place: the discovery of agriculture. With this came a complete change in the way humans lived their lives, the effects of which were felt at every level.

Instead of spending a small part of our day gathering food that was readily available to us, whether that was roots, berries or nuts, we now worked for most of the day, toiling in ways that didn't suit our skeletal structure. We began sitting down, discussing what and how many crops we should grow, and where we should grow them. We felt in control – the masters of nature! But then, of course, came pestilence or inclement weather, so we had to think of ways we could try to control that. For the first time in human history, a certain rigidity and feelings of expectation crept into our day-to-day lives. And, despite the increased 'security' our new life gave us, it introduced more fear. After all, if we were really successful, other humans would come and try to steal our crops. Psychologically, therefore, as well as physically, it was a huge and draining shift.

Socially, our easy days of chilling out – having a gossip with our friends, enjoying some jiggy time here and there – were over. Not only did we have much less free time to play and simply *be* with others, the context within which we interacted underwent a seismic shift too. Those who were 'successful' grew lots of food, which created a population explosion, causing added pressure to keep producing the goods to feed all those hungry mouths. We had officially stepped onto the treadmill of incessant workloads and a never-ending trajectory of growth. You can just imagine our prehistoric forebears saying to themselves: *Give it a few years of hard work, and then we'll have enough.* But salvation never came. We needed to keep growing just to stand still.

As time went on, we progressed from small bands to bigger tribes – to villages, towns and, eventually, full-blown cities. Then, of course, these larger masses of people needed organising, corralling into effective work and social dynamics. So in came the bureaucracies, the hierarchies and the dreaded tax collectors to fund the ever-increasing echelons of social organisation. Ever since the Industrial Revolution, we have moved further and further away from nature, living increasingly more in urban and (since the dawn of the internet) digital worlds.

Meanwhile, human beings' innate fight or flight response has remained the same. Even now, 10,000 years later, it's activating in us all just as it always did. As soon as the trigger is pulled, all of the processes I listed earlier automatically leap into action. The problem we face in this hyper-challenging world of ours is that we cannot turn this reflex off.

Outwardly, we have become more 'civilised', but biologically, survival dynamics are kicking into gear far more often than is either helpful or necessary.

And now, in the twenty-first century, the situation has become intensely acute. Technology has seeped into every aspect of our lives. We're in constant communication; our days are extended through artificial light to the point where true darkness is a rarity in our cities; stimulation comes at us 24/7 in every kind of sensory form. In the past twenty or thirty years, since the birth of the internet and the widespread availability and use of mobile phones, we've experienced a vast amount of change. We're now experiencing more stimulation in a day than we experienced in a month a hundred years ago. The world has sped up so much that our bodies' fight or flight response is no longer fit for purpose. Evolution has not been able to keep up, and our brain's alarm system – the amygdala – is responding to all sorts of everyday stimuli as if they were potentially life-threatening scenarios.

Potential triggers of our fight or flight response, in other words, are around us all the time.

As a result, our stress levels have absolutely rocketed. Instead of getting stressed once in a while, when we encountered a particularly dangerous predator, our stress response is now activating many times a day. If you find that hard to believe, just think what happens to many of us on a normal working week-day. We wake up to an alarm; rush to the office (via a commute where we're surrounded by other stressed-out people); get stuck in traffic or miss a train; have stressful meetings; make difficult decisions; struggle to meet a deadline; race home in time for dinner; watch a thriller or an action movie or rush to the next social engagement; bicker with our partner; go to bed late.

Instead of activating every time we encounter true life-or-death situations, our fight or flight response is firing every time we get an annoying comment from our boss, every time someone pushes past us on the underground, or we find the sink full of dirty plates. Even some slightly irritating behaviour from our child can be enough to set us off. That brilliantly cultivated stress response that saved our lives for 2.5 million years is now slowly corroding our way of life, and in many cases our minds and bodies too.

As each of us ages, what was intended to be a temporary, emergency response to stressful stimuli becomes a chronically ingrained feature of our lives – as does the inhibition of those biological systems mentioned earlier. Sooner or later (and increasingly it's sooner), we all develop what's known as chronic background stress, where ongoing stressors follow us throughout life, which has been shown to have profound physiological and psychological implications. The World Health Organization has called stress 'the health epidemic of the twenty-first century'. Instead of being our principal means of survival, our over-activated stress response is slowly but surely wearing us out.

And very rarely is a response intended only for emergencies a good idea as an ongoing default state.

As you'll see in this book, that overactive response affects immunity, reproduction, ageing, digestion, weight, sex drive, communication, relationships, productivity, creativity – and just about every other part of our lives. While we try to compensate by focusing on our outward appearance – going to the gym, dieting, using expensive face creams – the internal reality is very different.

How Does This Form of Meditation Help?

The chronic levels of stress we're seeing is one reason this form of meditation is such an essential tool for 21st-century life. The practice I teach is incredibly effective when it comes to delivering increased levels of physical and psychological rest and repair, enhanced neurological functioning and greater resilience – all of which means that your reactions to stressful situations, and the systems that cause your body's fight or flight response to go into overdrive, are more balanced.

You don't have to just take my word for it. Researchers at UCLA invited subjects into a lab and hooked them up to every possible monitoring device – a face mask (to measure CO_2), butterfly catheter (blood chemistry), pulse oximeter (oxygenation of the blood), EEG skullcap (brainwave output) and rectal thermometer (core temperature). In these not-so-relaxing conditions, participants began to say their personalised sounds in their heads, just as they would do normally.

What the researchers found astonished them.

Respiration levels dipped considerably, indicating deep levels of relaxation akin to a hibernation state. Blood pressure tended to normalise. Heart rate fell on average by five beats per minute. Blood chemistry changed for the better. Core temperature dropped by a very significant two degrees, an indicator of metabolic rate falling and the body going into rest and repair mode.

Most impressive of all, however, was what researchers saw happening in the brain. When the subjects started to repeat their sound, their brainwave frequencies calmed down from their previously revved-up states. They began producing highly coherent alpha wave patterns (a powerful combination of brain signals linked to deep physical and mental relaxation) in all areas of the brain at different points during the meditation. This is hugely significant, because alpha wave coherence helps us learn, be creative, memorise, and read the thoughts and emotions of others. In the beta state (the usual level of mind activity exhibited when you're awake), the brainwave frequency is higher, which means that the brain tends to get cluttered by thoughts, making it altogether less capable and perceptive. That's why achieving an alpha state, which techniques such as this form of meditation can elicit, is so important: because when the clutter is cleared away, your brain is able to work more efficiently. Receiving information when in the alpha state makes you far more likely to remember it, too, as a result of the dramatic increases in focus, concentration, memory, learning and powers of insight.

Of course, this all happened under extremely uncomfortable conditions – the effects of this form of meditation might be even more impressive when you're chilling out at home. From my own experience, and that of the thousands of others who practise meditation, the combination of these phenomena activates hugely significant changes within the mind and the body:

- Both body and mind enjoy significant periods of energy restoration, during which the brain – so often filled with a noisy internal monologue and obsessive worry – calms down, so you're no longer overwhelmed by the cacophonous nature of anxious thoughts.
- Your mind and body begin to purge themselves of the emotional charge associated with old hurts, pain and trauma, freeing you from the damaging weight of past experience.
- The corpus callosum (which connects the two hemispheres of your brain) becomes more active, allowing a greater flow of information between the two. The left side of the brain processes information in a very analytical way; it's focused on detail, and is very task-oriented. The right side of the brain processes information in a big-picture way; it's much more contextual, and tends to be more emotionally intelligent and collaborative in its approach. Better connections between the two leads to greater focus and heightened capability.
- The engine of your stress response, the amygdala, becomes functionally less active. So instead of firing at

any old trigger, perpetuating a need to firefight your way through life as if in constant survival mode, it begins to become more discerning as to what actually deserves a response.

- The hippocampus, part of the limbic system in your brain and responsible for consolidating information from short-memory to long-term memory, begins to grow, which gives you greater recall capabilities.

- The prefrontal cortex becomes much more active, so that your ability to learn new skills, prioritise tasks, organise information, engage in lateral thinking, solve complex problems and express yourself creatively all become heightened.

- Both right and left frontal lobes become more balanced, leaving you feeling more able to make rational, healthy choices for yourself in a calm state of mind.

- And, perhaps most significant of all, the ability to feel more connected to yourself and to others is improved. By enjoying a balanced flow of endorphins, and greater activation of your prefrontal cortex, you find that love, compassion and empathy begin to replace unnecessary aggression, anxiety or sadness.

The exact reasons Vedic-inspired meditation has such an impact are still unknown to us. Although science is slowly getting closer to being able to map the processes of the brain and their effects, we've still got a long way to go. We're also a little behind in our understanding of resonance and sound, and how these phenomena interact with our brain and wider nervous system.

While it feels appropriate that you can't patent forms of meditation, the absence of an obvious commercial opportunity means there aren't many multi-billion-dollar institutions channelling masses of research money into exploring its full effects in minute scientific detail. Despite this gap in scientific explanation, however, there is no doubt it does have a significant impact. The stories in this book are a testament to that.

THE POWER OF RESONANCE AND SOUND

When musicians play together, they need to make sure they're in tune with each other. They all tune their individual instruments to the same pitch, and, since 1955, the international standard has been 440 Hz. But actually, this may not be ideal, because many experts feel a more natural intonation is 432 Hz. Listening to music at 440 Hz can feel less relaxed than the harmonic quality of music at 432 Hz, which many say feels warmer and richer.

Likewise, the mode of music can be important. The ancient Greeks were big proponents of this. For example, Aristotle claimed a symmetrical scale called the Dorian mode settled the mind and Plato advised people to listen to music in that mode during times of war and crisis. It's been known for decades that the music of Mozart has a more powerfully active impact on our brainwave function than other forms of music.

Another interesting fact is that the earth's magnetic field resonates at 7.83 Hz, (the Schumann resonance). If you listen to sounds at that frequency, it has a very calming, soothing effect on mind and body.

What these examples demonstrate is that sound, or resonance, can powerfully affect how our brains, bodies and minds function. This is why the sounds I give my students are very carefully chosen, and it's why they work so well; our minds and bodies instinctively react to them in a positive way, without the need for effort or thought.

How Do I Teach?

Most of the time, I teach meditation on a three-day course. The beauty of doing the course in such a condensed format is that you're up and motoring almost straight away. Over seven to eight hours spread out over those three days, I give my students all the information and understanding they need to be able to practise confidently on their own, no matter what their starting point.

On the first day of the course, I have an hour-long appointment with each student, during which I give them each their personalised sound and some initial instructions on how to use it, so they can immediately get going. There's nothing like diving in and experiencing the depth and beauty of this practice for yourself. I then use the following two days to build on those first instructions by helping you to really refine your meditation, also providing you with tips on how to integrate it seamlessly into your life. I then teach students how they can tactically use their meditation to overcome many of the challenges they may face. For example, I can teach you how to use it to get through interviews and presentations without getting nervous, or how to prevent jetlag when travelling. These sessions are really relaxed, and last about three hours each.

By the end of the course, you'll feel really confident in your meditation techniques, with all the tools you'll need to implement it in your daily life.

How to Make Meditation a Part of Your Life

Practising this form of meditation is, as I've said before, an effortless process, which makes it really enjoyable. And because it releases lots of endorphins, all those happy hormones will serve to put you in a really good space, both within the meditation and in your everyday life. Combined with the deep rest and relaxation you get when you do it, you'll quickly find it a refreshing and energising way to start or end your day, and you'll be much clearer and sharper in everything you do afterwards.

As a general principle, wherever possible, the most productive way to meditate is for twenty minutes, twice a day. If you can do this, and make meditation part of your routine, the benefits will include a greater sense of connectivity (to yourself and others), an increased sense of joy in life, and the gradual unravelling and healing of past hurts and painful memories.

Of course, there might be times during the day when you feel like you need a bit of a boost. Maybe it's a job interview, or you have to do some public speaking, or you're about to go to a tricky family gathering, or have a difficult conversation with a friend. In those situations, do what works best for you. Say you usually meditate in the morning and evening (which is what lots of people like to do) – change it around and do your meditation when you need to be extra-calm or on top form. On your way to that interview or party, or backstage before you go on to speak, find somewhere to sit down, close your eyes and repeat your sound. You don't have to worry about mastering different techniques for different situations; simply use your personalised sound in the way that you've been shown, and *voila*! Twenty minutes later, you'll be much calmer, clearer, and ready for anything.

This form of meditation is brilliant both as a *strategy* and as a *tactic*. A *strategy* is something you apply on a long-term and regular basis and is what ultimately delivers the biggest gains, whereas *tactics* are employed according to need, in order to respond to occasional demands – i.e. to help dig you out of a hole. The *strategy* of regular meditation means that you don't usually need to meditate *tactically*. It takes care of 95 per cent of your daily dramas by putting you in a much better place to deal with them in the first place. You'll also find that, because you're less cranky in general, what once would have been major problems now barely register on your radar. Sometimes, however, you need to listen to yourself. If some tactical meditation is what you need on the day, then go for it – make it work for you.

But How Will I Find the Time?

Many people who are stressed – whether by work commitments, family, or simply the sheer pace of life – often can't believe that they can spare even twenty minutes, let alone forty, in the space of one day.

What they're doing is assuming that, by meditating for forty minutes a day, they've 'lost' that time. In fact, by carving out those precious minutes for meditation, you'll actually be *saving* time. With a mind that's calmer, you'll be more productive, focused and clear about what you need to accomplish. You'll be able to prioritise more efficiently; you won't spend your day procrastinating; you'll make better decisions; and you won't feel overwhelmed. You'll be able to take care of everything you need to do but without fuss. For this reason, lots of people I teach say that meditation gives them *more* time, not less.

In any case, it's not the quantity of time we dedicate to aspects of our life that's important, but the quality. Is the time you spend with your partner super-high value, or has it diminished into the ordinary and familiar? Does your time with your friends or your kids fill you and them with a sense of love, life and laughter? Or is that time spent on autopilot, or spent looking at your phone?

Life is short, and how we allocate our time each day is crucial. It can be helpful to spend a few minutes making a list of what is most important to you. Is it love? Health? Wisdom? Purpose? Fulfilment? Adventure? Fill in the blanks, then prioritise. Look at the list and ask yourself: are you living your life in accordance with those priorities? Or are there improvements that can be made? Go ahead and start making them now, and know that meditation will help you realise all of them.

My students are pretty inventive about finding ways to find their twenty minutes twice a day. Since you don't have to be in a peaceful place to do it, it can be relatively easy to integrate into your routine. You're not trying to focus or clear your mind, so it doesn't matter if there is noise around you.

Here are some of their suggestions:

- On your commute
- In the back of a taxi
- During your lunch break – find a park bench or a café to do it, then have a sandwich after
- Fitting a cheeky one in between meetings
- In a smoking break (not whilst actually smoking, obviously . . .)
- While your child or baby naps
- Waiting for appointments (perhaps arrive a little bit early)
- On the bus on your way to see friends, or to a date (saves you getting nervous)
- Waiting for a train
- On the loo (not the most comfortable but great if you're at work, need to quickly de-stress, and can't find any-where else!)
- Waiting for a long download or software update
- Waiting for HMRC to pick up the phone
- Waiting for the bride to arrive at a wedding or in between ceremony and dinner
- At the cinema while you're waiting for the movie to start
- While you're waiting for dinner to cook (it'll stop you snacking before the food's ready!)

- During the time between ordering a takeaway and it arriving at your door – turning a time of hungry anticipation into something useful
- In the departure lounge waiting to board a plane
- On the plane
- If you're stuck in a lift and you're waiting for help (keeps the boredom or anxiety at bay)
- Waiting for colour to take at the hairdressers
- In the car (after work or a gym session, etc.)
- Waiting to pick the kids up from school
- Nipping into a local library or church on the way home from work

One student told me she had once meditated on the back of a scooter in Vietnam! (Although I'm not entirely sure how safe that might have been ...!)

Common Issues that Meditation Can Help With

This form of meditation is known to relieve many stress- and nervous-system-related disorders. Those with more obviously physical facets include:

- Digestive problems
- Cardiovascular issues
- High blood pressure
- Chronic pain
- Chronic fatigue
- Headaches
- Immune disorders

The most common mental health issues that people come to see me about are:

- Anxiety (as well as related disorders like OCD, PTSD or panic attacks)
- Depression (and related disorders like SAD or mood swings)
- Anger

And then there are issues more related to lifestyle, including:

- Insomnia
- Weight management
- Relationship challenges
- Problems in the workplace
- Addiction (alcohol, drugs, smoking)

We'll be looking at some of these in our case studies that follow, along with tips on how to use meditation to help overcome them. Before we do, however, I'd like to tell you my own story, so you can understand how I came to meditation, and what led me to become a teacher.

From Hedonism to Happiness: My Story

May 2006 was where it all began – the start of a long summer of artificial highs and very real (and very deep) lows. I was twenty-six and struggling in all sorts of ways.

I was running a music management company with my recently ex-girlfriend and her brother, trying to help bands break through to the big time – matching them to the right producers, finding record deals, co-ordinating PR, organising tours. Artificial highs came with the territory. The music business is fuelled by substances and stimulants of every kind and I indulged in pretty much anything I could lay my hands on. That was nothing new – I'd always been a party boy, up for anything, first in the queue for a new experience, the person people went to for a good time . . . and I did my best to deliver!

The lows were in every other part of my life. I was constantly hungover or on a comedown. What should have been my dream job was being poisoned by the toxic atmosphere in our office, because things had gone very badly between me and my girlfriend, and the lack of a big breakthrough with the bands was amplifying the strain. A few times we came so close to hitting the big time, but whenever we thought we were about to make it, something would come along to sabotage it.

I felt like an utter failure. I was broke, stressed and stretched to breaking point. It got to the point when I was working almost 24/7, for our company during the day and then trying to make ends meet as a waiter in my local pizza joint, serving up Sloppy Giuseppes until midnight. I had no time to nurture a relationship that at the start had seemed incredibly fulfilling. I was too exhausted and stressed to make it work, and I felt trapped. Now that our relationship had failed, I was terrified that my dream job would begin combusting along with it and, to top it all off, I was suffering from chronic insomnia. I felt as if I was in a washing machine, stuck in a horrible cycle of sleeplessness and hopeless anxiety.

The summer wore on until it all came to a head one night when I found myself at 2 a.m. on my ex-girlfriend's couch, wanting to end it all. I was exhausted, totally frazzled, yet I couldn't sleep. I couldn't think, apart from awful, repetitive thoughts about how my life was going nowhere.

But I couldn't do it. Something inside me said: 'Hold on, you can find a way out of this.' And so, still feeling awful, I left the flat.

I walked the streets for hours after that. I felt like a failure for not even having had the guts to finish it. I was angry with my ex-girlfriend, yet overwhelmed with sadness that something so great had turned into such a bitter, ugly mess. Most of all, I was really confused; I didn't know where to go or what to do.

It was a very dark time. I was in despair about having to leave the industry that I loved and had worked so hard to be part of, but I didn't see how I could stay in it with my ex there too. I felt very heavy, burdened with worry and shame, and so I numbed myself with booze and drugs, trying to suppress the pain. I couldn't understand what was happening to me.

Then, come September, things lifted. My friends could see I was in trouble, and some of them took me on a surprise weekend away for my birthday, which brought the first smile to my face in months. Soon after, a big record deal for one of our bands paid me enough to extricate myself from the business, my life in London and the toxic relationship, and I could temporarily clean up the mess. I decided to go to South America to have a good time.

I did go to South America, but instead of partying, I ended up getting together with Kitty. I'd known her since I was nineteen, and she was the girl of my dreams. Five months later, I came back, in love and refreshed. But I was still a reckless, relentless party animal and a chronic insomniac. It was so debilitating to wake up every day with no energy and so little motivation. I'd always been a high achiever, but now it was impossible to get even the smallest things done. It was no good for our new relationship, either, because when we'd spend the night together, the smallest movement from Kitty meant I was awake until dawn.

I tried really hard to find solutions for my anxiety-fuelled sleep issues, which, now I thought about it, had been plaguing me for about seven years. I tried hypnotherapy, which I actually quite enjoyed, but it didn't help me sleep. I went to acupuncture and had one really great night's sleep afterwards, but then fell back into the same old groove of nocturnal despair. I went to reflexology and yoga, and although I always felt a spike of relaxation, I was still left buzzing at night. I got to such a point of desperation that when my friends told me they'd read an article that claimed colonic irrigation helped to cure insomnia, I went and had a hosepipe stuck up my bum a couple of times to 'clear myself out'. It turned out they were just winding me up! They obviously knew I'd go for it – I'd have done anything to get a good night's sleep.

It wasn't that I was particularly into complementary medicine, but I was very open-minded about finding solutions. When I was nineteen, I had been travelling through Asia when

I badly injured my knee. A medicine man on a remote island managed to fix me up in a way that totally blew my mind. He pointed this cigar-like thing at the area of injury, did some chanting, and wrapped a bandage infused with herbs around it. Within twenty-four hours, I was playing football and volleyball without any problems. I didn't understand how he'd done it, but I was so grateful that he had.

I'd obviously tried herbal sleeping tablets, but they made me feel awful the next day. Instinctively I was reluctant to go down the pharmaceutical route, which was somewhat ironic, because I was more than happy to pump myself with industrial quantities of illegal substances in the name of a good time. I tried all the earplugs and eye masks that I could find, but none really made a difference.

Instead of inducing sleep with external solutions, I realised I needed to find a way to make it come naturally. It was as if I was plugging the holes on a sinking ship with my fingers, when what I really needed to do was repair them – and understand why the holes were appearing in the first place. It felt wrong to be in my twenties and so beholden to all of these workarounds. I wanted to be able to sleep next to my girlfriend and be free to lay my head down however, and wherever, I wanted.

Nothing I tried worked. It felt like I'd explored every avenue, and was left wondering if I'd simply have to surrender and live with it.

When I was in South America, I'd come across a guy called Davide, who told me I should meet his friend Dan when I got back to London, and so I did. He was a really nice, cool, normal guy, and halfway through the night he started talking about meditation. It turned out he and all his friends were doing it, and it had cured three of them of their terrible insomnia. So, I thought: *That's a pretty decent statistic, maybe I should give it a whirl.*

For whatever reason, I sat on it for a couple of months. After all the failures, I felt disheartened to the point that I almost couldn't face yet another disappointment. And then, one night, I rocked up to an introductory meditation talk, did a beginner's course soon after, and got my personalised sound. During the first session, the teacher left me to meditate – and it was like nothing I'd ever known. I was floating in this lovely, dreamy state. Walking down the street afterwards I felt happy, energised, blissful – almost euphoric. And I thought: *If this is what it's going to make me feel like, I'm all in!*

Over the next couple of weeks, my sleep improved massively. That would have been enough for me, but I noticed other benefits, too. I was less stressed, and considerably more productive. Before I started meditation, I'd only work my way through about 60 or 70 per cent of my daily to-do list even on a good day, despite working until 8 p.m. each night. After that beginner's course, I managed to tick every item off by 6 p.m. – it was immense! What I found especially gratifying was that there had always been these tasks that I hadn't wanted to take on, which I'd keep pushing on to the next day to avoid having to face them. Now, all of sudden, I just got them done, and it felt so good. There was a hugely liberating sense of relief, because it meant I didn't have anything to sweat about when I woke up the next day. I could start afresh every morning, and I felt fresh, too.

I also noticed that I was becoming a nicer person. Much nicer. I began to chat to my local shopkeeper whenever I visited, and was really enjoying interacting with him at a human level. Before meditating, I'd never spoken to him; lost in my own little world of dramas and to-do lists. Now I felt connected – to myself, to others, even random strangers. It felt human, and I liked it.

At that point, I was running a business that was very successful but soul-destroying. I'd been thinking about becoming a maths or a physics teacher, but I was put off by the bureaucracy and lack of freedom to teach as you want. I've always wanted to do things in a way that makes sense to me, as opposed to trying to fit into a rigid system of others' making. Perhaps the idea of teaching meditation was already in the back of my mind, but I knew I was just at the beginning of this journey; I wanted to see how it went first, and what would unfold for me as time went on.

I spent that first year of meditating partying very hard, for the simple reason that I could. This amazing new tool of mine gave me a lot more energy; I could sleep with ease, and it also transpired that it was the best hangover cure ever (more on that later)! I was also kicking ass at work like never before. I felt like I was living the dream – getting the best of both worlds.

But something was changing in me. By now I was living with Kitty in Brighton, and she noticed the changes too. I decided that instead of using the meditation to simply work harder, and party harder, maybe I could do something a bit more constructive with this new life skill I had stumbled across and that was giving me so much more drive. I decided to go on a weekend retreat in Norfolk. I got on the train, feeling more than a little nervous about the kind of people I might meet, my rucksack full of snacks in case they were going to try and feed me any 'hippy shit'. I'd spent most of my life eating ready-made noodles, crisp sandwiches and other kinds of crap. The only vegetables I could even contemplate were ones that you'd find on a pizza.

I don't know why I felt such apprehension. The beginner's course I had taken nine months previously had been full of ordinary people, and the teacher didn't wear robes or wave crystals; he was just a guy looking to help those who needed it. It turned out that the weekend retreat was also full of normal people – actually pretty cool people; folks I'd happily go to the pub with. And I needn't have worried about the food either – it was absolutely delicious!

We were taught an add-on to our meditation practice that combined a very special, ancient form of yoga with some breathing techniques. When fused with the meditation, it had spectacular results. I could feel myself physically responding in weird and wonderful ways. By the final afternoon, I started to do my meditation and soon began to feel like I was floating in the middle of the room. Meanwhile, a very calm, very beautiful wave of love started building up inside of me. It crept through my torso, trickled down every limb until it finally filled my head. I began to feel very peaceful, and it was as if I was struck with this incredibly strong surge of love for everyone and everything in the world. The last time I'd felt anything approaching this was when I'd taken ecstasy, but even those artificially created rushes of love were nothing compared to this.

On many occasions since I'd started to meditate, I'd felt I was no longer bound by any care or worry. That feeling was now accompanied by a level of expansiveness I had never experienced before. It was immense.

This added dimension to the meditation was a true eye-opener for me. I felt sensational, both during and after the practice, and a thought kept coming to me: *I'm on to something big here.*

I went back to Kitty in Brighton and she could immediately see the change in me. I started describing my weekend to her, and how I was feeling. She stopped me and said: 'I've never heard you talk this way before. It's like you're seeing the world through the eyes of a poet.' It was true. I was seeing poetry everywhere I went. I spent the following week floating around the city, just glowing. It felt like everyone I encountered could sense it, and I couldn't help but smile, even at strangers in the street.

From then on, I started spending weekends with my teachers, learning about this ancient knowledge base from India. It's hard to explain just how transformational it was, and also how quickly and easily the change came about. For the first time since I was a young boy, I became interested in the welfare of the world – of society, of the environment, of other people. I'd always been very up on world affairs; I cared a lot about the state of things, but when push came to shove, I reverted to type and put myself first. I had done some pretty cool stuff for charity over the years, but, having done my bit, I would always go back to thinking about number one. It was as if there were two people inside of me: this really lovely lad that was drawn to doing something meaningful and making a real difference, and this other person that felt driven to be as successful as he could, whatever the cost. I began to see that the selfish side of me had dominated more and more as life had gone on.

The more I learned about this form of meditation, however, the more the other me was making himself known. Instead of caring only about myself and my own successes and failures, it was beginning to feel as if my welfare was a reflection of the welfare of the world. I wasn't separate from it any more, and that meant I couldn't really ignore what was going on. I could no longer pretend that someone else would take care of it, or (as I had in the past) believe that technology would solve all our problems. I became acutely conscious of the earth as a dynamic entity, and that I had a part to play in its future and wellbeing.

With the meditation also came a huge broadening of my awareness. I could understand now why people behaved the way they did, and why, on a larger scale, these sorts of patterns continue, even when everyone agrees that they are a barrier to progress. This new level of insight was enabling me to see through all of the complexities and get to the root of each issue – to see where the most meaningful changes could be made and where they were likely to be most effective. That was important because, for me, idealism without activity is a waste of time. Meditation had helped me change as an individual, and I wanted to help others do the same, both because of the difference it would make to their own lives and the contribution that it could make on a wider scale, to the world.

By now Kitty had learned to meditate too, and even though we (as well as all the people we'd met along the way) were different in so many ways, it had had all sorts of great effects on her as well. We couldn't help but conclude that the brilliant thing about this sort of meditation was that it didn't just deliver one set of identical benefits to everyone; it had a unique effect on each individual. I didn't yet understand how and why, but the anecdotal evidence was undeniable.

As we both felt this growing sense of connection with the world, we realised that there were a lot of places we wanted to explore. I'd been increasingly intrigued by India ever since we'd started 'zinging' (our pet term for meditation). I'd also been doing a lot of reading on cutting-edge physics, and was amazed to discover that most of what theoretical physicists were only now beginning to uncover had been understood by the sages of ancient India many thousands of years ago. I was itching to find out more.

We decided to move out, put our stuff in storage, and go to India. We bought one-way tickets to Delhi and resolved to make it up as we went along. And so began a two-and-a-half-year adventure around the world, during which we met many great meditation masters from across the continents. I spent six months learning the ancient secrets of Ayurveda at the world-renowned Raju family practice in Hyderabad, India, and learned the ancient language of Sanskrit in Sri Lanka. I left trails of blood climbing barefoot up the most sacred mountain in India to pour oblations onto a sacred fire, and was taken in by mountain-dwelling yogis to learn from them. Kitty and I trekked for three days through the Amazonian jungle to take part in ceremonies with its most revered shaman and, to my very great honour, received an invitation to go on pilgrimage with the Dalai Lama.

Along the way, we had many hugely profound spiritual experiences. I'm not generally in the habit of talking about them too much, because everyone's journey is different, and I'd rather let people experience it as it comes, free of expectation. They are also quite challenging to describe to those who haven't had such experiences themselves – they can seem rather fantastical unless you've been there yourself. Suffice to say, their sheer profundity changed me for ever.

During our time away, we'd sought out the very best teachers all over the world, learning all sorts of methods of meditation. It was fascinating to understand just how many approaches had been developed over the past 5,000 years. There are many forms of meditation that are all about denial, or that stem from monastic practices, like sitting still for twelve hours a day with flies on your face, not being able to brush them off, and I did them all. It was useful knowledge and valuable experience, but while I'm glad to have had the opportunity to see them first hand, they didn't strike me as being wholly relevant for people today. Vedic-inspired meditation, because of its simplicity, did, and so I decided to study and practise and learn to be a teacher.

I received my training from the pre-eminent master of Vedic-inspired meditation, considered a Great Seer by those in the know in India. He was incredibly knowledgeable and generous with his teachings. After that, I went to Bali for a three-month intensive course to complete my training with other leading gurus. It was the most eye-opening and awe-inspiring experience of my life, and also the most challenging.

By the end of the training, I was champing at the bit to get teaching. I still remember the first person I taught like it was yesterday. I had put posters up all over the Balinese town of Ubud for a course the following week, and it was not long before a woman called Mariko made an appointment with me via text message. All I knew about her was her name, but the night before our appointment I went to bed with a sound persistently flowing through my mind. When I woke up, it was still there. As I heard Mariko's footsteps come up the garden path, I looked up to see her walking towards the door and I smiled. The sound I'd been hearing was hers. I was a teacher.

It was a pretty arduous journey from hedonism to happiness, but I got there. I'd come a long way from that time at my ex-girlfriend's flat when I'd nearly ended it all. Back then, I felt desperate, bleak and out of control. By the time I became a teacher, I felt connected to myself, and to the world. I knew what I was about; I knew what other people were about; I knew what life was about. I was finally at ease with myself.

In the six years since then I've taught thousands of people meditation. While reaching out to such a high number of people feels like the best way I can help with some of the problems that we as a planet face today, the *quality* of what I'm teaching is also hugely important. Every year I go back to India for eight weeks to hang out with some of the most accomplished and inspiring masters, immersing myself in the most expansive experiences that this ancient knowledge base can provide.

I'm still learning, still growing. I'm not perfect and I'm not a saint. In fact, I don't even aspire to be a saint. I'm Will, a bloke from London who wants to share what I can with as many people as I can, because I know it works – I know it helps you be the best that you can be. Through this form of meditation, I learned how to help myself and find true happiness. In this book, I want to share with you my own insights on how to do just that, by showing you how to use meditation to cope much better with the stresses of everyday life, to heal yourself – body and mind – as well as to improve your relationships with others (and yourself). In doing all this, I will help you make reaching your personal best a reality.

MIND
AND BODY

What's your understanding of the links between your mind and your body? The concept of *mens sana in corpore sano*, or 'a healthy body in a healthy mind', has been around in the Western world since the days of the ancient Greeks and Romans, yet for some reason we always seem to like to divide the different parts of ourselves, separating them from the whole to analyse them on their own. We therefore tend to treat the physical symptoms of disease or illness in abstraction, rather than looking for the underlying cause of their presence in the first place.

Understanding how our mind and body are linked and affect one another is vital if we want to know how to live a balanced life, and to move towards a better state of physical, mental and emotional health.

Mind, Body, Balance

Before we start to look at the relationship between mind and body, a note on the difference between the *mind* and the *brain*. Your brain is part of your body; it's a physical organ, visible and tangible. Your mind is invisible, part of the realm of consciousness, of thought, perception, feeling, emotion, belief and imagination. The two are connected, and interact all the time, but the mind is not simply confined to the brain.

Your mind, just like your brain, is also connected to, and constantly interacting with, your body. So, when your mind is out of balance, it has a major impact on all your physical and mental faculties, and on your overall sense of wellbeing – and vice versa. We all know how feeling physically ill can make you feel mentally out of sorts, upset or even depressed.

Finding balance is key to leading a healthy life. Our mind and body are very complex, made up of many constituent parts that operate in different ways at different times. Think of it like an orchestra. When your mind and body are balanced, all the different musicians are playing their instruments in harmony with each other, kept in sync by the conductor – the innate biological rhythms of your body. If these rhythms are for any reason distorted, if the conductor misses a beat, and one of the members of the orchestra starts to play out of sync, what could have been a glorious piece of music starts to sound slightly jarring and uncomfortable. If the orchestra contains lots of players who are not in tune, or not in sync, then it begins to sound even less inspiring. It may soon get to a point where, as more and more players become confused about whom to follow and sync up with, the disharmony descends into a disorganised mess, the resulting noise barely distinguishable as music any more.

This is what it's like with our brains and our bodies. When every part is working as it should, balanced and in sync, we operate in beautiful symphony. If things are out of balance, however, then the resultant discordance can make us feel increasingly out of sorts and at odds with ourselves, until the harmony resembles nothing more than a babble of cacophonous noise.

Maintaining a stable internal environment is a very dynamic process, and our bodies are constantly monitoring and adjusting as conditions change to achieve what scientists call 'homoeostasis'.

Your Nervous System – The Great Connector

So how do our bodies find that homeostatic balance?

Well, your body, mind and brain are all connected by the nervous system. Your spinal cord is part of this, running from your brain to your sacrum (at the base of your spine) to transmit information to every single part of your body via all of the nerve fibres that radiate outwards from the brain and the spine.

The only way the brain can communicate with the body is through the nervous system. All our senses come via this incredible network of nerve cells, as does the way we express ourselves. When we have an intention or an emotion that leads to a thought or to speech, it is mediated via the nervous system.

The nervous system is therefore the conduit through which we interact with and experience the world.

It is of vital importance, then, that we know whether or not this conduit is working properly. Are those messages getting through? Or are there blockages inside the nervous system that mean those signals aren't being accurately communicated, getting distorted along the way?

Here's an old wartime story to show you what I mean. The commander on the front line decides this is the moment to advance. The message can't be written down in case the enemy finds it, so it has to be verbally conveyed. The commander instructs the messenger, 'Tell them to send reinforcements, we're going to advance.' The messenger runs as fast as he can to pass on the message to the next runner; he does the same, and so on and so forth. But the message changes slightly with each retelling, and is delivered to the auxiliary forces' commanding officer as: 'Send three and fourpence, we're going to a dance.' The auxiliary commander is so confused by this he doesn't know what to do.

A similar sort of thing is going on in the minds and bodies of people who are stressed – the messages transmitted in the nervous system are getting scrambled on their journey to the brain. For example, the body might say, 'I need some avocado,' but before you know it, you're eating a packet of crisps. The message has been garbled. Instead of hearing the body's call for a set of very specific vitamins and minerals, we've only understood the request for food.

If the nervous system is negatively impacted because it's

stressed, we're in big trouble. If it becomes chronically inhibited, through long-term chronic stress, then we're not going to function well at all, which is the case for many people nowadays.

THE AUTONOMIC NERVOUS SYSTEM

Whether or not you actually feel stressed is regulated by the autonomic nervous system, which is the part that organises all of the daily functions that keep you alive (like breathing, your heartbeat, and digesting your food) without you having to think about them.

There are two subdivisions of this critical part of your daily functioning: the sympathetic nervous system and the parasympathetic nervous system.

It's the sympathetic nervous system that sets off your fight or flight response, causing the body to tense up, sweat and secrete bile. The emotional and instinctive part of the brain also kicks in, which tends to make us edgy, aggressive and reactive.

In contrast, the parasympathetic nervous system acts as a brake and calms everything down. It conserves energy and performs essential maintenance functions during rest. It enhances digestion, settles your heart rate and allows your lungs, liver, kidneys and muscles to relax, among many other important functions. When active during sleep, the parasympathetic nervous system enables you to rest deeply, and is also essential for sexual arousal.

These two systems tend to operate in opposites, i.e. when one is active, the other is suppressed. You can literally feel when one or the other is particularly dominant. Ever wondered why your personality (or that of someone you're with) can turn on a sixpence – from nice, calm and happy to aggressive and hostile at a moment's notice? It's your autonomic nervous system that will activate these effects, and whether your sympathetic or parasympathetic side is dominating at the time will determine whether you're in nice Dr Jekyll mode, or more like mean old Mr Hyde. Once you understand this dynamic, you can begin to empathise with the people around you when they're in 'Mr Hyde mode'. That's another reason meditation is so brilliant (as we'll talk about in the relationships section of this book): it gives us the capability not to react to other people when they are being ruled by their sympathetic nervous system. We see the Hyde character, but can recognise that Dr Jekyll is somewhere beneath the surface, just waiting for the opportunity to emerge. In this way, we can avoid a situation where someone else's aggression activates our own sympathetic nervous system, and everybody's pissed off or agitated.

A Library of Painful Memories

The nervous system is also a warehouse; a library of all our memories of pain, stress and trauma. Every time you have a negative experience, your body has all sorts of reactions. The amygdala will go off, neurochemical changes will take place, and your nervous system will go into a different state of activation. At that moment, the nervous system takes a snapshot, almost like a screen grab, of all the information associated with the negative event, including room temperature, moisture, humidity, who you're with, any sounds you hear and colours you see. An impression of every single sensory detail is imprinted upon the nervous system, archived and flagged as being part of a stressful event. Then, any time any of those same elements reappear, the nervous system remembers the past stressful situation and prepares for a repeat performance by becoming just a little bit more alert.

Whereas this mechanism would be useful if it occurred only when genuine threats were encountered, nowadays we're experiencing these negative triggers all the time. This is because we live in a world full of stressed people. Whether it's hyper-aggressive world leaders driving the media to pump out fear-driven news coverage, or our demanding bosses who make unreasonable requests of our time, stressed because their kids are having problems at school, or their spouse is stressed because they're always working. It could be *your* spouse or partner feeling stressed; it could be *your* kid. It's a vicious dynamic.

In whichever form we encounter stress, we connect with it because we're feeling stressed too.

We've been encountering stress chemicals ever since we were born, and even before then, in the womb. During those forty weeks of gestation we are already getting our first impressions of the outside world, and our nervous system comes to some pretty big conclusions before we've even popped out. In those forty weeks, our mother has likely been exposed to a large amount of stress events, each of which will affect the development of the foetal nervous system. If that wasn't enough, we then have to go through the traumatic process of being born, from being in a nice little cocoon to this huge and unfamiliar world that shocks our senses. The umbilical cord – our last connection to the world we knew – is severed and we're suddenly on our own. We're dependent, but separated. As anyone who has heard a newborn's cries can testify, our first few days (and weeks, and months) in the world can be very uncomfortable and exhausting.

Even before we've put on our first nappy, therefore, we've actually gleaned an awful lot of information about the nature of the world, and these impressions will colour the way we process events thereafter. For example, as a baby, one of our principal means of getting attention is to cry, but sometimes our calls go unanswered. When we learn to walk, we fall over and hurt ourselves; dogs bark at us; Mummy might tell us off; or Daddy might not want to play with us when he gets home from work. We're very sensitive as young people, and each of our experiences really does matter.

This is because, whether we consciously remember it or not, all of this information is stored up inside our nervous systems. In the ancient East they called these formative experiences *samskaras*, from which we get the English word 'scar'. In the West, we call them *premature cognitive commitments*. Put simply, the unconscious memory of a past event causes us to jump to a conclusion about a present event, before we've got enough information to make an informed decision. This continues through our lives, causing us to filter information that suits our narrative, often reinforcing it. Our nervous systems, therefore, become increasingly cluttered with these incomplete conclusions that can put us in unnecessary opposition to people and things.

The more *samskaras*, or premature cognitive commitments, you have, the more regularly your nervous system will be on amber alert, which then puts your body and your brain on amber alert, too. At which point, of course, you become easier and easier to trigger. So, while many of the stresses we experience as adults are caused by triggers that we developed as children, to make matters worse, many of our adult stresses reinforce and confirm the validity of these childhood stresses.

Luckily, however, this doesn't mean that we're condemned to a life of repeating childhood stress and trauma. Techniques such as the form of meditation that I teach can have a significant impact on helping the nervous system to rest and repair. By doing so it can begin to overcome these premature cognitive commitments, thereby healing our bodies and minds in the process. I'll go into *how* in a moment, but first I want to talk a little more about what happens if we *don't* take steps to try to deal with these *samskaras*, these sources of pain.

Displacing the Pain

'Eventually everyone sits down to a
banquet of consequences.'
ROBERT LOUIS STEVENSON

A lot of the time, our painful memories are kept deeply buried; understandably, we'd rather not have to deal with them on a daily basis. The trouble is they have a nasty habit of presenting themselves when least expected later on in life, often in the form of physical or behavioural symptoms that appear completely unrelated to the past psychological or emotional trauma that is at their root. Such symptoms can be alleviated by treatment of the original trauma, indicating yet more links between body and mind.

As Suzanne O'Sullivan very compassionately explained in her 2016 book on psychosomatic illness, *It's All in Your Head*, many people who have been diagnosed with epileptic fits are actually having seizures brought about by trauma that they haven't been able to deal with. Because that trauma is being buried and not dealt with, it has to find a way out – and the way your body does this is through seizures, or some other physical or behavioural manifestation, such as addiction. It's an astounding insight, and one that we would be wise to understand in more depth.

So many of us are disassociating from our pain all the time – burying it, trying to pretend it doesn't exist. That's one of the reasons, I think, that smartphones are so popular, because when we use them we're able to disassociate from the pain of the present moment. If you stop and take stock of where you are as a human being right now on Earth, you might realise you feel a little empty, or at least not as fulfilled as you'd like to be. You might not feel as loved as you'd like. You might not feel you can love as much as you want to. You might not have the house/job/bank balance that you want. You might simply feel lonely. All of these feelings can be very painful. So, what do you do about it? You distract yourself. You go to work or, if work is the cause of the pain, you go to work and then distract yourself by chatting to other colleagues or surfing the internet or needlessly rearranging your desk. You might go for a run. You might go and get drunk. You numb yourself any way you can. This might seem like a good solution, but by numbing your pain you are really numbing yourself from who you really are, and what you really want in life.

Lots of us have feelings of shame because, deep down, we feel unloved or, worse, unlovable. It can be such a powerful feeling that we do everything in our power to suppress it, working really hard to make sure that everything seems fine on the surface, whether that's achieving professional status, having the nicest house, wearing the right clothes or editing our selfies to present a façade on social media.

It's all displacement – a defence mechanism to disassociate either from the pain of the present or the pain of the past. Eventually, however, this buried pain will manifest itself in one way or another. Your nervous system, and with it your brain and body, will become overwhelmed, creating a cascade of neurochemistry that causes the body to be in even more of a state of disrepair. Cells degenerate more quickly, and that puts the body as well as the mind under even more stress. That is when you get sick.

The Power to Change

This might all seem a bit depressing but, as I said earlier: don't worry, there is hope!

We used to think that everything about us was fixed; our genes, body and brain were an inevitability of our ancestry, we thought, and the effects of our upbringing were set in stone by the time we'd reached adulthood. We'd been dealt our hand and we just had to get through the rest of the game by making the most of it.

In the past few decades, however, rather than being governed exclusively by the genetic hand we were dealt at birth, and the upbringing that followed, it's become increasingly apparent that much of our health and wellbeing is within our control. We have the ability to nurture, not just live with, our nature. The underlying systems that govern our wellbeing are all malleable, and, to a certain extent, the way we feel is determined by our choices, whether they are consciously made or not.

In the 1970s, neuroscientists discovered that the human brain is neuroplastic, which means that it is constantly restructuring as a result of experience – building new neural networks, letting other, no longer useful networks fade, coming up with new ways of mapping things. How our brain reacts to and processes information is an ongoing, evolving and dynamic process.

Then, in the past fifteen years, we discovered something else. Although we all have our own genetic make-up, we also have something called the epigenome. This is a layer of proteins and enzymes that surrounds the genome (your own personal and complete set of instructions on how to build you as a person) and changes the way that your cells use those instructions. We have our twenty-three sets of chromosomes and the 20,000–25,000 genes that we inherited from our parents, but 95 per cent of them can be turned up or down like a dimmer switch, which means that most of what you inherited is not fixed at all: it is determined by how you're living your life (including factors like stress, diet, exercise and sleep). This means that, contrary to many people's opinion, we're not imprisoned by the genes that have been handed down to us.

Then there's the microbiome – the 100 trillion bacteria that exist mostly in our intestinal tract, found to have an enormous impact on our mind and body, sending signals to our brain via the nervous system, and in doing so influencing emotional behaviour and mental health. (I'll look at this in more detail a little later.) The microbiome determines how well we digest our food, but also our immune function, brain development and wider nervous system, as well as affecting the neuroplasticity of our brain.

These three discoveries mark a huge, game-changing shift in our understanding of the human body. We've gone from 'fixed brain, fixed genes; food is for calories' to 'your brain and your genes are like plasticine, shaped by your experiences; food nourishes our minds and our bodies with vitamins, minerals, proteins, enzymes and, perhaps most critically of all, good bacteria'. This new approach opens up a whole new raft of possibilities. Most importantly, it gives us the power to change.

The brain has the capability to retune itself in ways that could completely revolutionise how you think, and while this is very exciting, it has its upsides and its downsides. Through repeatedly inputting information, just as you do when learning a language or how to play an instrument, we can begin to master actions and memorise knowledge. We can recover from brain injuries and strokes. The sting in the tail, however, is that just as the brain can retain good information, it can also retain information that is less than healthy.

All your thoughts, actions and behaviours are firing specific neural networks in your brain. If they're occasional, they won't necessarily affect its function. But if you, say, smoke three cigarettes in the morning and have two glasses of wine when you get home every day, the neural networks associated with these actions become ingrained; you reinforce these behaviours and they stick. This is one reason changing habits can be so hard – they've been hammered deep into our neural networks and we have become dependent on them to feel better, each 'hit' triggering a little dopamine release that means we become even further hooked to the behaviour. Similarly, when we think something over and over again, we strengthen those connections within our brain, making it harder to avoid that kind of thought in the future. That's why we go over and over a particular argument with an ex, or keep replaying embarrassing memories right at the moment that we need some confidence.

The great news is, if those kinds of associations can be formed, they can also be dissolved. Whether you use meditation for spiritual growth, to reduce anxiety or to help with your relationships, the effect is the same. To use a technological analogy, think of yourself like a laptop. Every so often, to make sure the internal system is working as well as it can be, you need to defrag the hard drive and clear out any redundant files; you need to switch off the computer every now and again to help it reboot. Vedic-inspired meditation does just this. It will clear up the mess, bit by bit, on a daily basis, so that your nervous system can work at its most functional and operational level. Only then can work on our psychological and physical ailments really start, knowing that the two are absolutely and inextricably linked via the nervous system. Your brain will gradually loosen the neural pathways that trap you into habitual and restrictive thinking and form new ones that can make you feel much more positive and connected to the world. When you find new ways of being, and new ways of living, through meditation – perhaps changing some of your less than helpful habits – you are changing the way that your genes express themselves. And if you look after your microbiome (I'll explain how to do that later), you can go a long way to improving your mental and physical health.

Hormones, Stress and Weight

I really can't emphasise enough these links between our minds and our bodies. Everything we think and feel is transmitted to our bodies, and vice versa, and here I want to give you an example: how stress affects our hormones and our weight.

Hormones are chemical messengers in the body, created in the endocrine glands. They control most major bodily functions, from simple basic needs like digestion to complex systems like reproduction, as well as our emotions and mood. Unfortunately, our hormones are very easily knocked off balance; through lifestyle, diet, emotional or physical trauma, as well as genetic variants and epigenetic factors. If this happens, you'll soon feel the effects, either in your body or in your mind.

Stress is a particular disruptor of hormones. The fight or flight response causes our neurochemistry to react by *over-secreting* the hormones that will allow our bodies to either flee from or do battle with what it sees as an imminent threat (like the steroid cortisol), while *under-secreting* those that aren't essential to survival (such as sex hormones).

For this reason, stress is also likely to cause you to put on weight. If you experience intermittent bouts of stress, you secrete ghrelin, the hunger hormone, which is why you might find yourself reaching for a bar of chocolate or a packet of crisps in tense moments. This mechanism, combined with the extra cortisol that you'll also secrete (up to five times more than usual), will usually provoke weight gain – typically around your middle, because that's where cortisol particularly likes to deposit it.

Exercise will get cortisol out of your system by making something called adenosine triphosphate (ATP), which turns it into energy. But you have to be clever about this. You need to do enough exercise to turn those stress hormones into energy and get rid of them, but not so much that adrenaline and cortisol production are stimulated.

We know that diet and exercise alone don't necessarily work in terms of losing weight, because if your body feels starved it will shut down your metabolism to stay alive. You can really help yourself by lowering your cortisol production and absorption by meditating to soothe your nervous system and reduce your tendency to fight or flight. Even if your weight issues are genetic in origin, those genetic influences are malleable and can be managed if you keep your stress levels low and your microbiome healthy.

Apart from weight gain, here are some of the other effects that a stress-related imbalance of hormones can cause:

- Problems with periods: the suppression of hormones linked to reproduction can lead to disruption of the menstrual cycle. Prolonged exposure to stress can even result in infertility.
- Low sperm count, impotence and problems with ejaculation: most guys know that getting in the mood is infinitely less likely if they feel under pressure or stressed out, and chronic stress can play havoc with both sexual function and fertility.
- High blood pressure: this is caused by the over-secretion of vasopressin, the hormone that constricts your arteries when in fight or flight mode.
- Thyroid disorders: long-term high levels of cortisol will

cause your thyroid to begin shutting down in order to save your metabolism, so you don't burn out. A sluggish thyroid can lead to all sorts of problems, including tiredness and weight gain.

- Hypoglycaemia: occurs due to impaired insulin secretion, which means you're much more likely to develop diabetes.
- Premature ageing: high levels of stress-induced cortisol also results in low levels of anti-ageing hormones that would otherwise protect your DNA from the wear and tear of life.
- Digestive issues: stress causes us to release hormones that reduce activity in the intestines, resulting in sodium retention (which causes bloating), increased glucose levels, acid reflux and constipation. It also stops you extracting nutrients from your food.
- Depression: those who experience high levels of life stress are more likely to succumb to major depression. Stress is also implicated in triggering genetic predispositions towards depression. Sustained stress also depletes dopamine in our pleasure pathways, and noradrenaline from signalling the locus coeruleus of the brain. It also affects the synthesis, secretion, efficacy and breakdown of serotonin. An imbalanced profile of these three key neurotransmitters are intimately linked to most forms of depression (and anxiety).
- Calcium deficiency: calcium is another vitally important element in the body. After the menopause, many women suffer from osteoporosis, a weakening of the bones, which is linked to a lack of calcium. However, as well as bone strength, this mineral also has an impact on the thyroid, insulin secretion, energy production, nerve and muscle relaxation, the absorption of toxic metals and the digestion of fat. Stress siphons calcium out of your

body by excreting it in your urine. If you're regularly in fight or flight mode, much of your calcium will be going down the toilet. And if you're in the exhaustion stage of stress, which comes after you've been exposed to it for too long, calcium will build up in your joints, arteries, kidneys and elsewhere, which has been shown to lead to premature ageing.

So, stress causes weight gain, low energy, low sex hormones, ageing, poor sleep and psychological imbalance. Even chronic low-level stress causes a drip, drip, drip of stress hormone secretions that are like Chinese water torture to your brain and body. However, it *is* possible to bring balance back; through diet, moderate exercise, bodywork, emotional work and meditation. By calming your nervous system and making it less likely to go into fight or flight mode, you're much more likely to achieve a healthy balance of hormones and the right levels of calcium. And that's going to make you feel much healthier, more energetic and far happier.

Coping with Anxiety

Awareness about mental health seems to be growing at the moment, and I'm very glad about that, since one in four of us will suffer from mental health issues at some point in our lives. In the UK, the biggest single killer of men between the ages of twenty and forty-nine is suicide.

By far the most common problems that I see in my work are anxiety and depression. I believe that this is at least partially caused by the fact that we are vacuuming up stress and stimulation every single day of our lives, becoming ever more crushed by the demands of the modern world. I'll explore depression later, but here I want to talk about anxiety, which is a very real issue, and one that can feel utterly crippling to those who are living with it.

From a clinical perspective, there's a difference between fear and anxiety. Fear is what we feel when we're faced with a genuine threat; whereas anxiety is more of a subjective perception of threat that we can't see, hear or touch, but which feels very real to the person experiencing it.

Feelings of anxiety and fear are caused by the activation of our fight or flight response by our hyper-stimulated amygdala – in particular, by a trait known as hypervigilance, which prepares us to run or fight even before we have definite confirmation that actual danger is upon us.

If our brain continues to experience this level of

hypervigilance, and neuroplastically wires it in, we may begin to experience what's known as 'trait anxiety'. When we reach this point, our brain responds instinctively to even non-threatening external stimuli by creating a perception of fear that feels very real, even if the danger is not. This perception is so strong that people with anxiety often find their brain casting around, trying to justify why it's in such a state of agitation. This is where problems like health anxiety come in – people believe there simply *must* be something physically wrong; what else could be causing them to feel so awful?

It's often not long before we become physically and mentally exhausted by the constant sense of vigilance that we feel is required to deal with all the potential threats in the world. These feelings of apprehension and dread that can accompany anxiety often prove to be alarming, overwhelming and sometimes even paralysing. The problem is that this can easily become a conditioned response, so your mind, body and nervous system will automatically start reacting to a perceived unconscious threat even before you've become consciously aware of it.

You can't respond rationally at this point, because the corresponding alert signals reach your amygdala before they're processed by your cortex – the part of the brain where we get a lot of our conscious experience from. The amygdala is so sensitive that if you subliminally flash a picture of something fear-inducing to someone with an anxious disposition, their amygdala immediately goes into overdrive. An anxious person's amygdala is ready to pounce on any fragment of information and twist it into a signal for red alert, often without them even realising what the trigger was.

But why would someone be so anxious in the first place? The most likely cause would be a traumatic event that's been stored within the nervous system, often from when they were younger, or even in the womb, as I talked about before.

Having said that, sometimes chronic levels of stress can over-whelm our nervous system so much that it causes us to develop chronic anxiety despite the absence of any significant trauma in our lives.

When we're under constant demand, our reactions to stimuli become exaggerated. For example, for some of us, just drinking caffeine or watching television can push us over the edge into feelings of anxiety. Add to those social commitments, dietary stimulants, extreme gym routines, work and other life respon-sibilities, and you're left with a lot of potential triggers.

Noel

'My mind was always in anxiety mode.'

When I first met Noel, he'd been in an almost continual state of stress for a very long time. His fight or flight response was primed like a loaded gun, ready to go off at any moment, and his nervous system had all but burnt out. He'd been working and playing hard, staying up partying late into the night and putting a vast amount of pressure on himself to succeed both professionally and personally.

Obviously, if you're filling yourself with intoxicants or nar-cotics, it throws you off balance. Along with the harmful and potentially lethal side effects that all drugs possess, however, is the less obvious harm they do to your body's natural sleep patterns. This is something I have experienced first hand, and the damage it can do shouldn't be understated. Biologically, we're programmed to go to sleep very early, so there are lots of functions that take place inside the brain from around the 9.30–10 p.m. mark, and they're crucial for maintaining a healthy system. They only engage, however, if you're asleep during those times. By cutting down on sleep, you're effectively indulging in a subtle form of violence on your mind, body and nervous system. We're adaptable, so having a few late nights and early mornings every once in a while is not too damaging for most people. Consistently not getting enough sleep, mean-while, will put every one of us under great strain. It's simply not a sustainable way to live and, eventually, physical or mental health issues will start to arise as a result.

I see this kind of behaviour in so many people that I meet. Lots of them are trying to find salvation, it seems, by run-ning themselves into the ground. It's almost as if they point themselves in a direction, and then burn themselves out in the attainment of that goal, without necessarily knowing if their romanticised notion of achievement will feel as good in real life, or whether that goal is even still relevant to them. They put these plans together and don't look back until they've reached the finish line, never once asking themselves whether this is still a race they even want to win. Cultural stereotypes reinforce this behaviour; 'no one likes a quitter' after all. Many people's self-worth is already so low that they simply keep on keeping on, never wanting to be seen as a 'loser' in the eyes of society, even when they are clearly struggling to put one foot in front of the other.

By the time I met Noel, he'd tried a lot of different therapies and was pretty sceptical about whether I'd be able to help him. We bonded over music, which was a good start, as it put him at ease, and then we got going with the meditation.

This is how he describes his experience:

> I never even considered that I wouldn't succeed in music. My dad had been a musician, and maybe because of that, the guitar was my passion from the age of eight. I was in bands all the way through school, and then I went to Liverpool to study pop music at university.

I ended up leaving uni to tour with an indie band, and later on, back in London, I got a job running a pub with DJs and bands. When my boss wanted to open a new venue, I went for it. Soon we had three venues. That lifestyle was 24/7, and the distinctions between social life and work life began to blur. I was invited to gigs, festivals, after-parties – nights that quite often wouldn't finish until around 3 or 4 a.m.

Because our venues were open sixteen hours a day, I was always on the go, and I wanted each one to be amazing all the time. I had that attitude about nights out, too, which fuelled me to carry on partying way beyond anything I could realistically handle.

Then I started to have panic attacks. I began spiralling in a really bad way.

I had this horrendous nightmare where I, along with all my friends and family, had descended into this horrible, addictive mess. Everyone was an alcoholic, a junkie, a heroin user. It was incredibly sinister.

I still don't know where that dream came from. I was only taking recreational drugs about three or four times a year, nothing serious. I was drinking a lot because of the nature of my job, but never to the point that it was an issue. (It had been a big problem for my dad, so I was very aware of it.)

My anxiety was building on a daily basis and then, one day, I was walking to the station with my girlfriend Fran, and I lost it. I just had this utter meltdown. I felt like a million-tonne weight was pushing down on me, pinning me to the ground. I've never been so scared of anything in my entire life. I couldn't face going forward, to work, and I couldn't face going home to be alone with it either. Fran was going to this super-important meeting, but I begged her to stay with me. It was like all my previous anxiety attacks put together, times a thousand, and totally, totally crippling.

From then on life felt like hell. The nights were the worst. I'd wake up between two and four in the morning, and from that moment on, I couldn't sleep. My mind would be in anxiety mode, racing with negative thoughts. It could be about a nightmare I'd just had, or it could be about work. (I'd been signed off by this point, and I felt guilty for not being there.) Occasionally, I might sleep until 7.30 a.m. I'd wake up and think: *I'm okay, I've cracked it.* But it was like someone revving an engine. The negative thoughts would creep back in and speed up, like helicopter blades getting faster and faster.

My GP said I was suffering from nervous exhaustion. My family isn't at all well-off but they'd always managed to get the cash together for private healthcare insurance, and so my mum persuaded me to go to a clinic and see another doctor, who said that my anxiety had tipped over into depression. I was almost pleased with the label because it finally explained why I felt how I did.

I started to go to the clinic three or four times a week, but when I was in the waiting room, I needed to distract myself. There was no phone signal, so I couldn't go on the internet. Instead, I'd read the paper from cover to cover. The first week of January 2016, I found an article on 'Ten Things to Do This Year to Feel Better'. One was Will's meditation, and it was like, 'if you suffer from anxiety, depression, stress', and I was like, 'tick, tick, tick'. When I told Fran about it later at home, she said: 'My friend's worked with Will for years; she says it's great.'

I didn't act on it straight away. I was doing other things – acupuncture, one-to-one therapy, group therapy, group CBT (cognitive behavioural therapy), this thing called psycho-drama, where you act out bits of your life. I was going on mindfulness courses, doing loads of yoga, exercises for PTSD (post-traumatic stress disorder), downloading all the apps, watching YouTube clips, doing three guided meditations a day – you name it, I was doing it.

But each time I did one of those things, I'd come out and feel worse than the time before. There was never a breakthrough.

Then my boss offered to pay for any treatment I needed. My paranoia about work immediately lifted, Fran spoke to her friend and a few days later we went to see Will.

I was very cynical. All the way there I was like: *Nothing's worked; this isn't going to work. This is hippy shit.* I considered myself an expert on meditating because of all the apps and stuff I'd done. I'd even tried generic mantra-based stuff like the '*om, om, om*' type of thing, so I thought I knew it all.

Anyway, I walked into this apartment and all my preconceptions were blown out of the water. I'd expected some old guy wearing sandals and robes, but Will was just there in a T-shirt and jeans. I saw these Beatles records on the wall and said: 'They're old American jukebox records.' Will said, 'Wow, you know your stuff,' and so we had a bit of a geek-off about music. I could really relate to him.

We sat down, he gave me my sound, and I was guided into that first meditation. It wasn't so different from other meditations apart from repeating this personalised sound very gently in my head, sort of letting it wash over me. But not only did I feel calmer in that meditation than during any of the other practices I'd done, but that feeling of calm stayed with me pretty much until I went to bed that night. It was the first time in five or six months that I'd had three or four hours of feeling pretty good. I got up the next morning and I had hope.

I'd been told to do it again that morning, on my own, and it was this self-sufficiency that was so appealing about it.

I didn't have to go anywhere, or plug headphones into my phone, or go and lie down on my bed, or sit on a yoga mat or anything – I just did it. I just sat on a couch, closed my eyes, meditated for twenty minutes, and that feeling of calm came back again.

I wasn't cured overnight, but things started to get better pretty quickly. The depression lifted within a week, my anxiety in about a month and then my confidence really started to come back. I could visit guitar shops, record shops, go for lunch by myself, sit in a café and read a book – things I just couldn't have done before.

When Will advised me to go on a retreat, I thought: *He's just trying to sell me this.* But then I thought: *It's done me so much good just doing this twice a day, if I go and do it for a weekend, who knows what might happen?*

When I came back, I was on a total high. I felt like the real me again. I rang my mum and then my dad and waxed lyrical about how much better I felt. My mum was totally overjoyed and started crying down the phone – she'd obviously been storing up a lot of worry about me. My dad was like: 'I can't tell you how happy I am that you've found something that helps. It's such a relief.'

Soon after that, I went and saw my dad and had a really deep conversation with him. I'd been very aggressive with him when I was younger, because I was so angry at his drinking, but on the retreat, I realised he'd obviously been in a really bad way himself. Now I could understand that he'd been drinking to numb his unhappiness. Instead of me treating him like an enemy, which had probably made it worse, what I really needed was to empathise. Having that conversation with him was very healing for both of us. Another really nice thing that's come out of all this is that my mum and dad, who've been divorced for years, have become good mates again, and my recovery gave them something to really celebrate.

I don't want to paint a picture of me suddenly being this angel who's seen the light, but things have changed massively for me.

I used to get up half an hour before I had to leave for work. On my way to the bathroom I'd be checking my emails on my phone. Now I get up and I give myself a good hour before I leave the house. I'll do my meditation and get myself set for the day. Then I hop on my bike and cycle to wherever I'm working that day. I quit my job, eventually, and though my new job is very different, I have just as much work to do. The difference now is that I don't have that sense of being overwhelmed that I used to find so debilitating. I no longer have that manic, punishing drive to be the best all the time.

I try to meditate at the end of the day, before I leave work, then I'll cycle to wherever I'm going that night. I produce a music podcast, rehearse with my band, go to the cinema a lot, eat out quite a bit, go to shows – all without those moments of panic or anxiety. It's great.

If you imagine me as the side of a record, getting to the end of side one, and that needle just hitting the centre, still going round even though there's nothing going on – that's the space I used to be in when I wasn't working. It was always on my mind. Now, I imagine my life as more of a CD. When I leave work, I just press pause. Then, when I go to work the next morning, I come back to it and press play again.

The first time I met Will, I asked him why he meditated. His response was so simple, and yet it really struck me: 'I meditate because I want to feel great every day.' I thought: *What? I can feel great every day? That just isn't possible.* But it is, and I do.

Calming Noel's Nervous System

Noel's experience was pretty extreme, but no more so than a lot of the people I see. And whether you're someone who lies awake at night fretting about what's going to happen at work the next day, or someone who's tipped over into panic attacks, the techniques that can help you are the same. Working with Noel was all about calming down his nervous system and his amygdala, little by little, every day, and helping him to reconnect with himself. Once that happened, he was able to regain his stability and self-confidence.

So how did we calm down his nervous system? Well, firstly, by allowing his mind and body to rest at a level that was far deeper than anything he would experience during sleep, we were able to break through the programming that was causing him to be conditioned with continual alertness. By repeating his personalised sound, the prefrontal cortex of his brain was able to enter an extremely coherent alpha state (as I explained in my introduction to this kind of meditation), and that kind of high-level brain patterning very significantly reduces anxious thoughts and sensations.

Meditation also brought balance to his production of neurotransmitters and hormones like serotonin, which are implicated in anxiety disorders. His breathing became deeper, and so his respiration was more efficient, which brought a greater sense of calm and control. And, finally, he could sleep. He'd been so very much in need of this for so very long and I was overjoyed for him when he developed a healthy sleep rhythm again. (I'll talk about how to use meditation to improve sleep a bit later on.)

Once all that was happening, it became possible for Noel to see a way out of the terrible state that he'd been trapped in. Many people, when their anxiety is deeply ingrained, almost secretly feel like their anxiety is keeping them safe and secure. It's a cognitive distortion, just like the anxiety itself. By bringing about greater alertness, meditation gives you enhanced capability to detect genuine threats, and quicker reaction times mean you're better able to take corrective action if you really are under siege. When genuine danger isn't there, you can allow yourself to rest. The extra confidence that comes with being able to detect and respond to challenges and threats means that decision-making becomes easier, you're less preoccupied and restless, and you have more energy.

As Noel found, the more you practise meditation, the more its calming effects spill over into the rest of your life. As well as soothing an overstimulated nervous system, this kind of meditation starts bringing fundamental balance to the responsiveness of the amygdala. That's probably why Vedic-inspired meditation has been shown to be at least twice as effective as other relaxation or meditative techniques in reducing the symptoms of anxiety.

> 'When you become centred, the balance of power shifts from the amygdala to the prefrontal cortex, so that you govern your emotions rather than the other way round.'
> RAY DALIO,
> FOUNDER OF THE INVESTMENT FIRM
> BRIDGEWATER ASSOCIATES, USA

Coping with Panic Attacks

Noel vividly describes his panic attacks. A lot of people I see have had them, and I've suffered from them in the past myself, so I know how terrifying they can be – that awful, rising sense of paralysing fear that makes you hyperventilate or even feel as if you're going to die. Panic attacks are the result of a massive activation of the sympathetic nervous system, sending the mind, body and emotions into crisis mode.

They also arise from elevated anxiety levels, usually brought about by psychological stress and adrenal exhaustion. After you've had one or two, the problem is then compounded, since the fear of having another one is enough to make you even more anxious, which will only make their occurrence more likely. It's a horribly vicious cycle.

When the stress response is engaged, you take short, sharp breaths in preparation for danger. And when that stress activation becomes chronic, you tend to only ever use the top third of your lungs, creating a permanent state of hyperventilation. This results in a poor exchange of oxygen and carbon dioxide in the bloodstream. A deficiency of carbon dioxide can lead to panic attacks, insomnia and extreme fatigue; and a lack of oxygen will deprive your organs and muscles of resources that are vital for their effective functioning. This low-level hyperventilation will lead to increased heart rate, palpitations, and a sense of anxiety combined with a feeling of being out of control. I often teach people suffering from anxiety and panic attacks a supplementary ancient breathing technique that can really help keep things calm in those first few months while you transition to a more even keel. For more information on this, see www.theeffortlessmind.com. Another technique that I have found useful in combatting such attacks is the Adrenal Hands Technique.

ADRENAL HANDS – A TECHNIQUE FOR CALMING SYMPTOMS OF PANIC

Lie face-down in a comfortable spot, or stand behind a high-backed chair, and lean forward and rest your hands on the seat.

Ask someone close to you to place the palms of their hands on your adrenal glands, which are just above your kidneys, in the middle of your lower back area.

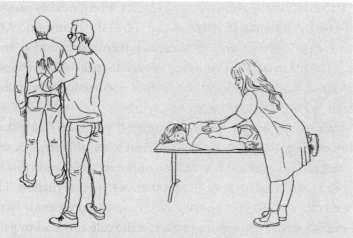

Breathe in deeply through the nose, and exhale slowly through the mouth. Aim to do this for five to ten minutes.

The warmth and contact of someone's hands in the area around your adrenal glands will help you calm down and feel less panicked. Allied with the breathing exercise, this is very soothing.

Internal Imbalance

Although Noel told me that he felt it was his nightmare that had kick-started his breakdown, my view is that, instead, there was a rising level of internal imbalance within his nervous system, and the dream was just one manifestation of that. His brain was trying to process the emotions that he was experiencing, so while he assumed that the anxiety he felt was because of the nightmare, there was actually a bigger story unfolding. In addition to the scary content of the nightmare, the anxiety he was feeling was also because of a clash, or dissonance, between how he was behaving and how he saw himself as a person. It was as if his mind wasn't able to compute the disparity, and so it called into question his entire worldview. Logic disappeared.

He couldn't make sense of the situation that he found himself in, and so his anxiety spiralled.

This problem of cognitive dissonance – that discomfort that you have when there's a conflict between your beliefs/what you know to be right and your actions – is something many people feel. A good example of this is smoking: although you know it's bad for you, you still do it. Another is going out with the intention of not getting drunk and waking up with a terrible hangover. This form of meditation will help with this by freeing you from the conditioned responses that you've built up over the years and make it possible to take actions that are more in keeping with how you fundamentally feel as a human being. By systematically putting your brain into a high state of connectivity, you can build new neural pathways and begin doing things differently.

In the longer term, once Noel's nervous system had calmed down, meditation began to work on deeper levels so that there were far fewer neurotransmitters of anxiety rushing around his brain and body. His hormonal balance was reset to more natural levels, and his brain could start developing different inter-neural linkages. In the end, he could start to really change the way he lived his life.

Improving Your Relationships

I'd like to add one more thing that I think is important: the impact that Noel's recovery had on his relationships, particularly with his dad. How we feel in ourselves makes a big difference to how our interactions end up playing out with others. When people practise techniques like meditation, they are much more in touch with their own feelings and those of others, which often means the dynamics of their relationships improve significantly. They're in a good space, so the other party feels like they can trust them, that they're not going to be attacked, and that they will be dealt with reasonably.

One of the ways meditation helps is by expanding your awareness beyond your own self. By calming down the activation of the nervous system and thereby reducing that fight or flight response, it takes you out of the 'me: must survive' mode. When this happens, it allows you to see that you are part of something bigger – a team, a species, a world – not just a lone individual. It also enables a greater flow of endorphins and activates the part of your brain that correlates with the emotions of love, compassion and empathy. That was what allowed Noel to understand his father's drinking, and gave him the courage to talk to him about it.

Dealing with Depression

Depression often goes hand in hand with anxiety, and so many of the people I see are suffering from it in one or other of its different forms.

They're not alone. Depression is a global epidemic. A recent World Health Organization estimate put it as the leading cause of ill health and disability worldwide, with an 18 per cent increase in rates of depression between 2005 and 2015.

Living with depression is awful, and it can seem almost impossible to find a way to break out of it. Anyone who's suffered from it, like Estrella, who tells her story below, will tell you how negative thoughts and inclinations consume you, and you feel a great sense of grief about what life has become. This is often accompanied by feelings of guilt that you're somehow responsible for your situation, or for not being able to get out of it, and an overriding sensation of hopelessness and despair.

Estrella

'Working with my monster.'

On the night I met Estrella, she was dressed smartly, her make-up immaculate. I could see, however, that she was very thin and tense and clearly in distress. She arrived late, her shoulders hunched, and she was very worried about not being on time.

Later on, I'd find out that it had taken her hours to get to the introductory talk because she couldn't bear to take the Tube, which would cause her to become overcome with fear. By that point, she'd been suffering from a deep depression for thirteen years.

I'm from Barcelona, and I come from a beautiful family. I have two brothers and a sister, and we're very close. I've always been the clown – the happy one, the funny one – and that's such a responsibility, really, entertaining the family. It's like a full-time job.

I think I've been an amazing actress all my life – pretending, not doing what would make me happy, but doing what people expected me to do. I always worry about other people; I always put them first. When I was a kid, we lived next to an organisation for deaf people, and when I was sixteen, I asked my mum if I could do a signing course. My mum wanted me to study for a degree instead. We fought for a year and a half, and in the end, I gave in and agreed to do it.

I started to study social work, but then later I said to my mum: 'I'm doing my degree but now I'm also going to learn how to sign.' As the year went on, I started to study signing a bit more, I did less for my degree and ended up leaving university. My mum was really unhappy, but I carried on with my sign language course. I was top of the class, loving it.

At the end of the course, there was an exam that would lead to positions as professional signers. There were four places available, and there were almost thirty of us in the class. I was thinking, *I'm definitely going to get one*, and everyone else thought I would, too.

When the day of the exam came, however, I had a panic attack. We were all sitting there, getting ready for it, and I started to feel as though I was dying. I couldn't breathe. I

felt my tongue swell, I was shaking. I thought I was in ana-
phylactic shock, so I went to my teacher and said: 'I have
to leave.'

I didn't just fail the exam, I felt like I'd failed myself, my
family – everyone's expectations. It was the first time in my
life that I'd done something wrong. From that moment on,
I felt this heaviness, and thought that nothing was worth it.
I started to bully myself, provoking more panic attacks. As
soon as I felt good, I went back to the moment when I had
the panic attack and felt it all over again. In Spanish, we say
morbo – meaning you like the pain. It was self-sabotage. I kept
wanting to go back to the painful state.

I think I was grieving. I definitely felt the kind of pain
you feel when someone dies, though I think now it was the
actress Estrella who was dead. I couldn't pretend to be that
funny person any more, the clown, not when the real Estrella
was such a mess.

I kept studying, went on to do two degrees, and got my
driving licence. I was focused, but during this time I didn't
care about meeting people. I thought that if I didn't get close
to anyone then they wouldn't expect anything of me and I
wouldn't fail them. I was alone for most of the time; I just
wanted to do things by myself.

In the first year of my depression, I lost my sense of smell,
and then, four or five years into it, I began to experience
paranoia. I thought that if I told people how I felt, it would
be like feeding a monster inside me; it would get bigger
and the depression would get worse. If instead I starved the
monster, by not telling anyone about it, doing nothing, the
monster would die.

But, in fact, the monster was growing anyway.

I had lots of panic attacks during those years, on a daily
basis. At that time, I was walking everywhere. I couldn't

take the Tube; I couldn't take the bus. Even if I had to cross
the whole of Barcelona, I would walk. I was avoiding living
like a normal person. I closed myself off from any normal
interaction.

After my second degree, I stayed in Barcelona and got a
position in sports reporting on the radio. I was successful, I
was growing, but the monster was growing as well and I was
still having panic attacks. From the outside, I was successful,
happy Estrella, enjoying life. But I weighed 45 kilos, I was
so pale, and I was losing so much hair, because I was grieving. It was a long, long grieving process, and my body was
feeling the strain.

One day my radio station sent me to London to see how
the city was changing in the run-up to the Olympic Games.
I had decided that this was a battle I needed to win, and so,
that first year in London, I tried everything – acupuncture,
Bach remedies, camomile, valerian. I started to practise a
bit of yoga at home by watching YouTube videos. My aim
was to get better, but as soon as I felt some relief, I started to
sabotage myself, so it was kind of pointless.

I was at a large press reception at a big hotel when I suddenly realised I was happy. I wasn't used to it, so I provoked
a panic attack to go back to my normal state of being.

And then started the worst years of it all. From that day
onwards, I couldn't feel anything physically. If you touched
me, I couldn't feel your hand. It was a bit like being a ghost. It
was terrifying; the room would spin and noise would bother
me a lot. I lost my sense of smell, and I couldn't feel pain. I
think my body was switching off.

Despite all this, I never cried. In all those years, I
never cried.

I was exhausted. There were nights and nights and nights
with no sleep and no food, and I was working so many

hours. I don't want to sound dramatic, but I really thought I was going to die. I went back to Barcelona and I hugged everyone, because I believed it would be the last time I would see them.

One day, at a yoga class, a girl mentioned meditation. That night, I went home and had a look online. I just clicked on the link to Will's website and booked myself in for an intro talk. I swore to myself that this was the last thing I was going to try.

The talk was in a room above a pub. It had taken me ages to get there; I got lost, and I was panicky. I stood in front of the door wondering if I should go in or just leave and give up. There I was, with my make-up on, my Spanx holding everything in, perfectly presented but a complete mess inside. But something made me climb those stairs.

When Will started to talk, I thought: *This is it. I think this can help me.* I booked a slot on the next course available.

It was raining the morning I went to see Will. I took the bus, not the Tube, because I still couldn't. The journey took me three and a half hours.

You remember how I hadn't cried at all for almost thirteen years? The day I did that first meditation, I cried like a baby. When I went outside after our session, I could smell the rain, for the first time in years. It hit me so powerfully that I just burst into tears. I went to the bus stop and just sat there, crying and crying. Then the sun began to shine, and I could see the sun, and smell the rain, and I said to myself: *That's it. I'm going to try.*

The first four months weren't easy. At the beginning, my meditations were so deep that I felt as if I'd almost left my body behind. I started to feel so good that it scared me. I wasn't ready to feel good just yet.

The second year of meditation, I felt more confident in

being happy. I was starting to be very, very happy and I liked the feeling; it was becoming more familiar. And now, in the third year? I feel great.

This morning I realised that I was late, and so I had to get the Tube. I just got on it, on my own, at 7 o'clock in the morning! It was crowded, but I was fine, and I was so happy! I've changed, and that monster inside me has changed: he's become a friend.

The Chemistry of Depression

There are many reasons for depression. It can stem from a chemical imbalance, from trauma, or from a combination of conflicting wishes and desires, environmental pressures, societal pressures, imagined consequences or the pressures of having to cope. In that way, depression can 'come from' the mind or from the body. As we discussed at the beginning of this section, the two are intimately connected, and each reinforces and reflects symptoms in the other.

I'll talk about the mental trauma that Estrella had gone through in a moment, but I also want to explain the possible chemical reasons for the negativity and apathy that she was feeling. Depression is linked to the unhealthy production of (or compromised receptivity to) certain neurotransmitters and hormones which are vital to psychological wellbeing, and which become destabilised by the chain reaction of physiological responses we experience when the stress response is regularly activated.

Most people with depression have high levels of glucocorticoids, the stress-induced steroid hormones that go to your brain and inhibit anything not deemed useful for raw physical survival. Under threat, feeling joyful is completely superfluous – you can worry about getting happy later.

The chronic release of glucocorticoids also results in a shrinking of the hippocampus, the area of the brain that processes memory, so your ability to remember information is compromised. And the cortex, responsible for motor skills and abstract thinking, tends to be considerably less activated, resulting in apathy.

Recent studies have also shown that, in some patients, depression could be linked to inflammation. Stress disrupts the balance of metabolic processes, producing a raft of destructive consequences, including the elevation of inflammatory responses, such as those mediated by histamines. Histamine is one of the neurotransmitters that's produced when the body encounters a foreign body (most people associate it with allergies – pollen being the foreign body that leads to hay fever), and patients with depression have been shown to have higher levels of histamine/inflammation.

The growing body of evidence highlighting the interaction between mind and body suggests that it's not enough to simply tell people with depression to 'cheer up' or that 'it's not that bad'. Because the causes of depression run in both directions and are manifestations of each other, a more holistic approach, such as this form of meditation, which takes into consideration biological, environmental and psychological factors, is much more likely to make a difference. I'll explain how it can help in the treatment of depression in a moment, after I've looked at some of the other features that might have contributed to Estrella's depression.

Rewriting Your Storylines

Estrella's depression was triggered when she found herself unable to take her exam. We all have our storylines, which can come not only from our own experiences and 'inner conversations', but also from societal or familial patterns. Powerful cultural influences further condition and sometimes limit the way we interact with the world.

And, of course, there are the traumas and events that leave their mark, which sear their way into our subconscious and leave scars. As I discussed on p. 44, our nervous systems are so delicate for the first three years of our lives, and even later, when we're children and teenagers, the smallest thing can become part of a storyline. Sometimes we are aware of these storylines, but very often we are not; they are buried in our unconscious and from there affect how we feel and behave. However, one of the particular properties of the unconscious is that it does an excellent job of ignoring reason, logic and conscious efforts to change it – and our storylines are therefore very difficult to unwind through 'regular' (by which I mean conscious) means. We can understand logically that we are as good/clever/worthy as most people, but that is not enough to make us feel genuinely self-confident. There are very few ways to 'unwind' the unconscious messages, but there is more and more anecdotal evidence that Vedic-inspired meditation, which impacts how different systems in our brain and our nervous systems interact, is one of them.

In that exam room, two of Estrella's storylines kicked in, in full force. There was the one that whispered: 'Follow your dream, it's more important than staying at university'; and the one that was handed down to her by her family, the one that said: 'You have to succeed at university.' This clash of storylines was so strong that the *psychological* pressure tipped into *physiological* pressure – her sympathetic nervous system reared up and her body reacted by producing a trauma-inducing overload of stress-related hormones such as cortisol. Her amygdala started going crazy, and this resulted in a panic attack.

When you experience that level of crisis, it's both physiological and neurological. Your body has effectively gone into trauma, and that can change the dynamics of lots of bodily processes. Now that we understand neuroscience, and the effect of stress on our epigenetic profile and the microbiome, as I briefly mentioned in the introduction to this section, we know that big switches can occur very quickly once trauma has set in. That trauma – a combination of conflicting wishes, messages from the surrounding environment, imagined consequences or the pressures of coping – can lead to psychosomatic disorders and outcomes.

Self-Sabotage

Estrella hadn't worked through this internal conflict, and it was still unresolved, so the pressure built up until it manifested itself in the bodily sensations of a panic attack. Estrella talks about 'bullying' herself, of 'self-sabotaging' her own attempts at happiness, sending herself back to a miserable state so there was no fear of disappointment. So many people find themselves resorting to this comfort zone, or, rather, *dis*comfort zone, because it's familiar; living with the pain seems easier than trying to get better (the path of least resistance). Also, because our society is so geared towards success that, in a way, it gives us a 'get-out': 'I can't compete with everyone else because I've got this thing going on that I can hide behind, so I don't have to measure myself like everyone else does.' And once it becomes familiar enough, we get used to it; it feels normal.

Presenting a Persona to the World

Estrella describes feeling like an actress, presenting a persona to the world, and this is not uncommon. We expend so much energy projecting what we hope is going to please others that we leave few resources for our internal selves. So many of us blunt our emotions and invest all our energy in trying to please people, to live our lives the way society tells us to, that it leaves us feeling hollow inside. It means there's a truth we don't want to face, and we'll practise any level of disassociation to keep the plates spinning, to keep this persona going. It's not sustainable. At some point in life, the plates and the persona come crashing down, and you're suddenly faced with the truth you've been trying so hard to bury. It's often the case that the harder you try – the longer you've been spinning those plates – the harder the fall that ultimately occurs.

Delusions, Distortion and Defeat

To top it all off for Estrella, and for many people who suffer from depression, there's a self-defeating delusion that often accompanies this disorder. Your brain has been hijacked by the autonomic nervous system for so long that an overwhelming sense of doom begins to emerge, and gradually there are all sorts of internal signals telling you to give up. This is amplified by an unhelpful contribution from the amygdala, which has learned to become highly stimulated when it detects any kind of sadness. The result is an empathetic sadness, which, like listening to sad music, feels strangely compelling. The sadness becomes a source of comfort, of familiarity, and risks causing you to hold on to the emotional triggers that have gripped you for so long.

And, finally, there's that sense of defeat and helplessness that so characterises depression. There's a perception that everything's out of control, that you might as well give up trying to find a solution. This cognitive distortion means you lack both the clarity of perception to see that things are not actually as bad as they seem, as well as the motivation to try to change the situation, because you've become programmed to assume the worst.

How Meditation Can Help

Finding *internal* security rather than security from external sources is incredibly empowering, and that's why meditation is so valuable, because it acts as an instant internal anchor. Once Estrella had that foothold, she could break the vicious cycle of depression – where the stress of the condition intensifies the symptoms, making it even harder to find a way out.

So how did meditation help Estrella to combat her depression? Well, it acted on a number of different levels.

Firstly, the resonance of her personalised sound would activate the parasympathetic nervous system, helping to initiate the relaxation response and calm the sympathetic branch, i.e. the part that gets activated during fight and flight. This helped bring balance to her nervous system, which meant that her thought processes were less likely to get hijacked by irrationally negative perspectives. Reducing the frequency and intensity of the stress response also meant a reduction in the stress chemical cortisol.

As I mentioned before, those who are experiencing depression usually have an amygdala that is functioning abnormally. Through the power of sound, this form of meditation has been shown to normalise the activity of the amygdala, so that for Estrella it stopped becoming hyper-aroused every time she saw something sad. Her cerebral cortex and left prefrontal cortex were more activated, bringing her a greater sense of positivity. And there would have been far fewer of those pesky glucocorticoids inhibiting the function of her hippocampus, reducing her energy levels and generally wreaking havoc throughout her body. In their place would have come a more balanced production, uptake and disposal of neurotransmitters, especially noradrenaline, serotonin and dopamine, meaning she had a balanced complement of happy hormones lifting her mood.

To top it all off, like Noel, she could now sleep.

In this way, Estrella's vicious cycle of symptoms and stress was replaced by a virtuous cycle, where everything started to get a little better, and then spiralled upwards. This gave her a sense of empowerment and control, because she could now see how an action that she chose to take (meditation) had an impact on how she was feeling and behaving. Her painful memories – of being out of control when a panic attack struck, her failure in that exam room and those feelings of despair – all those old scars, or *samskaras*, were eventually cleared out of her system until she was no longer trapped by the negative impressions of her past.

I want to add something about Estrella's 'monster'. In the West's highly Christianised worldview of good versus evil, we're all about embracing the good and rejecting the bad. However, from the Vedic point of view, there is considerable value in accepting that we all have a shadow, a dark side. If you can accept and be at ease with all sides of yourself, even those you don't want to be particularly prominent, then you can feel a certain level of peace in your heart and in your mind. As Estrella intuited by embracing her monster, this can be useful. As long as you're in rejection or denial mode, you will never make meaningful progress. It's only when you accept or acknowledge something about yourself that you can begin to do something about it, and this can be the first step for anyone who's trying to overcome depression.

THE FIVE TIBETANS

The Five Tibetans are a series of five dynamic yogic exercises that originated in the Himalayas around 2,500 years ago. They take only a small amount of time and effort, yet dramatically increase physical strength, energy and flexibility as well as mental clarity.

These exercises relieve muscle tension, as well as toning and strengthening all of the main muscle groups in the body and improving cardiovascular tone. They will leave you feeling energised, rejuvenated, calm and relaxed and are even reputed to stem the ageing process!

Practising the Five Tibetans before breakfast gives you a great energetic start to the day and really helps to lift your mood. It's one of the most balancing forms of exercise there is, so it simultaneously leaves you feeling calm and uplifted, leading to a truly effortless mind! Check out my instructional video at www.theeffortlessmind.com for more information.

Managing Anger

Anger might seem like a very different problem to anxiety or depression. It's often interpreted as a personality flaw, or the inevitable consequence of strained circumstances. But whether we're just a bit of a grump, or have reached the point of alienating those around us with uncalled-for bursts of rage, our anger is born from the intimate connections between mind and body. Many people see it as simply an emotional response, but the truth is that it comes from both a physical and a psychological place.

Once again, it's down to fight or flight. The flood of stress and stimulation that we experience as part of modern life causes us to unwittingly perceive all sorts of everyday challenges as threats. Our limbic system, fed by memories of pain and injustice, kicks in, triggering our emotional centres and jolting our endocrine and autonomic nervous systems into fight mode. The heart starts thumping to stimulate blood flow in our muscles, and the flood of adrenaline and noradrenaline racing through our systems causes mind and body to become overwhelmed.

This creates a vicious cycle whereby the more overwhelmed we feel, the more our innate aggressive tendencies start coming out to play. Our body is being prepared to fight itself out of mortal danger, yet when there's no foe to do physical battle with, this energy needs to be vented elsewhere. Our first response may be to try to suppress what we're feeling, holding down our irritability and frustration like the lid on a pressure cooker. The more these feelings escalate, however, the more we struggle to contain our rising emotions.

For a time, we may succeed in stewing in our own juices; too annoyed to rationalise our feelings yet simultaneously too aware of their ridiculousness to justify expressing them. Yet, without a way to diffuse toxic emotions, eventually, the lid will blow. Such outbursts of anger or rage can get very ugly, leaving all parties feeling diminished by the experience. Anger, like depression, feeds itself; if it becomes a chronic feature of our lives, then we may find ourselves with an anger management issue – one that's further fuelled by the frustration of not being able to control our emotions.

It's worth mentioning that anger can help us face danger when we really are threatened, and it is a critical capability to have in our repertoire. However, most people experience anger as a result of matters that are inconsequential or out of their control – like slow-loading web pages, which are guaranteed to get even the most chilled person angrily chewing on their keyboard. When we get angry about the genuine injustices in the world, our negative emotions will get in the way; because we are no longer utilising the logical reasoning that makes problem-solving easier, they will prevent us from tackling the problem constructively. Instead, the inappropriate activation of fight or flight creates a build-up of charged energy and emotion that we don't know what to do with. This then finds expression through resentment and a desire for revenge. These only feed the ego and, as this tendency develops, it may become a dominating force in our lives.

The ego is an enormous topic that could quite happily have a book of its own, but, simply put, it refers to our sense of individual self, of being separate from everyone and everything in the world. Ego, therefore, puts self-interest before any other concerns. As well as raw, physical, survival needs, we also have psychological needs, and if our ego doesn't feel that these have been met, then we feel injured, wounded, diminished or insulted. In most cases, though, we can't manipulate the scales of justice and we can feel incredibly frustrated by this lack of control, this inability to overcome perceived wrongs.

Once angry and frustrated, the ego can either retreat or seek revenge. When this happens, it changes our brain chemistry and creates neural pathways that are counter to our sense of wellbeing. We are effectively locking ourselves in a prison of our own making, and the more disenfranchised we become from a person or a group, the more we start to filter 'their' actions in a way that proves they are being unfair to 'us'. It's an incredibly toxic dynamic.

Anger is also extremely bad for our physical health. There's a direct correlation between anger and unsustainably elevated heart rates, as well as high blood pressure, both of which compromise our cardiovascular health. It can also affect our immune system and leave us wide open to all sorts of diseases.

The Vedic approach understands that emotional predispositions like anger ultimately stem from fear. Calming down the sympathetic nervous system through meditation so it can start to purge itself of *samskaras*, those long-held psychological scars, will help an individual let go of fear and, ultimately, the anger that is expressed as a result.

Without a healthy strategy to cope, such as Vedic-inspired meditation, we can't avoid taking out our frustration on the people around us. Usually those closest to us bear the brunt of our anger, whether that be a partner, family member or a colleague at work, and at some point, they're likely to find our impatience and irritability difficult to stomach. And why wouldn't they? Who wants to be on the receiving end of regular impatience and irritability? Deep down, we know this. After an outburst, the realisation dawns that we've responded more aggressively than we needed to, which piles on layers of guilt and shame to every unnecessary eruption, only adding fuel to the fire of our rising anger.

And, of course, if you're constantly having angry outbursts, you run the risk of losing the respect of others, including friends and loved ones. People will be reluctant to spend time with you because they are embarrassed by your behaviour. They will also be less likely to take you seriously because you're always overreacting. In the worst-case scenario, they can become intimidated by you, and start to modify their behaviour in order to minimise the risk of provoking your wrath.

Aggressive behaviour, therefore, becomes damaging and, in extreme circumstances, even abusive. If you've got to the point where others are tiptoeing around you and making endless concessions to the whims of your temper, something needs to drastically change. Unfortunately, our patterns of behaviour can become so ingrained that by the time people seek help with anger management, their relationships are often damaged beyond repair.

Arjun hadn't got to that stage yet, but he knew he had a problem. I first met him at one of our introductory talks, and I could tell he was seriously agitated. He kept fidgeting, looking down and to the side, impatience written all over his face. He was incredibly sceptical, and asked very searching questions. As the talk went on, however, and he started to realise that this wasn't the esoteric nonsense that his inner cynic was expecting, I began to see the lovely, slightly scared human being hidden behind all the armour. By the time I'd finished speaking, you could tell he was quite buzzed up, with this gorgeous grin on his face. He was obviously a great guy and I couldn't wait to work with him.

Arjun

'I got pissed off a lot.'

At my previous job, I got pissed off a lot. I don't know what it was; I used to get angry all the time, usually at the little things. People annoyed me (that was number one), my managers annoyed me, my work annoyed me. Then, when I got angry, I'd have these outbursts. Many times I was dragged in front of my director at work and, you know, told off.

Actually, it wasn't just at work. It was at home too.

I smoked a lot of weed, because it's supposed to mellow you out – it was more when I wasn't smoking it that I had problems. Everything used to annoy me and really frustrate me. Life in a big city is like that – it's all hustle and bustle, road rage ... It can be too much.

Meditation was something I'd been interested in for a while. I love my music, and I used to hear a lot of people talk about it in songs. I'm a big rap fan, and artists like Damian Marley, Nas and Akala mention meditation all the time.

And so, one day, I just Googled meditation and the first website that came up was Will's, so I decided to have a quick look. I read what it had to say and there was a part that said: 'It just takes twenty minutes a day,' or something like that, and I thought: *What's twenty minutes? It's nothing.* Then I read the section full of other people's reviews on the courses, and I was just like: *Wow! Can something that you do for just twenty minutes really change your life?*

I had all this stuff going on and so I thought: *You know what? I'm just going to do it. Free introductory talk – why not? I'll go just to see what it's all about, to see if it's real.*

What I first noticed at the talk was that Will was really

happy. I don't think I'd met anyone as happy as Will in my whole life. The vibe he gave off was so positive, and I remember thinking: *Is this guy high or something?* At the end of the meeting, though, I came out thinking: *I want to be that happy!*

Before I went on the course, my colleagues were convinced that I'd be joining some sort of cult. So, at our first one-to-one meeting, I asked Will straight away whether that was what this was. He just started laughing and said: 'I'm glad you asked me that. No, it's not a cult.' But still, even when he gave me my personalised sound, I was thinking: *Cult, cult, cult.* I couldn't understand how that one sound was going to really change my life, but decided to just go with it.

So, we had a meditation session. I felt much calmer, but I didn't know if my body just wanted to be in that state of mind, or whether it was the meditation causing it. I found the rest of the course really enjoyable. It was somehow comforting to see people who were having issues too, and good to know their reasons for doing the course. A lot of people suffered from lack of sleep, work stress, anxiety, and because there were all sorts of different motivations for being there, I didn't really feel out of place when I mentioned my anger issues.

During the group meditation, I experienced something much more than when I'd done it on my own, something much more powerful. I instantly felt much more relaxed. On the evening of that first day, I went to a friend's party, and I ended up talking about the meditation all night. Everyone was looking at me as if to say: 'Oh, God. What are you doing?' I could tell they thought I was crazy.

When I went back for the second day of the course, I was a bit hungover. Will told me that meditation would help with that, which I was glad to hear. In my life, drinking happens on a regular basis, so a hangover is a useful thing to know how to handle.

After the course, I started meditating on my own, which initially was quite hard, because I had to get up earlier to do it before work. Then I started doing it at work, which was better. I'd take twenty minutes for meditation, and then forty minutes for my lunch. Soon, there was a real change in me. In fact, other people noticed it before I did. Everyone at work was saying: 'You're *so* much calmer.'

I noticed that things that might have bugged me before now didn't. There was a girl I had this crush on, but she told me she'd got someone else, and even though I wanted to blow up, even though I wanted to be mad, I just couldn't. I was like, 'Oh, all right.' If she'd said that three months earlier, the shit would have hit the fan.

So now I feel like I've definitely calmed down. I'm not as aggressive; I'm more of a joker. I also listen more when people are talking, and I definitely pay more attention to what they're saying. Before, I was impatient, always wanting people to shut up so I could say what I wanted to say, but now I definitely find myself engaging with people more. I've always been confident talking to people but now I feel like I can talk to anyone; it doesn't matter who they are, or what their background is – I feel I can connect and have a real, meaningful chat with them.

My mum has noticed the changes most. She's always saying: 'Are you still meditating? I hope you're still doing it, it's good for you.' Although there are still a few outbursts, she's definitely seen the difference it's made, and she seems really happy for me.

I do think meditation's been a lifesaver for me. In terms of my career, I don't think I would have got my new job if it wasn't for that. I got it six months after I started to meditate.

It was a gruelling interview process, it was tough. It was a management position, so I told them at the beginning: 'I meditate. I'm very quiet and calm with people.' In the type of environment I'm in (corporate financial services), you have to be calm and collected. Before, I wouldn't have been ready for this, because my colleagues do annoy me, don't get me wrong, but you can't really start swearing at them. I was in a management position before, but I was threatened with 'if you keep being argumentative, we're going to demote you'. I was, like, 'hell no!' My pride would not let me get demoted. I had to leave.

I meditated hard just before each interview, and it was weird, because when I went in for the final interview I mentioned that I meditated and one of the guys doing the interview was like, 'Oh my God, I've just started meditating too!' It was a connection! I smashed the interview and got the job and I know it's because the meditation helped me be my best.

Meditation puts my life into perspective a bit. Sometimes, when I'm feeling drained, I go and meditate. Afterwards, I feel like a new person.

It's still really hard to explain it to other people, but I think if everyone did it, the world would probably be a better place! It's just getting people to take that initial step out of their comfort zone, and convincing people that it's not weird, or crazy. They always want to know what your sound is, and then they ask: 'Does everyone get the same sound?' I asked Will that too. He said definitely not – he would have been found out a long time ago if that were true!

Meditation is definitely one of the best things I've ever done, and I'm guessing it is going to open up many avenues and doors to my potential. It's something I'd encourage anyone to do. I reckon it'll take me far in life.

Managing Your Anger

Managing anger is a very difficult thing to do, and it's hard to know where to start with addressing the problem when you're feeling frustrated all the time. Research has shown that 'venting' – going off on rants, slamming doors, or, like Arjun says, swearing at people – actually perpetuates your anger. This is because we reinforce the negative response every time we give into it. It causes those neural patterns to fire in a particular way, increasing the likelihood of you resorting to this response in the future. Trying to repress anger, however, is even worse for your health, and does nothing to relieve it over the long term. (We all know that *I wish I'd told that horrible person exactly what I thought* feeling, which can torment us even years later.) If you suppress your annoyance, the perceived injustice of the situation may provoke angry feelings later on, leading to bitterness and resentment. Even if your anger isn't justified, pushing it away if it's rising up repeatedly will mean that your frustration only builds until you're truly furious and miserable.

So, if they can't hold it in, and they can't vent, what does a person who has a tendency towards anger do? They can't be expected to consciously control it; their unconscious physical and emotional reactions are just too powerful. It's hard-wired in. Natural selection determined that those with the most instinctive response – within one hundredth of a second – had the greatest chance of survival. This is because any delay is going to massively reduce your chance of reacting quickly enough to save your life. And – I can't stress this enough – it's automatic.

Say a woman at a party is chatting to someone, and suddenly her heart starts to race. She feels panicky – but has no idea why. Much later, she realises that the person's voice was similar to that of someone who once assaulted her. She doesn't consciously process the similarity; all she feels is the panic and fear that results from the connection her unconscious mind has made. It's the same with someone who gets angry all the time. Those perceived threats go deep, and the response is absolutely involuntary.

The involuntary nature of anger can mean that conscious attempts to remedy the problem, such as therapy, are sometimes only partially effective. Often, the patterns and emotions driving our reactions are stored deeper than we are able to reach by ourselves. Dealing with the neurological and physiological patterns and imbalances that underpin the reaction, alongside any therapy that you feel might be helpful, is much more effective. For the anger to subside, we need to delve into the unconscious and let the distortions unwind themselves naturally and organically.

By learning to meditate, that's what Arjun began to do. He started to calm his nervous system, and this began to calm his overactive fight or flight response. His blood pressure started to fall, his heart rate steadied, and he felt less edgy. And once those steroid hormones (made by his adrenal glands) that had been in overdrive for so long started to normalise, he was able to look beyond his annoyances. He was more able to distinguish between non-threatening and threatening situations and, as a result, was less threatened by life, and therefore less hostile towards it. The overactivation of the amygdala that many angry people suffer from leads to an inhibition of the prefrontal cortex (the part of the brain that's responsible for rational choices and control) and the activation of the limbic system, which is far more emotional and instinctive. Vedic-inspired meditation calms down the amygdala and activates the prefrontal cortex, which means you react in a more rational and less explosive way.

This kind of anger management should enable Arjun to build more refined patterns of behaviour, enabling him to tread more lightly through life. By meditating twice a day, he'll build up the emotional bandwidth to deal with the rising tension in any given moment, but also, on a subconscious level, begin to let go of the sadness and other emotions which are ultimately fuelling the anger and discord.

His personal and working relationships will improve as a direct result of greater empathy, awareness and understanding, and he will become more trusting due to his enhanced ability to read situations and people with much more clarity.

If you're someone who experiences a lot of anger, it's also worth thinking about your triggers, or pressure points. If, for example, you have a family occasion that you know is likely to lead to feelings of anger, or you're going to meet a friend who tends to rile you, do a tactical meditation beforehand. This way, you'll go into the situation in a much calmer state, prepared for what you might be faced with. (I'll talk more about this later, in our section on dealing with workplace confrontation.)

If someone you know is feeling the need to vent their anger, rather than indulge this unhealthy behaviour, help them express their feelings in a constructive way by asking them to tell you in no more than five minutes what happened that made them feel so upset, how it makes them feel and where in their body they can feel the tension. When the five minutes are up, you can discuss if there are ways to make them feel better.

TAKING A PAUSE: AN ANGER DISSIPATION EXERCISE

When you feel your anger rising, place your fingers around your wrist, with your index, middle and ring finger on your pulse, which can be located on the inside of your wrist bone (see diagram). The index finger needs to be about 4 cm below the line where your wrist meets your hand. Feel the artery pulsing beneath your fingertips. According to Ayurveda, it's best if women place their right hand around their left wrist, and men place their left around their right.

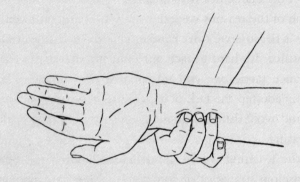

This creates a feedback loop whereby your tactile senses are tuned into your cardiovascular system, which will really help to dissipate the emotion.

Now, while you're feeling your pulse, really begin to breathe into your chest. See if you can feel your ribcage expanding, particularly at the back and to the side. Count to four on every inhale, and again on every exhale. Do this ten times, putting as much of your focus as you can on your breathing, your chest and your pulse.

I recommend practising this each morning or evening for the next week, so you know what to do if you are triggered.

Playing the Blame Game

People who are angry often blame other people for their problems. When our temper is close to the surface, it suddenly becomes the world's fault that everything around us isn't organised to our particular preference. If only our children were better behaved, or our bosses could see that our opinion is the correct one, or our frazzled partners put more effort into calming us down. Our anger becomes about everyone else but us, and no matter how unreasonable we may have been, ultimately we feel the blame lies with an external source.

One of the reasons we like to point the finger when we are angry is because we can't handle the sadness that underlies our annoyance. It's hard to face our own internal reality, so, as an avoidance tactic, we end up apportioning blame. This way, we can sidestep the task of addressing how we fundamentally feel, and avoid thinking about exactly why we find our lives so frustrating.

Vedic teaching would say that blaming other people is an unconscious strategy that comes from your ego's sense of separation from others – shifting the responsibility of your problem onto someone else, taking an internal flight from the issue. However, we can't heal until we accept the difficulties that go on in our lives and acknowledge that some part of us has agreed to take offence.

The Pitfalls of Pride

It was interesting to note Arjun's comment on pride. Angry people tend to use pride as a hiding place. You may recognise in yourself, or someone you know, the tendency to become unnecessarily angry over perceived disrespect or a lack of deference from others. Here, our pride has become so important to us that we become annoyed if others do not recognise our self-constructed – and often completely illusory – sense of status. We can even feel pride in our anger when it becomes an effective (albeit blunt and messy) tool for getting our own way.

If we manage to leverage our anger in a way that makes us feel triumphant, we may become proud of our victories. Pride, however, is divisive, and often creates an 'us and them' mentality that leaves us feeling defensive and vulnerable. While it can promote low-grade happiness, this is often accompanied by the twin expressions of arrogance and denial. Pride prevents us from accessing our best selves, causing us to settle for second best when, deep down, we know we're better than that.

Playing such a zero-sum game of conflict and desire to assert our control also means we feel diminished every time we 'lose' – amplifying our need to 'win' at all costs. Just like a self-conscious teenage boy may throw a punch at someone who jovially mocks him – deathly afraid of being made a figure of fun – we can lose our temper when our pride has been shaken, and feel the need to reassert our dominance.

That's not to deny the importance of being assertive. It's essential to stand up for ourselves, and to address the wider injustices we may be exposed to. I'm certainly not suggesting we simply roll over and accept truly *un*acceptable situations. As the very wise Jewish theologian and philosopher Abraham Joshua Heschel famously said: 'The opposite of good is not evil, the opposite of good is indifference.'

Our problems arise when we find ourselves being governed by emotional outbursts (which hold us down), rather than being calmly assertive (which elevates us and sets us free). Meeting injustice reasonably and with a sense of calm is far more constructive than fighting it with vitriol and violence. Even if we feel our anger is justified, we need to acknowledge that this is simply our limbic brain talking, stoked by memories of past pain and trauma. Approaches like those of Gandhi, Martin Luther King or Nelson Mandela, on the other hand, will create real and meaningful change. To effect change, or right a wrong, we need to first transition to a more sustainable place of equilibrium – one in which constant vigilance, division and aggression play no part.

Meditation can be an important part of such a transition, because it helps balance us out and gives us the capability to meet the challenges of life with more proficiency, wisdom and, ultimately, more success. It also increases your awareness, making it far easier to pick your battles. You'll know, almost instinctively, when to walk away and when to stand up for what's right. By increasing your empathy and compassion, meditation helps you to understand that when people are being unreasonable, it's because they're stressed and they're simply venting in your direction. Once you begin to perceive this, you stop taking things so personally. And if it's not personal or a matter of great importance, then often all parties will benefit from you directing your energies to something creative and constructive, rather than digging in your heels and initiating a stand-off.

It's only when you recognise that someone has genuinely crossed a line that you need to step up and assert yourself. Knowing deep in your heart what boundaries should not be transgressed gives you the confidence and clarity to ensure you are never taken advantage of, or let something truly important to you slide. And the more you meditate, the more you can trust that discerning voice inside that says: 'That's not acceptable.'

Forgetting Painful Experiences

Arjun wondered if he was angrier when he wasn't smoking weed. Here's what I suspect was going on. We know of 100–300 neurochemicals within our brain, and we're discovering more all the time. They are the chemical agents of change that help the body and brain do all the things they need to do. The brain produces these molecules and knows exactly where and in what quantities they should be sent in order to create the optimal response. Around every cell there are loads of receptors, purpose-built for each of the different neurochemicals. The neurochemical will act as a key that fits into the lock of the cell, opening it up to create a physiological response. The receptor then sends a signal to the brain to say: 'Yes, I got the stuff, thank you very much,' and that's how we maintain our natural home-ostatic balance – that constant, stable internal environment.

One group of neurochemicals that we produce are called cannabinoids. They're there to help us forget painful experi-ences. Many of us, however, find ourselves still struggling with painful memories long after the event occurred, and we resort to different ways of numbing ourselves. Cannabis is a particular favourite of many people because THC (tetrahydrocannabinol, its main psychoactive constituent) has a molecular structure very similar to the cannabinoids we naturally produce. On a superficial level, people smoke weed to get high. Biologically, however, the chances are that they're actually smoking because they like the freedom of not feeling the physical manifestations of unconscious pain.

Caffeine, cannabis and cigarettes (not to mention amphet-amines, opiates and medication) mimic what we naturally produce. We're doping ourselves with them because it appears we're not producing enough by ourselves, or we've become desensitised to them. This is because our old enemy – stress – changes our hormonal profile, as we've discussed before.

The problem is that these *exogenous* chemicals (that come from outside, as opposed to the *endogenous* ones that we produce ourselves) aren't flawlessly structured molecules, and they affect us in a different way to the ones we naturally produce. We take them in arbitrary quantities; they go to arbitrary places in the body; and quite often they get stuck in the receptor site because they don't perfectly fit. When this happens, your brain either turns down its production of that chemical or turns down its sensitivity to it. Either way, that's a problem, because then we end up with imbalanced hormonal chemistry, and this leads to imbalanced systems all over the body.

Arjun was clearly smoking the weed to calm himself down, but he was on a rocky road. His brain would have ultimately become desensitised to it, and it would have taken more and more to have an effect. By far the most sustainable, long-term solution would be to continue meditating until he has dealt with whatever pain he is unconsciously trying to block out.

Grump Overdrive and Blood Sugar

I'm really delighted to hear that Arjun thinks I'm so happy. He's right, these days I'm pretty chipper. But I used to have a lot of anger, and would get grumpy very easily. When I was travelling in South America with my girlfriend Kitty, she observed that I if I didn't eat something every four hours or so, I'd start getting cross. Which was problematic when we were trekking in the middle of nowhere – you couldn't exactly go to the local shop and buy a chocolate bar!

Thinking about it I realised I'd always been like that – I'd go into grump overdrive. After about a year of meditating, that became less and less a feature of my personality. As time has gone on, I can now skip meals happily without ever getting cross, because my blood sugar is much more balanced.

HOW TO MEDITATE YOUR WAY OUT OF A HANGOVER

Like Arjun, a lot of people are pretty interested to hear that meditation can help with hangovers - whenever I mention it in a teaching session, I see ears prick up all over the room! I'm not advocating getting drunk on a regular basis, but if you do find yourself feeling a little worse for wear after a late night of drinking, this is how meditation helps.

First off, one of the reasons hangovers feel so miserable is that you're sleep-deprived. You don't experience a proper sleep cycle when you've been drinking. Meditation, however, gives you twenty minutes of very powerful rest – the sort of rest you're unable to achieve when you've got alcohol in your system.

On top of that, drinking significant quantities of alcohol puts your organs and nervous system into a state of quite severe fight or flight activation. This is why many people experience 'the fear' after a night of slurringly telling friends how much they love them and wiggling about on a dance floor. Meditation helps calm that fear down, easing off all those paranoid thoughts.

And, finally, by calming your nervous system and therefore making you produce fewer stress hormones, meditation frees up other parts of your body to process the booze out of your system. Rather than focusing on getting rid of those stress hormones, your liver can get on with detoxing last night's tequila.

I should also add that meditation is fantastic for helping with problem drinking, because it helps you to calm down the anxiety and the overactive nervous system that may be behind it, as well as the unconscious triggers which cause you to want to numb yourself from the pain or exhaustion that you're feeling.

Beating Insomnia

I had a vast amount of sympathy for David when he came to me suffering from insomnia. I know from my own experience how awful it can be not to be able to sleep, and how it seems to drag down every other part of your life.

David and I weren't unusual. Sleep deprivation is a huge issue these days. A hundred years ago we used to get around nine hours a night; now we're down to seven and a half. That simply isn't enough. Even more concerning, however, is the major decline in sleep quality, which is actually far more detrimental to our overall wellbeing. I'll talk about why in a moment, but first let's hear from David about what his lack of sleep meant for him.

David

'Being able to sleep felt like a miracle.'

I'm married, with two kids, and my business is in Russia. The past few years have been very stressful. There was a point when I could have lost everything, and I went to a very dark place. I felt a lot of stress, a lot of anxiety, and I panicked. Maybe when I was younger I'd have thrived on all this, but as you get older, your mind and body aren't geared for it. Physically, the messages were crystal-clear – I had a horrific sleep disorder, and it had been going on for a year and a half.

I could fall asleep, no problem, because I was knackered and living mostly on adrenaline, but then I'd wake up and be bouncing off the walls. I'd be in a semi-sleep, sort of half awake, half asleep, with my mind just churning meaningless nonsense. On and on it would go, whirring all night long. If I did fall asleep, I'd be met with anxiety dreams, which were about being chased or busting for a leak and not being able to find a loo. Stupid things – like being constantly late; or missing something. Sleep should be when you rest, but I found it so stressful that I actually began to dread going to bed.

I felt powerless, and that was just soul-destroying. Sometimes I'd get up, go downstairs, sit in a chair and read, or I'd wake up and take a sleeping pill. Every so often I'd take one before I went to bed, because I was just too tired to deal with it. But sleeping pills aren't really a solution, not for the long term. You don't wake up after you've taken them feeling in any way refreshed. And then at 6 o'clock in the morning the kids would come in and I'd have to get up and function again. It was so horrible to have to strain to interact with my children; I felt like my humanity was slipping away and I was becoming a zombie.

Every time I travelled for business, it was worse, because moving across time zones would totally finish me off. Sometimes I'd wake up in the morning in some random hotel and I'd just say: 'Sod this,' and stay in bed.

I tried everything, from hypnotherapy to a sleep doctor, who referred me to a clinic, where they tried to force antidepressants on me. I thought: *No, I'm not depressed. This isn't right.*

I wasn't depressed; I was high-functioning, but short-tempered. I was getting through the days, but without sleep, you don't repair. And it had a very big knock-on effect on my confidence and on my ability to cope with stress. Suddenly I wasn't able to speak in public, which I have to do a lot, so I was really at my wits' end.

After about a year of this, I was on an evening out and met a friend of a friend. I began to tell him about my sleep problem and he said: 'Let me stop you there. This is what you've been through. This is how it started. This is what's happened. You've been here. You've tried that. That didn't work. And now you're taking sleeping pills every night.'

He was a Vedic meditation teacher, based in Paris, and he told me he dealt with this sort of stuff all the time and that I should definitely go try it.

When I went to see Will, he seemed remarkably confident that it would work. After all I'd been through, I really couldn't believe it would be that easy.

Within forty-eight hours of learning to meditate, my sleep problem had vanished. It was that quick; it was that powerful. I was suddenly feeling relaxed and calm. Meditation seemed like a very natural thing to do, and I loved it.

Being able to sleep felt like a miracle. I felt so grateful. If I had to rate it, I'd say my sleep pattern had been a two out of ten; meditation moved me to an eight. It had been agony before, and now I felt wonderful when I woke up in the morning.

I really feel as if I now have a tool for dealing with insomnia. There have been times since I started meditating when I've had the odd night of sleeplessness, but then I'm able to say: 'You know what? I've got the solution to this.' So I sit up, meditate, and then go straight back to sleep.

I haven't had to do that now for months. I feel so relieved. I also know that even if I don't get enough sleep, I can get the rest and repair I need because I can meditate there and then, and once more in the morning to get myself refreshed.

And that, of course, takes away the anxiety of not being able to sleep in the first place, so you go to bed more relaxed knowing you've got all the solutions in your back pocket.

Dealing with the sleep issue was the main positive effect of the meditation, but I use it as a tool for many other things now, especially for coping with stress and anxiety. I'm a guy that's quite impatient, moving a hundred miles an hour the whole time, and so I struggle to stay in the moment. I'm very aware of my limitations, and I'm always wanting to improve as a father, a husband and as a businessman.

As a father, I can say that I'm much more present. I feel those special moments with my kids a lot more, when you have a surge of overwhelming joy and it just hits you. Those moments of awareness have increased dramatically for me. I work from home, and if I've had a hard day, sometimes I'll hear the kids come back from school and I want to run downstairs and see them. Now I stop myself and think: *You know what, you can feel you're anxious; you can feel you're stressed – just go and meditate.* Then, afterwards, I can go and see them and be really present and full of love for them.

If they come upstairs anyway and interrupt, you can easily get back into it, because it doesn't require any focus. The kids come in and I'll say, 'Dad's meditating. Just give me a minute,' and they'll go. It's very easy to roll back into.

My wife says I'm a lot calmer, which is really nice to hear, and I'm so glad she's getting to benefit from it too. One of our kids has just been diagnosed with ADHD, and that's a whole other ball game of parental challenges, yet I feel like this is giving me the tools to help me deal with that. I very rarely get to boiling point now, which is a huge relief for everyone.

As for business – well, I'm far more in tune with other people. I can read others a lot better, and that helps with business as well as my relationships with colleagues. I think it's about stepping back and not constantly looking about. That's the key: taking it down a notch. It's about connection; it's about presence. It's about being with someone when you're with them. And when you feel yourself drifting, you're able to go: 'Now hang on a minute . . .' Meditating gives you a lot in terms of the enhancement of your connection with that person, and your emotional intelligence develops as well.

There's so many of us suffering from all sorts of mental health problems in this crazy world we're living in. My sister's been suffering from depression for years, and going to see Will to learn the meditation has been the only thing that's helped her. She's now completely over it. I wish I could say the same for my contemporaries, guys who are nearing their fifties. So many of them could use it. It's a very competitive world, and we're all suffering from these lifestyles that we've created for ourselves.

It ebbs and flows, of course. It's not as if every meditation is amazing, but certainly after every meditation I can say, 'I needed that,' and be truly grateful I found it.

Why Can't We Sleep?

David's experience is one that's common to many of us – lying there, mind whirring into the small hours, then staggering about the next day, 'high-functioning but short-tempered', as he puts it. He was suffering from a fairly acute level of stress, and for good reason. Running an international business while looking after two young children, one of whom has a behavioural disorder, was never going to be a walk in the park.

For someone like David, who had been living an adrenaline-fuelled life for decades, it's particularly hard to switch off. The wear and tear on your body is very significant when your adrenals are chronically activated by running on the hamster wheel of life, and, as you get older, your stamina decreases, which is why he and so many of his contemporaries are finding that their lifestyles are becoming a real challenge.

We all have our dramas in life, and to some extent we're all suffering from a chronic level of background stress because our nervous systems are struggling to adapt to all the energy and information that we're bombarded with every day.

When we go to bed at night, our brain detects that we are lying down, and it goes into rest and repair mode. It's then that it starts desperately trying to unload some of the over-stimulation we've experienced during the day. This stimulation is vented via electrical activity in the brain, causing our neurons to get excited, and this results in that all-too-familiar feeling of a whirring mind. And if your amygdala's been activated by any other stresses, you'll have lots of anxiety-inducing neuro-transmitters flooding your system – particularly between 2 and 6 a.m. – leading to those fretful early mornings.

What Happens When We Sleep?

Aside from the horrible frustration of insomnia, why is a good night's sleep so important? According to the NHS, most of us need around eight hours of sleep a night to function properly – but it's the quality that matters most. The NHS also warns that regular poor-quality sleep can put you at risk of developing serious medical conditions, affecting your body, mind, emotions and behaviour.

Put simply, you've got no chance of functioning at your best without sleep. So much is going on while you're getting those all-important ZZZs, so to miss out on this time is to be severely deprived.

As you sleep, you alternate between REM ('Rapid Eye Movement') and non-REM sleep. During REM sleep your eyes (as suggested by the name) move quickly in different directions, something you may have noticed if you've ever observed someone else sleeping – it can make it appear as though their eyelids are flickering. This is when dreams typically happen, because your brain is active, and your unconscious is busy creating weird and wonderful imagery.

Non-REM sleep has four phases, and you'll go through each phase during a typical ninety-minute 'sleep cycle', and ideally you would experience between four and six of them in a good night of shut-eye.

- Phase 1 usually occurs between sleep and wakefulness. Your eyes are closed but you could easily be woken up. This is a transition stage where brainwaves and muscle activity begin to slow down, getting ready for the next stage.
- Phase 2 is what's known as light sleep, when your body prepares for deep sleep by slowing your heart rate and dropping your body temperature. Muscles relax further and electrical activity in the brain reduces. We spend around half of a night's sleep in this state, and we return to it several times throughout the night.
- Phases 3 and 4 are called slow-wave sleep (or deep sleep), and are the most restful forms of sleep. Phase 3 oscillates between slow-wave delta brain patterns and faster frequencies. Phase 4 is almost exclusively delta. It's these phases which most restore the body, as we repair and regrow tissues, building bones and muscle. It also strengthens the immune system.

The balance between each sleep phase is important. REM sleep consolidates emotional information and, along with slow-wave, helps you to better retain perceptual information. The slow-wave, deep phases of the sleep cycle are also essential for rebooting all your physiological systems. This is why poor sleep quality can have a knock-on effect on immune function, digestive function, weight, the quality of your skin and memory.

However, it's much more nuanced than simply having up to six near identical sleep cycles. In the first two to three sleep cycles, we spend most of our time in non-REM sleep, whereas we spend most of the final two to three cycles in REM and shallow phases 1 and 2. The more non-REM sleep stages only tend to occur in the earlier part of the night (let's say 10 p.m.–3 a.m.), whereas after that we typically have more REM sleep. Could this be the reason a number of cultures have expressions like 'an hour before midnight is worth two after'? It's something that you can empirically test yourself. Have three days where you go to sleep at 10 p.m. and wake at 6 a.m., and have three days where you go to bed at midnight and wake at 8 a.m – if you're like the many people I know who've tried this out, you'll find the earlier routine far more refreshing!

Good-quality sleep has a significant effect on your brain's prefrontal cortex, which is responsible for processes such as judgement, planning, decision-making and problem-solving. The brain is incredibly energy-intensive, using approximately 20 per cent of your daily energy supplies. A night spent tossing and turning will leave you feeling foggy and drained because deep sleep is where this energy is restored.

Importantly for those of us with anxiety and depression, sleep is a time where you turn off the production of some stress hormones – particularly glucocorticoids. Not getting enough sleep makes you more susceptible to feeling stressed because there's an excess of steroid hormones floating around your system. Sleep deprivation also results in much higher levels of cortisol the next day, so you start off at a disadvantage. And on top of that, sleep disturbances interfere with your dopamine levels, so all in all it's a pretty grim picture when you don't spend enough time in the Land of Nod.

On top of all this, David was right when he talked about being able to get rest and repair, even when he isn't asleep. Rest is really vital, and I don't just mean when we're snuggled up and snoring, because it allows your body and mind to regenerate. The problem is that most of us simply don't know how to rest properly. We can stay in a chronically activated state all day long, and just don't have time for pure rest, except in emergencies, and then that's often only because we're forced to, because of illness. Many of us have experienced the sensation of having an hour or so to ourselves, sitting down, and then realising that our foot's tapping, or we can't stop thinking about the washing-up. We simply don't allow ourselves to relax.

Resting is an action, and is a vital part of being able to perform optimally and live life to the best of your abilities. I used to think to myself, *I can rest when I'm on holiday*, and I hear people echo that sentiment a lot. We work ourselves into the ground for most of the year, and then take a week off in the hope that this gives us an adequate amount of rest to get us through the next six to twelve months. We go on holiday and hopefully come back refreshed, but how much work do we come back to? How quickly do we feel like the holiday dividend is gone? Practising this form of meditation, on the other hand, is like going on a mini-break twice a day!

How Meditation Helps

The kind of meditation I teach will help you get this all-important rest in two ways. Firstly, it will help you sleep by working at the level of the nervous system, cleaning out all the noise, stimulation and daily stresses, and calming down those adrenals. The result is that your neurons will no longer be over-excited, so when you climb between the sheets, they won't be racing around – and neither will your mind. When you do finally nod off, it will induce a lot of slow-wave sleep – those all-important third and fourth stages of the sleep cycle during which the body regenerates and restores. So, your sleep quality will be vastly improved. As the NHS says, quality is more important than quantity, so don't worry about aiming for a specific number of hours. Trying to hit an arbitrary target is likely to stress you out more; just focus on what works for you.

Second, if you're meditating twice a day, then you're putting yourself into a state of deep rest. Even if you haven't had a good night's sleep, you'll be able to take whatever the day has to throw at you. A good twenty minutes of meditation can feel as regenerating and refreshing as several hours of sleep – and what's more, you don't have to be in bed to get it. You could be on the Tube or a bus, in the park or at your desk. One of the best things I've heard from so many people I've taught is that they've 'forgotten what it feels like to be tired'!

If you can make meditation a part of your regular evening ritual, then that's really going to calm you down before you go to bed. I actually recommend doing it before dinner if you can – that way you can enjoy a nice, energised evening as well as a restful slumber.

Phones are disastrous from a sleep point of view because the blue light they give off can inhibit the production of the sleep-inducing hormone melatonin and disrupt your circadian rhythms (the 24-hour internal clock that controls your sleep patterns, temperature, hormone regulation and appetite). They also emit electromagnetic radiation, which really isn't a good thing to have washing over you all through the night.

To make sure of a good night's sleep, create a digital-free haven in your bedroom. To help get your body's natural rhythms back on track, try not to look at screens (computer or phone) for the first and last hour of the day. This will also reduce anxiety levels – no more stressful emails from your boss to contend with as soon as you wake up or right before you hit the hay. Invest in an alarm clock (sunrise alarm clocks are brilliant) so that you can keep your phone out of the bedroom.

A YOGA *NIDRA* FOR SLEEP

Here's a simple awareness exercise from the wider Vedic toolkit that I often recommend for people who find it hard to get to sleep. It takes about seven to eight minutes.

Get into bed and lie on your back with your eyes closed, feet shoulder-width apart, arms a little away from your side with your palms facing upwards (this pose is known as *Shavasana* in yoga).

Take three deep breaths, letting out a good sigh as you exhale. Feel a wave of relaxation run down your body from the top of your head to the tips of your toes.

Now, without moving, gently take your awareness to the following body parts:

Right thumb, right index finger, right middle finger, right fourth finger, right little finger, whole of the right hand, lower right arm, upper right arm, right shoulder, right side of your chest, right hip, right upper leg, right knee, right lower leg, right foot, right toes.

Now be aware of the whole of the right side of your body.

Gradually move your awareness to your left thumb, left index finger, left middle finger, left fourth finger, left little finger, whole of the left hand, lower left arm, upper left arm, left shoulder, left side of your chest, left hip, left upper leg, left knee, left lower leg, left foot, left toes.

Now be aware of the whole of the left side of your body.

Now be aware of the whole of your body.

Be aware of the very thin layer of contact between your body and the bed, of the air temperature on any exposed part of the skin.

Finally, without opening your eyes, just be aware of the room around you. Picture the furniture, remember the textures and materials in your surrounding area.

If you have made it this far without falling asleep, keep your eyes shut and wait for a lovely deep slumber to envelop you.

Obviously, it's not easy to read this at the same time as trying to do it and fall asleep, so if you've got a partner who can read it aloud to you, great. If not, you can find a guided exercise on my website: www.theeffortlessmind.com.

Tackling Addiction

As you'll have read earlier, I've overindulged in the past, and many people who come to see me are smoking, drinking or taking drugs just that little bit (or a lot) more than they'd like. Sometimes they use meditation as a preventive measure, to treat addiction before it becomes a real problem. Others are in recovery, and want something to complement other addiction programmes that they're on.

The first thing I want to explain is how the brain responds to the activation of its pleasure pathways, and the role of reward mechanisms in all this. The neurotransmitter dopamine is a key factor in our sense of pleasure. If we lack dopamine stimulation, we feel unhappy and depressed, and this is often the case when we're stressed.

When something new triggers a pleasure sensation, we get a nice big hit of dopamine. After that, however, it's not so much the reward itself that triggers the dopamine release, but the *anticipation of reward* that gets the brain eagerly firing with expectation. This means that any thought of the stimulus will trigger an appetite for more – especially true if you're feeling a bit unhappy or unfulfilled.

If, due to the stresses and strains of life, we find ourselves with low levels of dopamine release, we're much more vulnerable to finding something dangerously delicious and falling into the cycle of dependency.

This cycle exists because, if we keep taking the substance that makes us feel good, triggering dopamine release, our dopamine receptors will turn down the volume on their sensitivity, otherwise the signals bombarding them would become overwhelming. At the same time, the brain will be tricked into responding to the overabundance of supply by turning down its own production of dopamine.

This leaves people in an ever-increasing spiral of wanting more of the thing that makes them feel good. Sooner or later, they need it to just feel 'normal', rather than euphoric. The lack of certainty, or even risk, surrounding said vices – 'I think I'll have enough cash; I think I'll be able to find a dealer; I don't think I'll get caught, I'm sure it will be all good' – can make them all the more addictive, adding to the thrill by creating an intensity to the expectation and subsequent dopamine release.

Interestingly, a history of stress (in the womb, or as a child) will make us much more susceptible to developing a dependency later in life.

Why? Firstly, stress will inhibit the production of many important neurochemicals, which will lead us to seek replacements from recreational substances and prescription medicines. Secondly, it makes us much more vulnerable to developing addiction by creating a greater contrast between how we felt before we took the drug/had the drink/played the video game and the lushness of the subsequent high. It also makes us more likely to keep administering until we've crossed the threshold of addiction.

That's why, if you're going to treat addiction, you need to reduce stress.

Before doing this, however, you need to take the first, most challenging, step of admitting you have a problem. Remember, too, that denying an addiction exists might not be a conscious choice you've made. When you consume intoxicants, they create cognitive distortions that twist your perception, as well as how you read situations and events, and the more damage we do to the prefrontal cortex of the brain (via stress or substance abuse), the more difficult it becomes to see and think clearly. Addiction also changes your brain function, so you find it easy to justify the addiction and the often anti-social behaviour it inspires. Think of the smokers you know who cling on to the fact that someone they heard about smoked all their lives and lived to a hundred. In their minds, that becomes the likely outcome for them too, even though all the evidence suggests otherwise. It's an amazing bit of neurological jiggery-pokery.

Dylan

'I'm not a man of willpower. But I haven't drunk since.'

Dylan didn't think he had a problem with drugs and alcohol, and that wasn't why he wanted to learn to meditate, but he later found that it really helped with that aspect of his life. People often come to see me without a specific issue they're trying to address; for them it's more that they have a feeling that things aren't right, or that they could be improved. They might not even be able to articulate what the problem is, but things begin to shift when they start doing this practice, and then, with the benefit of hindsight, issues become clearer.

It was very random how meditation came to me, or at least it seemed to me at the time. I was at my niece's second birthday party when one of my brother Alex's friends came up to me and said: 'I was thinking of you the other day.' He told me he'd been on a meditation course, and that the guy who had taught it was interesting and accessible, and he thought this might be something that might be up my street.

Now, I'd never spoken to him about anything like this, but I had been considering going on some sort of mindfulness course because I felt increasingly scatty, kind of disconnected. I'm the sole founder of a successful business, so my work's always been quite stressful. We've grown a lot over the past ten years and I employ about forty people. The novelty had now worn off a bit, and so I was starting to realise that it was perhaps a bit more stressful than I'd initially thought. Often, I'd get to the end of the day and someone would ask me, 'How was your day?', and I wouldn't know. It would take me a little while to think about what I'd done, and even then I didn't even necessarily know if it was a good day or a bad day. Did I achieve what I wanted? Did I even know what I wanted to achieve in the first place? Was I happy? Was I sad? It was all just kind of passing me by. It's remarkable how much we think we value life and then it just washes over us.

At that point, I was drinking a lot. I was smoking loads of marijuana and snorting a fairly obscene amount of cocaine – generally leading what I'd call a highly functioning debauched lifestyle, which is the most dangerous sort. When you're able to lead that life and manage it, you're in real trouble, because you feel sort of invincible.

If I'm honest, I was using the drugs and the drink partly as a general lifestyle choice, and partly because, as everyone says, it's rife in the industry that I work in. Actually, I've smoked weed for the majority of my adult life. I started just before I went to university, enjoyed it a lot, and pretty much did it most nights after that. Although I always wanted to cut down, always wanted to quit, it never quite happened.

I told Will a bit about the drink and drugs, but I don't think I was really admitting to anyone the extent of it, and actually it would be wrong for me to portray it as a situation that I was actively trying to get out of. Quitting the drugs

wasn't my objective because I didn't think it was a problem. I was enjoying myself, having fun – even if all those
nights blurred into one, or I couldn't remember them in the
first place.

On the first day of the course, I remember being suspicious
of the other people on it, and of Will. I was a bit uncomfortable, somewhat alienated and ill-prepared, but when
we did the first meditation, I did feel very still, the room
felt quieter, and I remember thinking that it was having a
significant impact.

Will was making a lot of claims of the benefits of meditation, and I have to be honest, I thought it was all a bit
far-fetched. When I got home and did some research, however, I was surprised to find that what he said was backed
up by science. I was particularly taken by the research using
MRI scans, which showed changes in brain patterns and also
the growth of grey matter. Irrefutable stuff.

After that, I started meditating. Soon after, though, I got
arrested.

I'd been out with some friends, we'd got drunk and were
all about to go home when instead we decided to buy some
drugs. I cycled off to see a dealer and bought a gram of
cocaine and a bag of weed. Then the police pulled me over.
They arrested me, and we went to the police station, where
I was put inside a cell.

They told me I'd be out in an hour and a half, and if I'm
honest, my thought process on hearing that was: *My dealer
will still be up in an hour and a half and I can just buy some more
when I get out.* I knew my friends would be gone, but I was
like: *Well, I can just do it on my own.* I'd been doing that more
and more. If I suddenly realised I had a Wednesday night
free, I'd just sit at home, snort a gram of coke, masturbate
and write in my diary.

Anyway, I didn't actually get out until 8.30 the next morning, and I had a meeting with a new client at 9.30, so I had to cycle home, shower, change and then get to work. It was a pretty tough meeting. I couldn't stop sweating and, obviously, I hadn't really slept.

While I was in the cell, however, I had meditated. When I walked out, I was filled with this strange sort of clarity. I knew then that I didn't really have a problem with cocaine – it was the alcohol. I'd have a drink, and then another, and then I'd be a bit excitable and all the inhibitions would come down. That's what I liked about it.

So, in a way, I was drinking because I knew that after a few pints I would make a call to get some drugs. I said to myself: 'Well, you've got to stop drinking then, if you want to have any significant chance of sorting this.'

I haven't drunk since.

It was probably the biggest change I've ever made in terms of my lifestyle as an adult, but I haven't struggled with it at all. I've never even been tempted. And I'm not a man of willpower. I fail a lot when it comes to the things that are good for me and my own wellbeing – especially when the motivation needs to come from a deep place of self-worth. I usually struggle, but with this choice, I didn't – I just never drank again. As a result, I never bought cocaine or took ecstasy again.

Now, was this because I had learned meditation prior to getting arrested? Because I meditated in the cell? I can't tell what impact or what correlation those things had on my increased ability to resist the temptation of alcohol; all I know is I haven't had a drink since.

I'll reiterate: I'm not a man of willpower; I'm not a man who's been able to keep going with his press-ups in the morning or his yoga and all the stuff that we guilt ourselves about. I struggle. But this was the biggest change I've made in my adult life, and it came shortly after a period when I had been meditating.

Do I meditate religiously? The answer is no. Has it impacted me? Absolutely. When I don't do it for a while, I get re-acclimatised to a certain level of stress and I operate within that. Then, when I go back to it again, I definitely feel the benefits. I feel stiller, calmer, much more mindful and in the moment, and there's a reduced reliance on the immediacy of my emotional response. And I've also noticed that when I stop, I feel worse than I would have done before because I've become used to feeling good. My sense of normal has shifted upwards. If I then stop meditating, I feel worse than my newly acquired baseline, and it gives me a kick up the arse to get back up to speed. I now think that what I was doing with the marijuana and the booze and the drugs was numbing myself to avoid the pain, and the lack of self-worth. The meditation instead opens you up to feeling more, and generally that's a really good thing, because it also helps you process it and deal with painful feelings and to feel the joy of life much more. But it's not always easy – sometimes numbness feels like the path of least resistance.

What I think I've taken from this is that, before, I was very much of the opinion that I was me, and everyone else was not me. I was fighting my way through life, playing a game of me versus the world – not necessarily in a combative way, but my perspective was very much of singularity: there was me, and there was other people. Becoming more in tune with myself, and, dare I say it, more spiritual, I've been able to transcend that idea of myself as an isolated entity in this universe. It's made me see that, actually, far from being isolated, I'm very much connected. I'm part of a living, breathing ecosystem that is much bigger and more intertwined than it first appears. With that awareness (that I'm not just me and you're not just you) comes a sense that we're all one – with each other, with nature, with the universe.

I feel spirituality is an increased awareness of what love is, and I don't mean romantic love. I think it's that journey to realising that we're all interrelated and interconnected and part of one thing. And in that, and in our acceptance of and responses to other people's pain, you allow yourself to unlock a lot of love, and to project that love out. I'd say that transcendence is the acceptance that we're all from the same place, which means that you can give a lot more compassion and kindness to people. And to yourself, if you'll allow it. **9**

A NOTE ON MINDFULNESS

Many of my students come to me having tried mindfulness, or, like Dylan, thinking that's what I'm going to teach them. The aim of mindfulness is to be as aware of the present moment as possible. When people consistently practise mindfulness, it works well, but I think it tends to be a better fit for the monks on mountain tops that it was originally designed for. Monks don't need to exercise their analytical minds or flex their concentration capabilities too much outside of meditation, whereas the average, everyday person in the Western world has a brain filled with tasks, lists and focused activities. The last thing many people want is another focus-based activity.

The Vedic-inspired meditation I teach will deliver much enhanced present-moment awareness – in fact it's been shown to deliver greater present-moment awareness than any other technique! – and the beauty of it is that it enables your brain to relax into a coherent state rather than focus into one. This not only makes it much easier, but it also elicits more wide-ranging coherence within the brain and the nervous system. The personalised sounds allow the brain to truly switch off, reboot and top up with energy, which means the body is able to rest much more profoundly than when you use concentration-based techniques. It takes you to such a deep part of yourself that all of you is nourished by it – bringing about heartfulness, soulfulness, mindfulness and wholeness.

So, if you've tried mindfulness and it didn't work for you, give this form of meditation a go! You will be surprised by just how easy it is. And if you've tried mindfulness and liked it, but feel there could be more, it may be worth exploring Vedic-inspired meditation to see how much further you can take your practice.

Low Self-Esteem

One of the things that jumps out at me from Dylan's story is his comment: 'I fail a lot when it comes to the things that are good for me and my own wellbeing – especially when the motivation needs to come from a deep place of self-worth.'

Possibly the most surprising thing I've discovered since becoming a teacher is how ubiquitous low self-esteem is. So many of the people I encounter have it. This discovery made me think. I realised that I used to have it too, and it was low self-worth that drove a lot of my self-destructive behaviours. On a day-to-day level, it was why I found myself not wanting to pick up the phone to people – I'd much rather send an email. It was behind how I acted with the opposite sex, with my friends, and most certainly with my family. What was interesting is that no one who knew me would have had any idea that I had low self-esteem. After all, I was the guy who was throwing the parties, getting drunk and telling jokes. Why on earth would I have any self-esteem issues? But I did.

So, where do these issues come from? It could be because we had parents who made us feel that we didn't have as much of their love or attention as we wanted. Many people carry this idea that they're not worthy of love for the rest of their lives. Often, the way that their parents communicated with them has something to do with it: rather than being told that they've *done* a bad thing, they're told that they *are* a bad child. There's no separation between the event and their self-definition, because as children we believe what our parents tell us.

Our schooling is all about a very narrow set of parameters for achieving success, instilling in us the idea that we're not good enough unless we're top of the class. Later on, as teenagers, we start taking an interest in other people, and want to have relationships with them. But no one really teaches you how to do it in a healthy way, and so we end up experiencing random collisions with people that often don't turn out so well. If we've already got these storylines in our head about not being good enough – or of being bad, or a failure – then we take those into our relationships, creating a self-fulfilling prophecy. Our baggage and insecurity can prompt us to sabotage relationships or push other people away, and this only reinforces the idea that we aren't good enough when we're left alone again. Sometimes we're even dimly aware that this is what's happening, but we are unable to stop ourselves.

Dylan very clearly had self-esteem issues and, on talking to him more, it soon became apparent that some of them revolved around his elder brother, Alex, whose friend had told Dylan about meditation. I thought he might have an inferiority complex when it came to his brother, but I wasn't sure if it was because Alex was very successful in his career (although so was

Dylan) or – more likely in my opinion – it came from something that had happened when they were very young. Maybe his brother was the more 'successful' one in terms of getting attention from their parents, which then created a narrative within Dylan that caused him to feel unworthy. Then, like so many people with self-esteem issues, he sought relief or release through sleeping with lots of women (another of his former strategies that we discussed) and using cannabis, cocaine and alcohol. It's all about suppressing the pain. Alcohol is an intoxicant that helps to temporarily liberate you; cannabinoids, as I discussed in relation to Arjun, make you forget pain; and amphetamines cause you to not really care. Sex is a great distraction, and offers a fleeting kind of acceptance – even if this often goes hand-in-hand with plenty of rejection.

Lots of us have numbing strategies that we use to avoid feeling pain, emotion, trauma, discomfort or shame. But whenever we use avoidance, distraction or disassociation as a strategy, we also numb ourselves from who we really are – and then we wonder why we feel less like ourselves as time goes by. Numbing is a two-way street: you numb the positive as well as the negative. It provides short-term relief, but long-term grief, because we eventually find ourselves mourning the loss of self.

Dylan is a very successful guy, and one of the things that's driven him is a desire to be accepted and loved. The problem was that he didn't love himself. Happily, I saw a definite shift in him over the first year to eighteen months of learning, during which time he did start to love himself, and value his decisions. His sense of self, and worth, were quickly coming from an internal place rather than external stimulants or sexual conquests. I was so glad to see this, because he's a really fun, intelligent guy who's not afraid to take risks. He's now learning to live with his own vulnerabilities, and that's going to make him the strongest, most well-rounded person he can be.

The Vedic method can give people like Dylan a practical tool for getting out of the cycle of addiction. Although we don't have any control over the things that happened when we were children, we do, as adults, through techniques like this form of meditation, have the power to change how we feel about them, so we're not forever stuck in victim mode. And once that happens we can reframe how we understand ourselves, our life, and the people in it.

How Meditation Helps with Addiction

Dylan started off by talking about drugs and alcohol, and ended up by talking about compassion and love. I don't think that's a coincidence. On the spiritual level, addiction can ultimately be viewed as a state of consciousness (more on this later).

On the physical level, one of the causal factors of substance abuse is a super-agitated nervous system, caused by high levels of anxiety and a hugely overactive mind. Sometimes these stem from trauma; other times, it appears to be the result of an accumulation of factors. As Dylan says, you can either numb this agitation through drugs or alcohol or soothe it with meditation. By doing the latter, you reduce anxiety, calm your body and clear out all the busyness in your mind.

I remember reading an interview with the musician Moby, who put it very well: 'One reason I drank was that my brain would get to a level of agitation, and one thing that was incredibly effective at diminishing the agitation was alcohol . . . [meditation] is an effective tool at diminishing agitation and because it was agitation that often led me to drink, its lack – the lack of restlessness – makes me less inclined to do so.'

The key to overcoming addiction is when the nervous system is able to break through chronic, ingrained activation – the one where your leg really starts to shake with nervous energy, or you start playing with your hands or your nails, or you compulsively check your phone. If you can break through that stage and let it really, genuinely rest, the nervous system will spontaneously start removing the memories of pain, stress and trauma and these emotional memories will begin to lose their hold over you. Once this happens, you're much less likely to trigger a craving for dopamine-induced joy.

Other sorts of memories will go, too. As soon as an addict is faced with a trigger that the body remembers as being intimately related to the process of scoring a hit (like a particular situation, person or feeling), their subconscious is consumed with a thirst that can only be quenched with their substance of choice. This is why someone who hasn't smoked for years, and now barely even thinks about it most of the time, can suddenly crave a cigarette when they have a glass of wine. Meditation will wash away the emotional charge of those environmental triggers that would otherwise cause us to self-sabotage and self-destruct.

It will also help the brain and body's self-repair mechanisms to kick in. The greater levels of rest that meditation brings, as well as the reduction in cortisol levels, help the cells and tissues to regenerate and new neural networks to form. It also catalyses the reactivation of your prefrontal cortex, which makes you more rational and less reckless and impulsive. In this mindset, it becomes much easier to make good decisions and avoid the destructive path of least resistance.

The personalised sounds we use help develop resilience and robustness within your nervous system, so that the outside world doesn't seem so overwhelming without the numbing effects of a drug. It also initiates a lot of endorphin release, which makes you feel good naturally. The deep state that meditation takes you into – a state of transcendence (which I'll go into later, but, in a nutshell, means going beyond your mind and everything else into a place of bliss) – is much more sustainable than what you might have experienced through drink or drugs, and one that you come out of feeling uplifted rather than hungover.

Going deeper still, the Vedic understanding of dependency issues is that they are, at their root, a symptom of an addictive state of consciousness, or what some might call 'an addictive personality'. That's why addiction is so hard to beat; the trait is so deeply ingrained in our consciousness that it can almost be seen as a part of who we are. It's as fundamental as that. You may be able to beat one addiction, but you just end up switching to another, whether that be from cocaine to cigarettes, or sex, or shopping. You might have progressed to a slightly less destructive addiction (and there's no denying that's a huge achievement), but you're still carrying that 'addictive personality' – that part of you that always craves something after the first taste.

When you systematically start experiencing transcendence, as you do with deep forms of meditation, your addictive personality begins to dissolve. The cognitive distortions that developed as a result of the addiction will begin to lessen, and in their place comes an ability to interact with people in a much more fulfilling way. Patterns of self-sabotage begin to diminish and you tune into who you really are and what you're about. After a few years, you find yourself feeling significantly healed, and this is noticeable in the lack of addictive traits in your life. To explain why, I'm going to use a metaphor.

Think of a painting, covered in layers of dust and dirt that have accumulated over decades. A restorer comes along and, little by little, very gently starts to clean away those layers, dissolving the dirt to reveal the true beauty of what's underneath. Meditation means that you can be your own agent of restoration, taking your individual brushstroke of consciousness and merging it with all the other brushstrokes of consciousness to reveal the whole picture. Memory is such a powerful force within the human physiology that it holds onto your patterns until they are released. If you keep dipping your brush into the turpentine, your patterns will start dissolving, even the strongly addictive ones – the stains that are really hard to budge. So, in addition to reducing the primary addiction, meditation clears away the addictive state of consciousness, or addictive personality.

The Statistics

If you're more into statistics than metaphors, here's some scientific evidence. Harvard-trained psychologist Charles Alexander reviewed nineteen studies of meditation over a 22-year period. In seventeen of those studies there were significant reductions in the use of cigarettes, alcohol and recreational drugs when people practised meditation using personalised sounds.

An eighteen-month study of alcoholics showed that those who meditated had an abstinence rate of 65 per cent, which was far superior to standard counselling (25 per cent). When it comes to the tendency to overthink and over-worry about things, meditation using personalised sounds has been shown to be 250 per cent more effective at reducing anxiety than any other methodology.

As a final point, I'd like to say plain and simple that it's always worth engaging in a twelve-step programme as well, because that is a fabulous support aid for people with dependency issues, helping them to acknowledge that they are in recovery, and to feel part of a community. It also helps you to maintain vigilance against complacency, which can often trip people up as they journey through recovery. There's never any need to take an exclusive approach to getting better.

Getting Your Digestion in a Groove

Getting Your Digestion Into Shape

To me, digestion is one of the most fascinating processes of the human body. From an Ayurvedic point of view, if you get someone's digestive system functioning at its absolute best, then they're going to be a supremely healthy human being. But people have all sorts of problems with their digestion these days, including IBS (Irritable Bowel Syndrome), acid reflux, food intolerances, constipation, indigestion, peptic ulcers and ulcerative colitis, to name just a few.

What's the reason for this? Yes, you guessed it. It's our old enemy: stress. Digestion uses up a lot of energy, so when our bodies are in the midst of a fight or flight response, our digestion shuts down so that energy can be diverted elsewhere. During an emergency situation, we don't need to worry about breaking down our lunch – we're much better off using that energy elsewhere to make sure we don't end up getting digested ourselves!

When we're stressed, we don't produce as much saliva. This is an issue, because saliva contains amylase, which helps to break down the food that we're chewing on. We also tend to chew and swallow more quickly, making it harder for the stomach to continue that process of digestion. Once the food arrives in the stomach, it's processed both mechanically (banged against the stomach walls to break it down further) and chemically, whereby a series of powerful acids and enzymes help to extract nutrients. Stress will disturb these processes, inhibiting the release of digestive juices, which can result in issues like ulcers, acid reflux and IBS.

Even when there's no acute symptoms or pain, if you have lots of gurgly gas, funky farts or smelly stools, you're unlikely to be digesting your food properly. And that means you won't be able to metabolise most of the nutrients the food contains. So, however healthy your diet is, you won't be getting much of the goodness out of it. If your digestion is up the spout, that healthy lunchtime salad will be transformed into a pile of toxic mush.

It's definitely worth noting how your body's digestive rhythms are functioning and taking corrective action. Meditation is incredibly effective when it comes to helping with digestive disorders because of the way that it allows us to deal with stress. (I'd always suggest consulting a doctor as well.)

Mia

'I basically did an experiment.'

Mia had been suffering from IBS for a long time before she came to see me. In fact, it had developed into something more severe – a condition known as IBD (Irritable Bowel Disease). The tricky thing for Mia, and many like her, is that scientists and doctors don't know what causes IBS and IBD. They know that many people report a similar set of symptoms, but from a medical point of view it's extremely difficult to pinpoint the source of these issues. Troubling disorders like IBS and chronic fatigue syndrome are simply not fully understood.

IBS appears to occur more frequently in women (although it may be that men are just more reluctant to report their symptoms) and can cause discomfort, pain and embarrassment.

However, doctors are rarely able to offer a comprehensive solution, because there doesn't seem to be a reason for the symptoms. Irritable Bowel Syndrome is in many ways simply an umbrella term for digestive issues that can't be attributed to any physical damage or disorder.

Like many 'invisible' illnesses (chronic conditions for which there are no outward signs of distress), IBS and IBD can be underestimated, trivialised and even mocked. But try telling the tens of millions of people around the world who have these disorders that they're exaggerating, and they'd be likely to have a few choice words to say to you . . .

Despite the lack of an identifiable cause, there are strong suggestions that IBS and IBD are correlated with stress. In some prolonged cases, doctors attribute the disorder to a 'worried bowel' and will prescribe counselling. Meditation, however, is the best stress reduction and digestive wellness programme that I'm aware of. The largest ever study carried out on meditation measured the medical records of 2,000 people using this technique versus a control group. The meditators demonstrated a 51 per cent reduction in incidence of gastrointestinal disorders, which I think we can all agree is pretty compelling.

Before I get into the nitty-gritty of how meditation helps, let's hear what happened to Mia.

> I used to have really bad stomach issues. I had IBS, which is what they tell you when they can't find anything else wrong with you. I went to the GP for four or five years, and then I stopped because they just kept telling me there was nothing they could do.
>
> I was generally fit and healthy, but I had excruciating stomach pain. It was like really, really severe menstrual cramps across my lower abdomen. It would fluctuate, but it was always there. I'd been given prescription painkillers,

using them if I couldn't sleep on a work night, until it got to the point where I was controlling the pain with them.

A friend told me he'd started meditating, and he thought that I should give it a go for my stomach issues. Now, I'm a scientist, a medical statistician, so I was naturally very sceptical. I quizzed him and quizzed him but he just said: 'You should go.' He gave me the details and I went along to a talk. I did think it sounded interesting, but I didn't think I had time to actually learn.

Then I got salmonella, which caused awful pains in my stomach, along with fever and blood in my stool. I was doubled over in acute pain every day, and so they referred me to hospital for a colonoscopy.

It took three months to get an appointment. In that time, I lost a lot of muscle tone. I'd been so fit – playing hockey at a national level, cycling to work every day – and now it had got to the point where all I could do was go swimming once a week and cycle into work one day then leave my bike there and cycle home the next. I was so frustrated with life.

At the colonoscopy, the consultant said: 'Look, we'll wait for the test results, but it really looks like there's nothing going on. We're going to refer you to the IBS clinic for management.' And at that stage, I was like: *Where is that meditation course?!* This was two years after my friend had first told me about it.

So, I decided to take the course. And I basically did an experiment. I deliberately didn't change anything about how I ate, or anything else about my daily life – not my work, or my exercise regime. Clinical trials are part of what I do. I look at data and make inferences about how things are being used in the real world. I used to do it for intensive care in public health and now I do it for pharmaceutical companies. You know how on a pack of pills it might say something like 'these side effects happen to one in 1,000 patients'? It's people like me who compile those figures, so I knew how to conduct an experiment.

I thought to myself: *If this is going to work, it will take weeks, if not months.* Within just three days, however, the pain had calmed down.

I didn't believe it at first. It was like: *Okay, sometimes your body pretends it's going to calm down.* But my stomach had gone from excruciating pain every few hours to excruciating pain every second day, so rather than multiple times a day, I only had it three times that first week. Then a week went by, and the second week went by, and I thought: *Wow, this is really working.*

That was the first thing I noticed. I was having bowel movements that were regular and normal, which was fantastic, then I found that it was doing big things for my sleep. It was just phenomenal. It no longer took me two hours to get to sleep every night. My eating got so much better too. Now I definitely eat less fat and sugar, less processed food. I used to get colds and flu a lot, and that stopped. My acne, which was really bad, got better. My skin improved in general, as well as my hair and nails, which is funny because I remember Will telling us this would happen, and I totally didn't believe him!

And then the effects spread, moving beyond the physical. I'd never realised how dismissive I was of people, but I started to become aware of how I treated others. I mentioned it to my family and my friends, and everyone was like: 'Yes!' My brother said: 'Mia, the number of times we've had to apologise to shop assistants for how you've treated them . . .' I had no idea I was like that.

People in work have probably noticed that I definitely strop less, whereas before that was one of my instinctive go-tos. I didn't think I was stressed at work until my old

manager gave me some stuff to read about time management, and slipped in a sheet about recognising stress in
yourself. He casually brought it up two weeks later at our
line management meeting and I said to him: 'I think I'm
stressed.' He said something along the lines of: 'Well, now
that you realise it, we can deal with it.' It's so strange that I
hadn't seen it before.

I think I'd suffered mildly from depression for years,
but never medicated, never really talked to any health pro-
fessionals about it, and I think it's really helped with that.
Meditation is really steadying in that way; I'm able to recognise myself going towards that space much more easily, just
to talk about it. In general, I'm able to deal with emotional
situations so much better. I've had some pretty epic emotional rollercoasters in the past year, and I've just accepted
that there are going to be days when I'm going to feel shit,
but it's fine. I don't panic and think it's going to be for ever.
It's about not wallowing in that feeling, but acknowledging
it, and working through it, and not allowing it to dictate your
day. That's been a huge plus.

The IBS clinic was quite happy to discharge me, and noted
that it was as a result of meditation. I have clinical friends
that I've spoken to about it, and from their point of view,
they're not surprised that a more holistic approach, for want
of a better expression, works. Sometimes it works better in
conjunction with medication, sometimes not. I don't think
the medical world is completely against that idea.

You might have thought that my scientific mind might
sometimes feel at odds with the meditation. Or that I might
mind having something work when I don't quite know how
it works, but actually, it's created an interest in me to do
research, because I want to know if I'm an anomaly, or if
this is what happens when you put meditation in the world

at large. For me, it's something unexplained, so I want to see if the answer can be found. I'm working with Will to put together the criteria, then we'll conduct a study that's wide-ranging and in-depth enough to use as a basis for recommendations that we can make to the medical profession.

So, yes, I've gone from being this complete sceptic, waiting two years to do it, to conducting research in the area. My friends think it's absolutely hilarious – literally, of all the people, I was the biggest sceptic. But now I'm actually really excited about my little meditation journey. I'm like: *What's going to happen next?*

Restoring Digestive Balance

Let me explain what starting to meditate will have done to Mia's body and mind to restore balance. Through bringing down her stress levels (which she perhaps wasn't aware were so high), it will have:

- Helped restore biochemical balance to her digestive fluids, resulting in a fuller complement of hormones to make sure the different digestive players could do their bit.
- Brought blood flow back to the gut area so nutrients could be distributed, and waste disposal processes be fully active.
- Aided repair of damaged tissues and cells so that they could function correctly and stop causing her so much pain.
- Worked on ensuring that she didn't respond as automatically to psychological stressors so that the driving force behind compromised digestive functioning was calmed to a much more manageable level.

Another effect of the meditation that Mia noticed was that her eating habits changed. She could feel when she'd eaten enough, so she didn't overeat. Meditation tends to give you more of a refined palette and, by clearing through those blockages in your nervous system, means you're able to understand what your body wants in the way of nutrients. Because you're dealing better with stress, you're less likely to be reaching for fatty, sugary food, which is what your body craves under chronic or intermittent stress. You don't have to be a rocket scientist to figure out that if you avoid putting so much processed stuff into your belly, your digestive tract is going to be healthier.

If you have great digestion, then you're going to extract every worthwhile vitamin, mineral and nutrient out of the food that you eat. You won't create unnecessary toxicity, and waste products will be eliminated easily, rather than getting stuck and being absorbed into your system.

Digestion and Ayurveda

Ayurveda really recognises the importance of food, and has a very sophisticated understanding of how the combination of different ingredients has an enormous influence on our bodies. Ayurveda approaches health in a very holistic way, and focuses on creating positive health as well as treating disease. It also emphasises the role of consciousness in maintaining good health. The approach is very different to the Western method of simply using one ingredient or chemical to 'solve' a physical or psychological issue, such as taking artificial serotonin for depression or salicylic acid to help with a headache.

Here's an example: proponents of Ayurveda have known for thousands of years that if you suffer from various aches, pains or fevers, then crushed willow bark will sort you out. The ancient Egyptians and Chinese also used it, and Hippocrates often prescribed it for headaches. Then, in 1897, a Western scientist realised that the anti-inflammatory agent salicin was the active ingredient in the bark. Very quickly, the ingredient was isolated and synthesised as acetylsalicylic acid, which was artificially manufactured, put into pills and marketed as aspirin.

However, what's not found in aspirin are all the other ingredients in willow that go along with salicin. Unlike aspirin, you can take as much willow bark tincture as you like and it won't hurt you. If you overdose on the synthesised aspirin, however, you'll have adverse reactions such as stomach bleeding or gastric ulcers. That's because, throughout millions of years of evolution, nature has developed as a solution to the intricate interaction between living species, but by taking aspirin we're ingesting the isolated ingredient without all those other buffering ingredients that nature provides to deliver the most holistically beneficial outcomes. It's as if we've seen a play, identified the lead character, then decided that the performance would be better without any of the supporting cast. The result is usually a lot less impressive, and we'd soon get overwhelmed by the constant monologuing.

We live in a culture of active ingredient mentality, whereby our thinking is largely confined to cause and effect. Doctors and scientists tend to isolate the cause of anything negative and then address it as a solitary issue, which so often does not represent the whole picture. The Ayurvedic approach, like this form of meditation, is *all* about the whole picture – mind, body and spirit. It would suggest that if we can just tap into our body's natural creative intelligence and give it the resources it needs to find balance, it will allocate its own chemical resources in a way that is superior to anything the pharmaceutical giants can give us, because we have the world's greatest pharmacy right inside us all, regulated by the neurotransmitters in our brains.

Most medical interventions by Western pharmaceuticals or

surgery are designed to make symptoms go away. The Eastern worldview, on the other hand, is much more about looking at what's causing those symptoms in the first place. Rather than waiting until your body tells you it's crunch time and then having to spend a lot of time, energy and money digging yourself out of a hole, why not just develop a simple daily meditation routine – the equivalent of brushing your teeth – which will create solid foundations to prevent you from getting into that situation in the first place?

I'm massively excited about the research that Mia's doing with us. There's so much more to discover. For example, did you know that 90–95 per cent of your happy hormone serotonin is produced in your gut? There may have been a very strong link between Mia's depression and her sub-optimal digestion.

Ayurveda is a fascinating subject, and a much bigger one than we can go into here. For those of you who are interested, I've given a list of further reading at the end of this book.

A SECOND BRAIN

We now know that because the microbiome has so much DNA within its 100 trillion bacteria, it may well have a significant impact on how you're operating epigenetically (how your inherited genes can express themselves differently). So, all of a sudden, digestion isn't about just extracting kilojoules from carbs - it's the engine of our entire experience!

As the Vedic civilisation understood thousands of years ago, we now know that we actually have loads of neurons in the intestinal tract (400-600 million). That's where having a 'gut feeling' comes from. And it's also one of the reasons eating a greasy burger makes you feel rubbish - because it's basically like shovelling rubbish into your (second) brain.

Vedic-inspired meditation can help you be much more in tune with the needs of your body and mind, and develop a strong and healthy relationship between the two. So much in life hinges on relationships that work well, and thrive. In our next section, we're going to look at exactly that, with tips on how to make those all-important connections with the people around us work as well as they possibly can.

RELATIONSHIPS

Our relationships are at the core of our lives. Whether they're shared with partners, friends, family, children or parents, improving them is something that the vast majority of my students want to do. Even many of the high-flyers who initially suggest they're coming for work reasons usually confess at some point that they're having a few issues with their partner or their kids, and ask if there's anything they can do about that. Everyone wants to know how to enhance their relationships at home, because, as I know only too well, when that side of your life is out of kilter, everything else starts going wrong too.

Romantic Relationships

Love: the most captivating, enchanting and compelling force we can experience in life. That magical, barely explainable feeling of joy at the mere presence of another human being, combined with a belief that no one as wonderful and beautiful as them has ever lived. Love has been the inspiration for some of the greatest songs, books, poetry and movies ever produced. It's a glorious thing, and when it's at its best, it opens us up to human experience in a way that nothing else can.

Sadly, many relationships break down at some point, or stumble on longer than they should, making both parties unhappy, and I'd like to look at why that is. One of the answers from the Vedic point of view is that we live in a world in which many people were brought up by stressed parents, and who are now stressed themselves, struggling to get by under the strain of life in the twenty-first century. This often leads to neediness. So few of us are truly content within ourselves, and if we have needs that weren't met by our parents when we were growing up, we carry this want and disappointment with us into adulthood. We all have our insecurities, our need to be reassured, our hang-ups about body image – and often we look for a solution not in ourselves, but through the conduit of a partner who's magically going to make us feel okay. If we haven't found fulfilment inside, on our own terms, then while it is easy to *take* love and use it to shore up our shaky sense of self, we will find it very difficult to *give* truly unconditional love to others.

If one or both of you are in this situation, there's going to be trouble. This happens an awful lot, and I doubt there are many people out there who don't have some experience of it. The *raison d'être* for many relationships comes from a place of pain, stress and trauma, and the desire to move beyond those things without first addressing the core issues that are at the heart of them.

The simple fact is that your partner isn't always going to be able to meet your needs, because they've got their own life full of their own pressures and stress. When they inevitably fail to meet your needs, you feel hurt. You find yourself offended by the fact that they don't hear you; they don't understand you; they don't put you first. It goes back to the baby not being heard, to the child whose father was always reading the newspaper instead of giving them attention. When your partner is exhibiting the same behaviour – watching the TV or checking social media rather than listening to what you are saying – you find yourself thinking, *Well, sod you then*, and you start to withdraw.

Equally, you might be in a relationship because you're looking for someone to distract you from looking inwards. Some people bounce from one partner to the next for this very reason. Others simply use the fantasy of meeting Mr or Mrs Right as a means of ignoring an inconvenient truth – that they don't yet feel whole inside themselves. We can, in the early days, project an unachievable ideal onto our partners, and feel immense disappointment when they inevitably don't live up to this impossible promise.

If you combine this with the stresses of life, where bills have to be paid and endless daily tasks taken care of, then as the relationship goes on, things can begin to get on top of you. All those glorious love chemicals – oxytocin, serotonin, dopamine – become less prevalent, and in their place come the stress chemicals – adrenaline, cortisol and noradrenaline. You find yourself more on edge, worrying and fretting, sleeping badly and snapping at your partner, who's likely tired and stressed themselves.

The result is a love that's often smothered by a deluge of petty demands and grievances, blown out of all proportion by the background of stress that so many of us live with. And once we're clouded by resentment or complacency, we stop viewing our partner as a full and separate human being, and at an unconscious level may begin to see them as an inconvenient or irritating appendage to our own lives. It's from this place that the more serious and hurtful neglect in a once devoted, tender partnership can take place.

Does any of this sound familiar? I appreciate it all sounds a bit doom and gloom, and what I've just said might be a (slightly harsh!) generalisation, but if we're being honest with ourselves, these patterns are very common in many of our relationships, even if for the most part they are ticking over okay. And yet relationships offer us such amazing opportunities for love, laughter, learning and shared experience, so surely we want to make them the best they can possibly be? If we can learn to recognise these unhealed aspects of ourselves, and grow into more well-rounded, fully functional human beings, then we can offer a love that is much deeper and much more uplifting, both to ourselves and to others. We can begin to experience the fullness of a love that is unconditional, rather than needy, and this is where this form of meditation can be of such immense value to each and every one of us.

Using Meditation to Boost Your Relationships

It's simply impossible to spend most of your time with someone and never get wound up by something they do, at which point your less than pleasant side can emerge. You may snap at your partner for making an honest mistake, and they may push away any later attempts to make up because they're still annoyed with you. In the end, the atmosphere can get a bit toxic.

A daily meditation practice can help with this situation. By calming down your overactive amygdala, and pulling back that hair-trigger fight or flight mechanism, you become less reactive and aggressive. Your moods are calmer and more balanced, and you won't fly off the handle over silly little things. The parasympathetic nervous system, which acts as a brake and calms everything down, is activated, and you become much more relaxed. When your system is balanced, you're calmer, more resilient and more loving. This means your past traumas don't infect the present moment – or at least not as much as they did before – and you become less needy. This form of meditation is all about finding fulfilment from within, having accepted that trying to get it from outside sources or other people is unsustainable.

As I've mentioned before, we have two sides to our brain. The right hemisphere processes information by looking at the big picture. It contextualises, and results in collegiate and collaborative behaviours; it is emotionally intelligent. The left hemisphere, on the other hand, has a fixed narrative. It's focused and intrinsically competitive; it's task dominant. It can and does work to the exclusion of the right side, and the common good. EEG scans show that Vedic-inspired meditation increases the connectivity of the brain, allowing you to be more in touch with everything you're thinking and feeling. You can find new ways to express your thoughts and feelings, in an easy-to-understand and articulate way. You begin to be able to communicate with greater emotional intelligence and articulacy, rather than just talking about trivial things, ultimately giving you greater capacity to love.

On top of this, enhanced activity in the prefrontal cortex gives you increased access to empathy and compassion. With these feelings brought to the fore, you'll have a much better chance of understanding why the people around you are behaving the way they are. This will allow you to forge deeper and more positive connections, in spite of your (and their) imperfections. When you're no longer locked into self-interest mode, you can happily put other people's needs before your own. It also makes you more aware of yourself and of others. You're more likely to be conscious of other people's needs, and of when you might be upsetting someone, so you can nourish that relationship with what it needs at that moment, rather than just doing what suits you, or what has simply become habit.

All this will stimulate more positive emotion, make you feel more creatively expressive and will give you the physical, mental and emotional energy needed to be able to invest in the relationship on a regular basis. (This is vastly preferable to coming home knackered from work and needing to distance yourself from your partner.) You'll go from just taking what you need from the relationship to feeding it what *it* needs; nurturing it, rather than treating it as a means of transaction.

These benefits will apply to *all* your relationships, not just romantic ones. Empathy, compassion and good communication are the cornerstones of every great relationship, whether that's with partners, children, parents, friends or colleagues. Developing these qualities is something we can all benefit from.

FOCUSING ON THE GOOD

If you're going through tough times in your relationship, here's a tip for taking the edge off things.

Before you start to get truly angry with the other person, try to focus on one good thing about them. It might be that they have nice eyes, or that they're always kind to children, or that they're a great cook, or that the way they're dressed today is lovely. It doesn't matter what it is; the important thing is to focus on that good quality.

Just that simple action will change your body language, making you less threatening to the other person, and therefore lessen the potential for conflict. It'll also distract you from whatever negative thing you were thinking about them and help to diffuse the situation. Win-win!

Sexing Things Up

As a society, we seem to talk about sex all the time, while simultaneously not talking about it at all. We really are quite bad at communicating with each other about 'the facts of life' (as your grandmother might put it). We've developed so many insecurities, bad attitudes and impossible expectations around the issue that we have a lot of hang-ups when it comes to our sex lives. In our Western culture, sexual imagery is ubiquitous, but it is very rarely realistic.

It's true that sex is the linchpin of many romantic relation-ships – the thing that brings us closer together, builds intimacy and strengthens our bond. It can also be, at its most basic level, one way to have a very good time. Despite this, recent polling suggests we are sleeping together less now than we have been in decades. We have contraception, liberal attitudes, and the average person's internet search history certainly *suggests* that we still want to be 'getting it on till the break of dawn', so what's behind this dip?

One explanation is that we simply feel too busy to have as much sex as we might like. Combined with stress, this will have a disastrous effect on anyone's libido. Stress can really knock our confidence, leaving us with a low opinion of ourselves and a negative body image. We take small, often imagined slights to heart, and stop viewing ourselves as someone people could find attractive. Naturally, none of this is going to put us in a romantic mood.

Neither will feeling absolutely exhausted. In this case, we'll probably prefer getting straight to sleep than engaging in any mutually naked activities. Furthermore, if our sleep has been affected or we are distracted by worries, it can be difficult to get in a sexy frame of mind. As everyone knows, feeling in the mood is essentially impossible when the only thing we can picture is that particularly hefty spreadsheet that's become the bane of our professional lives. Not to mention that it can be very difficult to even *like* our partners when we're incredibly stressed, let alone contemplate a bit of seduction.

As we've already seen, stress has an impact at the hormonal level, too. When you're in fight or flight mode, your body will make stress hormones, not sex hormones. As a consequence, we produce less oestrogen, androgens and testosterone and so it's no surprise that our sex drive becomes inhibited. To highlight how strong this effect can be, it has been found that social stress can suppress oestrogen levels in female monkeys as effectively as removing her ovaries.

In order for us to feel aroused, we need to be relaxed. As one of my favourite writers on this topic, Dr House, puts it: 'If we want the hormonal orchestra of our bodies to not sound like a brigade of six-year-old tuba players on LSD, we have to do everything in our power to live in a more parasympathetic state.'

Meditation works on three levels to balance out your sex drive: firstly, by keeping your stress levels in check, it allows your sex hormones to flow more naturally; secondly, your blood circulation evens out (because stress is no longer making your blood vessels constrict and contract), allowing you to respond more easily to arousing circumstances; and thirdly, the levels of relaxation you arrive at through meditation make you feel alive and emotionally open. I could add a cheeky fourth thing to that list: the increase in tactile sensation that comes with meditation, which can only be helpful when you're enjoying a lovely intimate moment.

THE TRIALS AND TRIBULATIONS OF SNORING

Anyone who's ever had a partner who snores will know what it's like: one moment you're lying next to someone you're in love with, and the next they transform into a creature so noisy and disruptive you can barely believe they're the same person. It's hard to keep that loving feeling alive when all you want to do is sleep, and their snoring means that just can't happen. For the snorer themselves, it can mean reduced quantity and quality of sleep, which can lead to grumpiness from their side too, as well as drowsiness, a lack of focus, or a lack of libido when they wake. (Sleep deprivation is associated with erectile dysfunction because it lowers the production of testosterone, so if you're a man, stress-related lack of sleep isn't going to help your sex life either.)

Plenty of snorers try everything to deal with it – noise-reducing headphones, nose-strips, lozenges, nasal sprays. But often nothing except the dreaded separate bedroom will make a difference.

Vedic-inspired meditation can really help with this, working on lots of levels, from reducing the fatigue that can lead to snoring, to giving you a daily relaxant, to washing away stress and so releasing the tension in your muscles and jaw so they're positioned in a less obtrusive way. You'll also begin to breathe much more deeply and efficiently.

So, if you're a snorer – do your partner a favour and come and learn to meditate. Or, if your partner's a snorer, send them along. It'll lead to silent nights – and much happier days.

Knowing When It's Over

Sometimes, despite everyone's best efforts, there's just something fundamentally wrong in a relationship. Not all relationships are meant to last for ever, and one of the very useful things about meditation is that it can help you identify when a relationship has exceeded its natural lifecycle. Part of this is recognising that, though something might be ending, this means there is now an opportunity for something else (hopefully better) to start.

Meditation does this first and foremost by boosting your self-esteem (as I talked about in Dylan's story). When you aren't so needy, you can feel more confident about letting something go that isn't working for you, and by increasing your levels of awareness and honesty with yourself, you can more easily admit to yourself that something isn't right. It's always going to be painful, and no one likes to see romantic love fade away. However, knowing when to end a relationship is just as important as knowing how to maintain one.

This is as true of romantic relationships as it is for any other kind of relationship. We've all had childhood friends who we thought would be our best friends for the rest of our lives, only to discover as adults that we have grown apart.

When we're locked in fight or flight mode, we fear change, we fear the unknown and we fear changing the nature of our relationships. The thought of suddenly being without your partner, however much your relationship may have soured, feels very scary and uncomfortable. So we cling on to them, hoping that things will get better. But if that person is no longer right for you, clinging on for dear life is actually going to have the opposite effect and suffocate the relationship even more. The lifeblood drains out of it and desperation kicks in. We cling and cling, like barnacles to a rock, and we don't let go until we are forced to, or until one of us is brave enough to say: 'This is scary, but it's time for us to end this.'

Sometimes we're reluctant to end relationships because we don't want to hurt the other person. A lot of people stay with their partners because they're scared of that. But you know what? It might be hurtful in the short term, but in the long term they'll be incredibly grateful, because the worst thing you can do to a relationship is to hold on for so long that you destroy the legacy of it. Instead of remembering the relationship as it was, good and bad, you hold on so tight that only the pain and its slow death are recalled. Also, if you know the relationship is wrong, isn't it unfair to deny your partner the chance to find one that's right?

In the West, we have a cultural fixation on longevity, with the ideal being lifelong marriage. That might not be the answer for you. Once again, it's about quality, not quantity, of time spent with another person that counts. If, through meditation, you feel more whole and complete as a person and you're not afraid of the unknown, then allowing relationships to end becomes considerably easier. The other person will be set free, and then you are also free, to spend time developing your ability to be more present and more attuned, releasing yourself from some of the pain that may be holding you back. Meditation will really tune you into what you're really about, what you're looking for and what's important to you. It will allow you to fill your life with quality relationships that are based on the expression of fulfilment, rather than used as a Band-Aid for your own insecurities.

Letting Go of Past Trauma

When I first met Anna, she was going through an extremely difficult divorce. While working with her to get through it, some very complex issues of childhood abuse came up. I feel it's really important to tell her story here because I want to show you that recovery *is* possible from almost any situation. Furthermore, with 31 per cent of young women aged 18–24 reporting experiences of sexual abuse during childhood (according to the NSPCC in 2011), this is an issue that society just can't keep sweeping under the carpet.

Anna

'I never felt safe.'

My mum's mother died giving birth to her, and she was sent to an orphanage where she was abused. The woman I call my nan adopted her when she was very small, but she struggled with learning and relationships. She fell pregnant at fifteen, and my nan took on the baby boy as her own. When she was seventeen, she ran away and married another guy, but he was very violent. They had a little girl, and she was so badly beaten up by her father that she too was given to my nan.

When my parents got together, they tried to get custody of

my mum's two previous children so that my dad could raise them as his own. It didn't work out, and so my elder half-brother and half-sister really hated me and my three siblings because, in their eyes, we were the lucky ones. To them, we were living a perfect life, and they went completely off the rails.

My mum had post-natal depression, and she just used to sit in the room and not speak to us. My dad worked very hard and drank too much, to cope. When he wasn't there, my mum was very spiteful. She just didn't know how to engage with us unless she was being mean to us. She would tell lies to my dad about what we'd done, so that we'd get a hiding for things we never did, because she enjoyed it when my dad was hurting us, and she didn't like it when my dad showed us affection.

Then my elder half-brother began to touch me inappropriately, maybe because he didn't consider me his 'full' sister. It made me uncomfortable, but I never said anything. We also had a male babysitter who sexually molested me and my elder brother. I felt confused and ashamed, but didn't feel I could tell my parents. When I was about fifteen, I finally plucked up the courage, but they didn't believe me – they just said I was making up stories.

And so we grew up in an environment where there was no self-esteem whatsoever. I never felt safe. I took on the responsibility of looking after my little brother and sister, who are nine and eleven years younger than me because I didn't want them to feel what I and my elder brother felt.

I remember looking at the walls of this house on a council estate, and thinking, *What the hell am I doing here?* I left home when I was about sixteen, and I found it hard, because I had such a bond with my younger brother and sister, and I felt like I was leaving my children to bad people. I felt incredibly guilty.

I met my husband about a year after I'd left. He was very charismatic, incredibly intelligent – the kind of guy who could make you feel like you were the only person in the world. I was seventeen, and he was like a knight in shining armour. I thought: *Wow, I don't need to deal with any of it; he can deal with it all for me.* My husband was like a rock for my younger siblings, too, and he took on a fatherly role with them.

But they had a lot of problems. My younger brother did a lot of drugs, and he was quite emotionally manipulative. Although there's such a big age difference, we have a very close bond, and, about ten years ago, I reached breaking point. An osteopath told me that the reason I was experiencing so much pain in my hip and back was due to the weight of responsibility I'd taken on for my family. It was having a negative impact on my body, and he sent me off to buy a book by a spiritual writer. When I read it, I suddenly realised he was right: I'd taken on all these burdens – and I wanted to shift them.

My brother soon noticed there was a change in me. He read the book, and he also experienced this internal shift. Soon we were reading lots of spiritual books, and then we came across this system that was all about employing certain techniques to expand your brain. We decided to try it.

It required us to sit for five minutes a day, and I thought you had to sit there very upright, with perfect posture, in the lotus position. Those five minutes would be excruciating. I'd sit there, hating every minute of it. I persevered for a month or two and then gave it up as a bad deal.

Then I started to go to Sufism meditation workshops once a month, and when I was there, I could sit in stillness. I had moments of no pain, and to me, that was heavenly. I was only doing the meditation twice a week and didn't want to do any more; I thought that was enough. That was before things started to go wrong in my marriage.

It was very subtle at first, but since I'd started meditating, I began to realise that I didn't want to take on the role of 'giver' any more. And my husband didn't like that.

We'd been together twenty years, and then, in the last two years of our marriage, he did some things that weren't very nice, like having an affair. Even before that, things were changing between us. He was in wealth management and he was hanging around with these billionaires, becoming very focused on money and power. We were in totally different worlds.

So we decided to get divorced.

Part of me was elated, because I felt a sense of freedom that I hadn't had since that brief taste between leaving home and meeting him. I was also overwhelmed. Suddenly I had to think about money and paying the bills for the first time in years.

It was a strange, very raw time. I wasn't just going through a divorce with my husband; I was struggling with one inside myself. I had no clue who I was, or where I was going.

At that point, I was extremely off-balance, engaging in hedonistic, self-destructive behaviour that was totally out of character, taking unnecessary risks and acting carelessly towards people. I didn't care about much at that time. I'd feel numb, and then suddenly incredibly anxious – from having a panic attack to feeling this incredible sense of restlessness. It was a crazy mix of emotions. Sometimes I couldn't breathe, or I'd have to pull the car over because I'd hear a song or recall a painful memory. I got very used to walking around London, crying. I don't think I'd ever cried that much in my life.

A friend suggested Will's form of meditation, but I said: 'I already meditate, I don't need to.' 'Yeah,' she said, 'but this is different.' She was really insistent, and I was at a loose end that weekend, so I went to check it out.

I really do think it saved my life. If I hadn't started to do it, I would have got really ill, because I was burning the candle at both ends. I just couldn't bear to be by myself, so I'd go out drinking. I wasn't sleeping or eating, so I think I would have crashed big time.

Within no time I was meditating twice a day, and instead of being something I forced myself to do, it was almost a relief, because it was forty minutes a day that I could switch off from it all and find a bit of peace. I wasn't sleeping, either, so that was also like my sleep time.

Within a few months, I found things a little easier, and by the end of the year, I felt a lot more stable. There's still a fair bit to shift. I'm processing emotions from old situations, traumas, memories, almost as if I'm detoxing those emotions, but I'm definitely getting there.

I'm trying to get pregnant at the moment with my current partner and I think the meditation helps because it prepares both your body and your mind for the experience. It also helps you prioritise. With this new perspective, I'm looking at my past in a different way, and I'm thinking a lot about who I want to be as a mum and what I'll learn from my child.

I feel very removed from my former life. I don't feel resentment; I forgave my parents a long time ago. I suppose my past is something I've worked with, and processed, and it's just a story now. I tried to understand why I had such a traumatic childhood for years, but then I realised that it just can't be understood, and so now I just accept it as part of my past.

Whenever I've done other meditations, it felt like I was snorkelling and looking down at the scene below. Now

I'm scuba diving, swimming with fish, going deeper and deeper. It's really exhilarating. Bit by bit, you learn to trust your increased lung capacity. It's like you've got more air to breathe – so you can get right down to the bedrock of issues that you've accumulated over the years. **"**

Working with Anna

It was really hard for Anna the first day she turned up to see me. She was in bits, crying uncontrollably. We spent the first hour together helping her find some semblance of centre again, and then I was able to proceed to giving her a personalised sound and guiding her into her first meditation. She really calmed down a lot after that, but she still needed a lot of support in those first few months. While I'm not a qualified counsellor (and I always invite people who've been through great trauma to seek professional help), every now and again you come across someone who's so troubled that you end up playing the role of confidant a little bit more, which can help them to change the way that they interact with their past pain, trauma and storylines. We were in contact once or twice a week for the first few months.

She also needed some help to find ways to reframe the situation with her husband; to see it as an opportunity, rather than as a threat or a loss. It was great that, within a few months, Anna had managed to do just that – and then she really started living life again. The way I saw it was that, because she'd got together with him at such a young age, before she'd emotionally developed into a woman, this was now her time to start experiencing what most people would experience much earlier on in life. It was such a privilege to see her being free, growing and finding her voice.

And then – once she'd had enough of stepping out and living

her wild youthfulness for the first time — it was my role to encourage her to move to a place of sustainability and balance, and to use the meditation as an anchor for that.

LETTING GO OF EMOTION – DAILY JOURNALLING

Each morning, as soon as you get up, start writing your thoughts and feelings down in a journal. It's really important that you don't edit or censor the material in any way; it needs to be a pure stream of consciousness. Even if it feels weird to write down some of the things that are going through your mind, celebrate that weirdness, because it's all about unloading that irrelevant content onto a page, and freeing up some bandwidth in your mind. Try and do this exercise for ten to fifteen minutes.

There's no wrong way to do this. Whatever comes out is representative of what's playing out in your consciousness in that moment. If it feels dark, or negative, don't worry. This is you giving expression to that voice that's coming from the shadows in a healthy way. If you keep these thoughts and feelings bottled up, they will only fester inside you. By letting them out onto the page, they are released from your psyche. You can learn to accept yourself and life's situations much more easily when you do this.

Allow yourself to be innocent, *not* all-knowing, to be vulnerable about any lack of knowledge you may have. Be inquisitive. Be open. Be observant. And be responsive. And then, when you're done, get on with your day. You can always burn the paper you've written on afterwards to let go of whatever negativity was written there.

Toxic Relationships

It was very clear from our conversations that Anna had some really difficult relationships with all of the people that were closest to her. Her parents hadn't believed her when she finally plucked up the courage to tell them about the sexual abuse she experienced, and as a child she couldn't help but feel not only let down by them, but emotionally detached from them too.

Her mother's mental illness, and her father's difficulty in coping with it, suggests that her parents were overwhelmed with their own worries. They lacked the capacity to deal with Anna's traumas, or indeed those of her siblings.

You could say the same about everyone else in her life. When she first came to see me, her relationship with her ex-husband was a disaster. They were still living together but they weren't talking. Their lack of communication and other relationship problems had become an enormous elephant in the room, and the atmosphere was extremely toxic. This put her under strain 24/7. She either had to be in this noxious, prison-like domestic environment, or be out and about knowing that she was purposely avoiding going home, because home didn't feel like home any more.

Becoming Self-Sufficient

If you're in a difficult relationship, the first thing to work on is yourself. Anna needed to focus on her own personal wellbeing, her psychological and physiological balance, and her emotional fortitude. This focus would allow her to be less governed by a sense of inadequacy, and less reliant on other people always being there to support her. She would no longer need to lean on people who didn't have the emotional strength or capability to really meet her needs. It was imperative that she got herself to a place where she felt more resilient, so the aggression of others could no longer trigger her so easily.

Meditation helped with this. It helped her access that place we all have inside, where courage resides – and she needed this courage to break free of the toxic dynamics in her life. In doing that, she became more self-sufficient, and as a result, more self-confident. I also hoped that by breaking through the stress, the pain and the trauma (and therefore finding her own sense of stability), Anna would end up being a guiding light for the rest of her family to take inspiration from.

Anna's relationship with herself was fascinating. She had so much heart and I could tell that she was such a free spirit. However, I did wonder if perhaps some of her free spiritedness was actually born from a need or desire not to commit, because to commit herself to something opened her up to being vulnerable. If that person let her down in the same way she'd been let down by everyone else – her parents, her half-brother, her babysitter, her ex-husband – then yet again she would be vulnerable.

Understandably, she found it very difficult to face her pain and trauma, and I saw her use lots of avoidance strategies. But she took the process step by step, and as time went on she got better at facing her demons, learning to accept them and move on without them.

Ending the Cycle of Trauma

Bit by bit, Anna has managed to deal with and recover from her past, and now she's a remarkably stable, inspiring and radiant being. So many people have come to learn to meditate because they're inspired by her demeanour, her sense of freedom and *joie de vivre*, and they don't even know her background. They simply think that she's a hugely inspiring human being. If they knew the adversity that she'd come from to get to that place, then they'd be even more wowed. She's an absolute superstar and I'm so proud of her. She's a living testament to how effective meditation can be in helping you transition from a state of chronic trauma to something that's far closer to what we'd all like to experience in life.

It's interesting that Anna now wants to become a mother. Before, I think she would have been scared of the commitment a child brought, but now she seems totally ready for it, and ready not just to be a mum, but a great one. She has worked through so much of her own internal pain that she now has wisdom, compassion, empathy and patience, and by freeing her nervous system of that trauma, she won't pass it on to *her* children – breaking the cycle that existed within her own family.

Breaking Free of the Past

Anna's progress was remarkable, but why did this particular form of meditation work for her when others hadn't? The explanation lies in how Vedic-inspired meditation helps people achieve a meditative state. Rather than trying to *concentrate* her way into it, she was getting there in a much more relaxed way – by simply closing her eyes and repeating her personalised sound, letting it resonate and do the work. This has a far more holistic impact on the brain and wider nervous system than methods that require you to do all the heavy lifting yourself. As a result, she could go much deeper; she could go beyond breath, beyond what visualisation could provide her with. With this kind of meditation, you can enter a state of complete transcendence, and when you do that, you rise above all of your past pain, hurts and trauma. Even if you just experience that state for a few minutes each day, it starts to loosen the grip that your history has over you. Unconsciously, you become free of it, and that's the key.

There are so many things we can do to consciously resolve

our life situations, but if we don't take care of our unconscious programming, we'll forever be at its mercy. That's why this form of meditation is so brilliant; it enables us to shake loose the unconscious bonds that are holding us back, and in doing so, it provides us with a level of freedom from our past. We are no longer trapped in the narratives we have internalised and telling ourselves for so long, giving us the chance to rewrite our story.

REGAINING YOUR SENSE OF CONTROL

Despite living in the first half of the twentieth century, American psychologist Abraham Maslow had a theory that I believe is very relevant to many people's problems today. He identified the importance of whether we have an external or internal locus of control, i.e. whether our sense of self is dictated by what other people think of us, or by what we think of ourselves.

Most people have an externalised locus of control, governed by other people's opinions of them, their job, how successful they are, how nice their house is, or how perfect their partner is (which is why social media platforms like Instagram or Facebook – both of which, I think it's safe to say, would have rather bewildered Dr Maslow – have been so enthusiastically embraced by so many, because you can edit your profile to show only the good bits of life). That doesn't make us happy.

An internalised locus of control is when you're so safe and secure within yourself that you live according to your values, while not requiring others to live by them, which makes you feel much more fulfilled. The wonderful irony is that people respect you much more too, because they can tell you're being really authentic and true to yourself.

Many of the things governing our externalised locus of control reside in our unconscious. The meditation I teach takes you beyond that – allowing your unconscious distortions to unwind – and this means you naturally begin to live your life as an authentic expression of yourself, rather than playing a role defined by other people.

The Importance of Adaptation Energy

'It is not stress that kills us, it is our reaction to it.'
HANS SELYE,
ENDOCRINOLOGIST

Before I go on to talk about other forms of relationships, I want to mention something that you might not have heard about before: adaptation energy. Put simply, adaptation energy enables you to adapt to changes of expectation or circumstance. Here's an example: you thought your partner would be there to help you paint the living room before your flat is due for a valuation, but they've been kept behind at work. Now you're left brandishing a roller alone, dappled with paint spots and feeling a little bit panicked. In this scenario, adaptation energy helps you cope with the changes of expectation and circumstance, so you don't find the situation as stressful.

The origins of the concept are particularly interesting. The term 'stress' as it is currently used was coined in 1936 by an Austro-Hungarian endocrinologist called Hans Selye. He borrowed the term from the field of physics, where the word describes a force that produces strain on a physical object – like bending a piece of metal until it snaps because of the force, or stress, exerted on it.

His key contribution to our understanding of stress was his conception of the stimuli that create a biological stress response, called 'stressors'. This distinguished stress as a purely internal experience that may be triggered by a given stimulus, depending on the subject's 'resilience'. If we're as resilient as a titanium turbine, it will take huge amounts of pressure for us to snap or bend. However, if we're as fragile as a carton of eggs, it really won't take much stress at all before we break. These stimuli could be positive as well as negative: for example, getting married or having a baby is both positive and stressful at the same time.

And this is where we come to adaptation energy. One of Selye's most interesting findings was that stress decreases an organism's ability to adapt to changes in circumstance. A lot of us find that our ability to deal with challenges and unexpected situations is much greater in the morning than later on in the day. It's as if the day's stresses and strains deplete our reserve of energy, so we become less and less resilient, and with that, less able to cope when the washing machine suddenly breaks down, or our child decides to have a tantrum at the dinner table. With less adaptation energy, our sense of perspective is eroded. When we're feeling resilient and happy, we can deal with our car breaking down without much bother, seeing it as a minor inconvenience. If we're strained and tired, however, the same event can feel like the end of the world – just another example of how the universe is working against us.

At some point in the day our reserves of adaptation energy are so depleted that even small changes of expectation cause us to experience stress. That's why if someone presents you with a challenging task to do towards the end of the afternoon, you just can't cope, and it ends up on tomorrow's to-do list. Or if you come home and your partner tries to be spontaneous, you end up simply growling at them. You're so attached to the idea of the evening you'd already imagined – perhaps dozing in front of the TV – that any suggestion of change feels onerous and stressful.

We increase our stock of adaptation energy when we sleep, which is why when we wake up after a decent night's rest, all those things that we couldn't deal with yesterday suddenly don't seem so difficult. Equally, if we don't get a good rest, our ability to adapt is compromised from the very beginning of the day. Unfortunately, as we've discussed, stress tends to have a negative impact on our quality of sleep. This creates a vicious cycle whereby we have less adaptive capability during the day, which makes the whole business of living a busy life feel doubly stressful, so it becomes even more difficult to achieve good quality sleep.

If that happens for too long, our ability to adapt to the varying demands of life becomes permanently impaired. This is the phase that Selye described as exhaustion, and ultimately results in the severe impairment of many of our physiological and neurological systems.

Do you have the adaptation energy to cope with the fact that your partner hasn't done exactly what you wanted them to do? If you don't, you're going to snap. The emotional reaction that comes with seeing the massive pile of washing-up that you were promised would be gone by the time you got home can be disproportionately intense. Then, you either have to suppress your annoyance or upset your partner by making it clear that you are pissed off. On the other hand, if you are calm and well equipped to cope with changing expectations, then the prospect of working through these little niggles is going to be much improved. Doing your evening meditation on the way back from work, or before your partner gets in, will get you in a much better place before either of you walks through the door.

BREATHING FOR CALM

If you've had a particularly bad day, or your partner, your flatmate, or your kids have done something annoying and you think you're going to snap, try this breathing exercise to restore calm.

Close your eyes and inhale. Count slowly to three or four as you do so, then gently exhale for twice as long as you inhaled (counting to six or eight). As you're exhaling, imagine all of the tension and stress that you're carrying melting away into the atmosphere. If you can feel the stress located in a certain place – in your chest, your stomach, your liver or your lower back, for example – then gently tap or do a clockwise circular rub on the area as you inhale and exhale.

Doing this for three to four minutes will slow you down and stop you saying something that both parties might regret.

How Do We Increase Our Adaptation Energy?

The ability to react and evolve is a vital part of a contented life. Nothing stays the same, and if we find it difficult to cope with change then our lives become dominated by stress and discomfort. Using meditation to increase your adaptation energy is one way to ensure you can happily adjust to a world in constant flux.

As I've already discussed, this form of meditation has a significant influence on our brain, and most relevant in this case is how it impacts the behaviour of our prefrontal cortex (which mainly deals with higher functions such as planning and personality development). This part of our brain interacts with our emotional centres and the limbic system, taming our impulses and helping us organise our feelings. Meditation appears to stimulate the prefrontal cortex, even to the extent that just eight weeks of the practice is associated with increased cortical thickness.

The promotion of our higher functions – the parts of our brain that drive our intellect and rationality – has a hugely positive impact on our adaptability. Rather than being driven by uncontrollable emotions and irrepressible fears, we can view a situation logically, and then work out how to solve any issues that arise. Say we've pinned all our hopes on a visit from a long-distance loved one, but something crops up and they can no longer make it. Rather than breaking down and viewing their absence as an unmitigated disaster, with meditation we can process our disappointment. We'll still be sad, of course, but we can think of solutions to the problem, and rationalise our emotions with the knowledge that we will see them again soon.

In addition to that, as we've already explored, meditation can vastly improve your sleep. With a refreshing night of shut-eye behind you, you're far more likely to be able to meet the challenges of the day with enthusiasm and adaptability. This helps you to become more resilient, and your reservoir of adaptation energy drains less quickly throughout the day.

Settling down to a morning meditation gives you loads of adaptation energy. Then, just as you begin to flag as the day wears on, you can do your second meditation and get another hit. Boom! You're back in the game. As I said at the start of this book, when I first started meditating I used to call it 'zinging', and I think that's a pretty accurate description of that extra charge, that extra 'zing' it gives you twice a day.

Being able to adapt is important for any kind of human relationship – romantic, parental or professional. Do you want to be a person who delays, ignores or reacts badly when change is afoot? Or the one coming up with solutions, finding ways to meet the new challenges with creativity and an open mind? With improved sleep and regular top-ups of adaptation energy via meditation, soon you'll be the master of change, adapting and responding optimally to any situation you face.

FERTILITY AND PREGNANCY

Trying for a baby can add a lot of stress to a relationship. I've worked with many couples who have experienced difficulties getting pregnant, and it's a particularly vicious cycle.

As I've talked about already – when we're faced with stressful situations, the fight or flight mechanisms within the body divert energy towards survival. Reproductive capability is one of the first things to go when chronic stress has become a part of a woman's life. Stress can also wreak havoc on a man's hormonal profile and have a negative impact on sperm production and quality. And, of course, not being able to conceive creates even more stress, which then compounds the situation.

By using meditation to break through chronic stress and calm the nervous system, women can help solve some of the problems that stand between them and pregnancy. With reduced stress and less anxiety, monthly cycles often become more regular, and the reproductive system begins to function as it's meant to.

Meditation can also help deal with the roller coaster of fertility treatment, and the pressure that this puts on relationships. And, if all attempts ultimately fail, it can also help couples come to terms with that and move forward, knowing that, while incredibly disappointing, there are many other ways they can fill their life with love and joy.

If conception is successful, practising meditation can make pregnancy a much smoother, less challenging process. I've now taught more than a hundred pregnant women, and they report that their hormones feel more balanced, they feel less stressed than they've felt during previous pregnancies, and they have considerably more energy.

The greatest gift you could ever give your child is to meditate regularly during pregnancy. It's a gift to yourself as well, to know that you've done the best for him or her, and to know that the next twenty years of your life are going to be much smoother, because you'll be spending your time with a calm and well-adjusted person.

I've now met so many children who've been born to meditators that I've taught, and they're always incredibly aware, calm and joyful. Their parents tell us that their babies never cried that much, sleep through the night, and then, as they grow into children, develop really well – emotionally, academically, creatively and behaviourally – so much so that the parents' friends, families, nursery and schoolteachers regularly comment on it.

Why does meditating have so much of an effect? Well, as I mentioned in my introduction to this book, our nervous systems come to a lot of conclusions about the world that we're about to be born into during those first nine months in the womb. Our foetal nervous system processes all our mother's stress chemistry while we're in there – all of that cortisol, adrenaline and noradrenaline races through us and has a very powerful effect on us and our development. One very sad example of this is in children of pregnant mothers who witnessed 9/11, who have been shown to have a much higher predisposition towards anxiety and depression.

Improving Family Dynamics

Parenthood is simultaneously one of the greatest joys and one of the greatest challenges of life.

The main things a child needs from its parents are love, presence and attention. This may seem simple enough, but they're not always easy to give. The stresses and strains of having small children add extra pressure to our already stressful lives, and it can often be hard to be at our best every moment of every day. Meditation allows us to free ourselves from stress and fatigue, which makes us more able to love and nurture our children. We have more attention to give, much more love to share and a greater capability to face the constant demands of parenthood.

Speaking of fatigue, one of the biggest issues that new (and not-so-new) parents face is lack of sleep, and as you've probably understood by now, meditation is great for helping with that. If sleep isn't an option because you are breastfeeding or the baby's up all night, it can be a very helpful substitute.

Parenting requires energy, and with meditation, we have more vitality – so we can keep up when our children have told us that the floor is now made of lava and we have to jump across conveniently placed cushions in order to slay the imaginary dragon. Meditation is also a great accompaniment to exercise – deep breathing oxygenates the muscle tissues better and gives you more energy – so kicking a ball around the park will become much less of a challenge as well.

We also develop more of the aforementioned adaptation energy, which for lots of reasons is very helpful for those who have kids. Parents are constantly presented with new demands, both in their lives and in the lives of their children, and with kids in tow things rarely go to plan. If we don't have much adaptation energy to rely on, then we're going to snap at our children. No parent likes upsetting their kids (even when they've done something truly naughty), so this just creates a burden of guilt. When we're feeling resilient and adaptable, however, then we can deal with anything a child throws at us – even if it's the dinner you just lovingly prepared.

Later on, as your kids grow older, meditation gives you access to greater levels of inner wisdom, and, as such, your guidance will be much more inspiring. Enhanced understanding and empathy mean that you can relate to your child more, even when they are being challenging (the teenage years, anyone?) or experiencing difficulties.

Meditation also helps with parental anxiety. Older children need the freedom to go out and explore the world so that they can learn to take responsibility for themselves and make decisions that lead to greater maturity. Being able to let go and allow them to do this is much easier if you're in a calm place yourself. Then, when they do start flying the nest, they'll find they have less to rebel against, and at the same time you'll find yourself becoming less and less prone to negative patterns of behaviour that may rub off on them. Instead, you'll become more of an example to be followed.

And, as an adult child of your own parents, you'll find, like Noel did with his father, that meditation will help to soothe any difficult aspects of your relationship with them. Your increased levels of empathy will mean that you come to better understand behaviour that in the past you might have regarded as difficult or hurtful, forgive it, and move on to a better way of being. This will lead to much improved family dynamics. Some people feel like they will never be able to forgive their parents for certain things that have happened and may struggle to find peace in this area of their life. More is possible than many people realise, as you can see from the great things that Anna managed to achieve.

Tom

'My son said, very quietly: "Love you too." And I was like: YESSSS!'

My first impressions of Tom are really memorable. He was a walking contradiction. There was something very light and friendly about him; he had a very open and relaxed manner, but I could also feel this heavy energy. He seemed to be stuck, and I could tell that he was probably a pretty moody individual. My heart went out to him because, prior to learning to meditate, so was I.

As the course went on I started to see that, underneath his outward coolness and bohemian openness, he was insecure; I could see the little boy in him who hadn't quite found what he was looking for when he was small. It could have been me speculating, but there was definitely a hole there. I knew that meditation so often helped people fill that kind of emptiness, and so I was really looking forward to teaching him.

And he *was* a real pleasure to teach, because he was so receptive. I'd like to think that being a musician enables you to flow with life (he's a music critic and a trumpeter), and he certainly seemed to do this with the meditation straight away. That's really helpful for people in their early days of the practice.

Over the years I've always wanted to learn to meditate, but I never found the right approach. I've always been interested in spirituality and in the counterculture of the 1960s and '70s, the beat poets and all that sort of thing. I tried learning Buddhist meditation a couple of times, did some drop-in courses, but I could never get the hang of it. I used to beat myself up about it a little bit, if I'm honest. But every now and then I'd look around to see what was available and this one time, about three years ago now, I found Will.

I went over and had a chat and thought: *Well, this is interesting.* I'd heard of Transcendental Meditation® before, but something had put me off it. Instead, this form of meditation just instantly spoke to me.

I didn't notice much change at first, but after the first couple of weeks, my wife Ali noticed that I was much calmer, and then after about six months there was a pretty profound sense of transformation, which I'll talk about more in a bit.

Around the time I was learning to meditate, things were a bit tricky at home. My daughter Katie had been diagnosed with an autoimmune disorder called ulcerative colitis, which causes all sorts of digestive issues. She was in a lot of pain and really unhappy, and it was heartbreaking to see. The doctors said there wasn't a cure for it, that it could only be managed.

All of this put a lot of strain on us as a family, especially between Ali and me. I responded to it by throwing myself into my work, sticking my head in the sand, going out a lot and drinking quite a bit, and she took on a lot of the responsibilities with Katie, like taking her to the hospital. She thought I wasn't coping with it very well, and I probably wasn't, to be honest. It put the worst stress on us we've ever been through as a couple.

I think it affected our son Jack as well, who was fifteen at the time. He and I just weren't getting on at all, and it was crushing. Dads and teenage sons are never going to be the easiest combination, but we were butting our heads together all the time.

I initially learned meditation for the purposes of self-discovery and personal development, and it was really delivering in ways that I found both surprising and delightful. But the more I read about Will's claims for what meditation could do and the scientific studies to back it up, the more I began to wonder if it might help Katie. We'd tried all kinds of other stuff, but none of it was really working, so I asked Will about it. He said he'd had some really good results with digestive and autoimmune issues, and so Katie started meditating when she was twelve years old.

Now, I want to stress that it's impossible to say for certain what effect the meditation had because of all the other things we were trying, both at the hospital and with complementary therapies, but now, two years later, she has no symptoms and no medication of any kind. She's completely free of it, full of life, and she eats whatever she wants. She's wonderful – so cheerful and funny. Meditation's given her more than just a way to beat the illness; she just seems so grounded now. She's going on fifteen but never seems to have too many dramas; she's simply happy and creative.

When we were at our worst, Ali and I had gone for couples' counselling, and it had worked really well. Being a psychotherapist herself, she'd been telling me for ages that I should give it a try individually, and after the success of the couples' counselling, I decided to do a year of counselling just for me. That, along with the meditation, was such a powerful combination, because it seemed to me that they were both helping you to achieve the same thing but from different directions.

After I'd taken up Ali's challenge and given counselling a

go, she told me she was going to learn to meditate. She's very pragmatic, so I was pretty taken aback by this, but pleased, too. She was having a really hard time at work, so I thought it might help with that. It did. She loves meditation and has benefited so much from it since then.

We're subsequently getting on much better. We've been together for twenty years, but since the meditation we've never been so close. It's wonderful. It's quite sickening, actually . . .

So that just left Jack. He and I were still not always seeing eye to eye, and he was having some tricky times in his life, mainly issues with his friendships. Then, last summer, he told me he wanted to learn to meditate. I was completely amazed – he's into hip-hop and computer games; he's just not that sort of person at all. I hadn't thought for a moment that a teenage boy would want to do it.

All the way through our hard times, I would say, 'Love you', just as he was going upstairs to bed, and I wouldn't get anything back. Then, after he learned to meditate, there were a couple of times when I'd hear him say, very quietly: 'Love you too.' And I'd be like (very quietly, so he wouldn't hear): *YESSSS!*

Now all four of us meditate. Often, Ali and I meditate together when we come home from work, while the kids do it in their rooms and each has their own little routine. We're now so much more content as a family. We give each other space, we don't get on each other's nerves, and even in a small house with only one bathroom, there's never any conflict.

Most mornings I get up at around five thirty – which is a massive change in itself. I used to stay up until then. Now I go to bed around ten, rise early and do some sun salutations and then some rounding (a technique I learned from Will, which is basically some yoga and breathing exercises and then a meditation). I get it done before everyone else starts getting up for school and college and work, and if I can fit it in every day for a week I feel a huge difference.

One of the main changes I've noticed about myself is my ability to take a step back from my emotions and not let them control me, to recognise that they are temporary, and not to get too caught up in them.

I used to be a big drinker, too, but with meditation, that started to fall by the wayside. I still drink a bit – I'm a jazz critic, so it kind of goes with the territory – but I definitely do it a lot less than before. When I was younger, I did a lot of partying, and I'd say that some of my first spiritual experiences were as a result of taking LSD. I'd always thought it would be lovely to be in a situation where you could experience bliss from within, without having to take in external chemicals, and that's what meditation feels like for me.

Perhaps because of this, my friendships are all a bit less fraught than they used to be. Actually, the meditation has enabled me to eliminate some fairly toxic friendships from my life, as well as improving the ones that are fulfilling and important to me. I think it gave me the clarity to see how things really were, and to ask myself honestly why that person was in my life. It gives you the confidence to be able to say: 'I don't need this.'

I have often in the past been quite a control freak, needing to know what's going on all the time, but now I'm much more relaxed about things, which I think has improved my parenting. I can trust my kids to be getting on with their lives without trying to control them. I worry about the state of the world, too – I'm sure we all do at the moment – but if I didn't meditate, I'd probably be crippled with anxiety by now.

I think Ali and I didn't fully acknowledge the depth of the shit we were going through until later, when it cleared up a bit. Then we were like: 'Holy cow – that was hard work, wasn't it? Jesus, you know, we did so well to survive that.'

Now I really feel that there's a sense of kindness, consideration, closeness, happiness, honesty and openness in our home, and that's just a really wonderful feeling. As a family we think this is to a very large degree thanks to our meditation practices. Impossible to prove, but we feel very strongly that this is the case.

Meditation for Families

Tom's story is a great example of how Vedic-inspired meditation can really help parents, kids and their family dynamics. If everyone in a family is feeling good – physically, emotionally and spiritually – then the relationships between them all are bound to be improved.

Because it's such a simple technique, children as young as five can benefit from it (we don't ask them to sit still and meditate but give them a 'word of wisdom' that they can use while at play). They learn and see results very quickly, too, because their young brains haven't got as much ingrained conditioning or trauma to work through. We do a shortened version of our adult course for adolescents, like Tom's kids, who use the 'sit down, eyes closed, repeat the sound' technique that adults do, but they only need to practise a minute for every year of their age (so a twelve-year-old would do twelve minutes at a time).

We only teach children if they've expressed an interest in learning to meditate and ask that one of their parents has learned the Vedic method, so they can give them the right support. Teaching them takes around an hour, and parents are present while we do it.

Then it's just a case of figuring out how to fit your meditation into a busy family schedule! As Tom explains, he gets up early to fit it in before the rest of the household wakes up, which is one approach. Other top tips from parents include tag-teaming, so one of you looks after the kids while the other meditates. Some meditate while their child or baby naps, when they're in the car waiting to pick them up from school, or once they've gone to bed for the night. Many parents tell me that they really treasure their twenty minutes as time for themselves, with no interruptions, as it gives them a little break from what can be a pretty intense environment, with lots of conflicting demands on your time.

Meditation and Therapy

Tom talks about the benefits of counselling and meditation, and he's right: embracing both approaches can have really powerful and complementary results. Therapy helps us by reframing some of our unconscious motivations and feelings so that we can really think about them. Meditation works in a more effortless way, skipping any conscious processing and instigating profound change through transcendence. If there's a possibility of doing both, they can make great bedfellows.

Finding Bliss from Within

The concept of finding bliss through meditation really strikes a chord with me. Parents, perhaps more than most, need to find ways of chilling out, and the prospect of finding something that can relax you and make you feel fantastic without involving late nights, bad comedowns or terrible hangovers is something that might appeal to many who want to be able to function when their kids wake them up at five in the morning.

But what *is* bliss? The best way I can think of describing it is that when you experience pure bliss, your mind falls completely mute, which is a truly beautiful state to find yourself in. Many people think that it's by quietening down the mind that we experience bliss, but it's actually the other way round. It is only once you've achieved a state of bliss through meditation, through reaching a state of transcendence, that the internal chattering in your mind is muted. It will stop incessantly searching for something more and simply settle into this beautiful state of 'being'.

Rounding and Retreats

Tom talks about including some 'rounding' in his morning routine. This is something that I teach on the retreats that I run, and it's an ancient Vedic practice that vastly increases the depth and efficiency of the core meditation technique. It involves a very gentle series of yoga postures (unlike anything you might find in modern yoga classes), followed by a specific breathing technique, and then meditation. At the end you get to lie down for a while, like you might at the end of a yoga class, to relax. It's all very easy.

This specific set of ancient poses and the breathing that follows prepares the mind and body for the deepest possible dive into meditation. The sequence is the key. The way it works is that every stretch causes the brain to fire in a particular way, so if you do the sequence as instructed, it's like coding in a cheat for a computer game – you instantly get to the next level. Doing just one round makes an amazing difference to how you feel; doing many of them, as we do on retreat, can be extraordinary.

If you're interested in finding out more about our rounding retreats, please see my website: www.willwilliamsmeditation.com.

Discovering What's Important

Although most of Tom's story is about the relationships within his family, he also talks about letting some of his friendships go. This comes back to what I mentioned before about discovering what is really important to you in life. You have to ask yourself what you're getting out of your interactions with people, whether that be your partner, colleagues or friends. Do you feel under pressure to keep the relationship going even though it all feels a bit forced? What do you think you're giving the other person? Are you a helpful presence in their life, or are you something of a burden because there's an awkward dynamic between you?

When you dip a dipstick in a car engine, there's a range within which you can consider the engine to have a healthy amount of oil. Every now and again, it's worth doing a similar test with your relationships and seeing what comes out of it. If there's not enough good stuff, then is there something that can be done about it? Yes or no? If yes, do you *want* to do something about it?

If the answer to both of those questions is yes, then great, there's the potential for a sustainable and fulfilling dynamic. Meditate, inject some creative energy into it, and enjoy the fruits of nourishing your relationship. But if the answer to either of those questions is no, then maybe it's worth considering letting the friendship go and making space for something new and more fulfilling.

Navigating Divorce

I remember the first time Nick got in touch. It was a Sunday afternoon, and I was just about to shut down my laptop and go for a walk, when an email popped up. I had a feeling I should look at it, and when I did I saw that the sender had recently been in a psychiatric hospital and had been in a pretty bad way for two years.

I asked him to call me and we chatted for a good while. We agreed that it would be good for him to join the next available course as part of rebuilding his new life, and helping him to become the best dad he could be. His wife had left him, and he was just about to go through a divorce, feeling devastated about losing his kids. Nick was a really touching mix of desperation and humility and my heart really went out to him. I wanted to help him in every way I could.

Nick

'I'd lost my kids.'

I was previously married, with two children. I work in banking and at the time I was earning more money than I've earned in my life. We had four foreign holidays a year, we had a nice flat in south London. I thought I had everything, and yet something was wrong.

My wife and I had been married for twelve years or so when we received news that her grandmother was dying. She went to Australia to say goodbye, taking our two-year-old son with her because he was too little to leave behind. My five-year-old daughter was left at home with me, and one day, I took her out. Then I started having what I now know was a panic attack.

It was the scariest thing I've ever been through in my life. I thought I was dying. Suddenly I realised that, at some point in the past six months, I'd descended into deep depression. For the next week I couldn't sleep at all. I was frozen.

I went to see a psychologist, then a psychiatrist, and they put me on all this medication. Now I think I was just overwhelmed and felt trapped. I was in this unhealthy relationship, I had two kids, and nothing was fun any more. I love my kids beyond belief, as most people do, but I just couldn't breathe. I was feeling very unhappy.

When my wife came home, I told her I was seriously ill.

'I don't have time for your shit,' was her response, and then I realised we had a real problem.

It got to the stage where I couldn't work any more, and soon my wife said she wanted me out of the house. So I had to leave. I was all over the place at this point. I went to my parents and then I went to a psychiatric hospital, where I had two separate week-long stays. They gave me a treatment plan, and then I talked to some psychologists. When I came out after my second week in the hospital, however, it hadn't really done any good. I didn't feel any better; I still had deep depressive, suicidal thoughts.

Just before I came out of the hospital, I'd quit my job. I just couldn't operate. And then I was served with divorce papers. I had no idea what to do.

I'd always thought about doing meditation because I'm

always on the go, and I thought it might calm me down, so I went online and found Will. I went along and spoke to him about what had happened, and he gave me my sound, but I couldn't really interact properly because I was so on edge and jittery. After that, I said to myself: 'Look, you've got nothing to lose, you're just going to do this every single day – you're just going to do it.' I used to get up every morning and I'd sit there, close my eyes, repeating this sound, with my head spinning. I was in such a state of panic that I couldn't concentrate on anything because my mind was so busy.

Soon I got into a routine, which I badly needed since I was no longer working. Every day I'd meditate in the morning, swim, and then go to the coffee shop.

And after about ten days of this, there were times during the meditation when I'd actually feel quite calm, maybe for a minute or so. I was like: *Okay, that's interesting.* And then, about two months later, I started seeing major differences. The anxiety had halved. I'd cut out a lot of the medication. I began to see a light; I began to enjoy things, small things. I managed to start going out with friends a lot more, and then the anxiety just dropped, and dropped, until suddenly I got to a stage where I could go back into the workplace. The medication also tapered off big time. So, within a three-month period, things had significantly shifted.

The meditation gave me a focus, and it also gave me an environment within which to relax. If I felt stressed, which I did on a daily basis, I could go into that zone. If my head was spinning with recurring thoughts, I could recharge my batteries. And it was the first time I'd ever been able to do that. My clarity of thought was just amazing – it was as if my brain had just sort of settled.

Before this I'd been very money-focused, very material-istic. Now I began to realise that if you've got your health you've got everything; it doesn't matter about wealth or anything like that. It was the first time I'd ever felt this, and this sense of calm. My time with my children began to be really fulfilling and it dawned on me that focusing on the present, on the small things, is the most important thing, rather than constantly worrying about what the future holds. My confidence levels rose, and I felt much more content in life.

The divorce was really horrendous (it went to court), but I was now in a very comfortable place mentally and physically to get through it. Unfortunately, I knew it was going to be a fight, even though I tried to do it on friendly terms.

As part of the divorce settlement, my now ex-wife got the right to take the kids to Australia. She went there for a year at first, and then stayed.

The old me would never have had the confidence to go out there on my own, but that's just what the new me did. I went over with no set plan, found a job, found a flat, and just like that I started my new life. As well as work, I go and swim at the beach three or four times a week, and continue my meditation. It feels like a fine way to live my life, and the main thing is I get to be with my kids and be the kind of dad for them I'd always wanted to be. I'm calm, present, and I have energy to give them.

I see them every weekend and on Wednesday nights, and I've actually got quite a good relationship with their mum now, because I've changed as a person and I know how to deal with her, whereas before I didn't. I take the kids swimming, and we play football and do stuff like that.

I think that, although they were too young to verbalise things, they must have known something was going on, but I'm glad that it happened four years ago and not now. My son's at the age where I'm teaching him to ride a bike, how to swim, and those are really important times to me.

I'm not sure the old me would have done that. I was nearly always working, or anxious. Before, I was always waiting for the next big thing, so I was missing out on everything that was happening now. One of the big lessons this experience has taught me is to enjoy what you have. So, in a sense, I'm really glad for what I've gone through, because it's made me realise what's important in life and what's not.

Now I feel I'm trying to pass these messages on to my kids.

One of the main reasons I got through the hard times was the support of my family and friends. Other things helped too, but it was the meditation that had the single biggest effect in terms of the physical and mental impact. It gave me an opportunity to calm down after that fraught period and brought me a completely different focus. Within the space of three months, I was a completely different person.

For me, it was all about hitting the pause button. Because of that, and because I now had the tools to calm my mind, I weaned myself off the medication and got through my divorce. I went to Australia when I was forty-four and built a new life for myself. I didn't really want to be there – I went there for my children – but you know what? It's worked out great.

Becoming a Great Dad

After our first session, I told Nick that because things had been so bad for him, he'd be wise to prioritise the meditation above all else. 'Do it twice a day, no f***ing about' were my exact words. I hoped my strong language would get through to him the importance of putting his health first during this critical phase.

I also told him to call me anytime he needed, and to send me a weekly update for the first eight weeks. He told me that he was experiencing a lot of anger, which wasn't surprising given what had happened with his wife and how let down he felt by her. I told him that the anger was perfectly natural, and though it might be around for a little while, it would eventually pass. If he wasn't meditating it would rot inside him for years and he'd probably end up carrying a lot of bitterness inside. That would affect him badly. It's the same for anyone going through a difficult divorce. You really need to do something like meditation to deal with the anger and pain, so it doesn't fester and make everything worse.

I'm very grateful that Nick listened. The wonderful thing about his story is that, not only was he able to transform himself into a better person, and therefore a better father, he also managed to let go of so much of the bitterness and resentment he was feeling towards his ex-wife, which was critically important for his peace of mind and his overall health and wellbeing. It was also crucially important for his kids to see that their mum and dad weren't at war with each other; that they could be cordial and co-operative and friendly. It's vital for children to see stability in their parents because it helps them feel safe, and by taking this journey of transformation, Nick was able to help bring that about. If at least one of you is in a calm, peaceful and non-reactive state, then it speeds the healing process up, and things don't fester in vitriol.

This is how things can go in relationships once there is a critical mass of stress. It's like being inside a nuclear reactor. Things can spiral out of control very quickly and before you know it you're faced with a meltdown and a lot of negative radiation. If even just one party meditates, by cooling down the nervous system (like the control rods in that nuclear reactor) and helping you to become less reactive, it prevents the process from escalating out of control. As we saw with Arjun's story, this form of meditation can be a great way of calming you down so you're less likely to go over the edge.

Your Relationship with Yourself

As we've seen with Anna, Tom and Nick, the biggest variable in all relationships is your relationship with yourself. When you're happy with who you are, you are much more likely to have happy, healthy relationships with others. If not, the insecurities and issues you have in the relationship with yourself are likely to colour all others – with family, friends and colleagues. The key to a healthy relationship with yourself is whether you feel comfortable in your own skin. Do you love yourself? Can you bear to be in your own company? Do you, like Dylan, in our previous section, have low self-esteem, or beat yourself up, indulging in an internal dialogue with yourself that you'd never tolerate from anyone else, or impose on anyone else?

Here's a self-love and gratitude exercise to help that relationship along.

BEING THANKFUL AND DEVELOPING SELF-LOVE

Each night, as you lie in bed before going to sleep, think of three things that have happened that day or three things in life for which you're grateful. It could be a time when people showed you kindness, a lucky break, or a delicious meal that someone prepared for you. It could be something that made you smile, something that deeply touched you, or something that inspired you.

To mix it up, you could also consider things you take for granted, like your health, your best relationships, the fact that you have enough to eat today, or that amazing possession that you've become so accustomed to that you've stopped appreciating it as much. You can even be grateful for someone who behaved badly, because it's helped you to clarify ways of being that don't work, and learn ways to do things that are more harmonious and inspiring. And, of course, if the practice of this exercise starts to make you feel good, you could even be grateful for being grateful!

Now, having expressed gratitude for three things to do with people or life, now find three things that *you* did really well today, and give yourself some praise for a job well done. Whether it was making someone a cup of tea, offering a sincere compliment, hitting a deadline, writing a really well-constructed email, or maintaining your integrity even when someone was encouraging you not to. You might even have tried something new that you've never done before. You could even congratulate yourself for simply doing your two meditations!

This is a brilliant exercise for lifting your mood just before bed. It is alleged to improve your biochemistry, and it will also help fire the neural networks in your brain that promote a more positive outlook.

If you feel like doing this in combination with the yoga *nidra* exercise on p. 113, do this one first, and then move straight into the *nidra*.

The best way to improve that all-important relationship with yourself, of course, is to meditate. It's not going to fix things overnight – after all, it's a relationship you've been in all your life – but it *is* going to make it better. You'll soon find that as your relationship with yourself improves, this will spill over into your relationships with everyone else, allowing you to focus on being the best you can be. In the next section, we're going to look at just that – whether it's being more productive in the workplace, unlocking your natural creativity or simply performing better in every aspect of your life.

BEING YOUR BEST: PRODUCTIVITY, CREATIVITY AND PERFORMANCE

*'I have so much to accomplish today that I must
meditate for two hours instead of one.'*
MAHATMA GANDHI

One of the major reasons that people come to see me is because they are experiencing problems at work. They might be having issues with a difficult boss, or they might *be* the difficult boss who's struggling with management. They might be having difficulties with concentration, recalling important information, making decisions, or coming up with new ideas. Instead of a specific problem, they might just be feeling as if they're not performing quite up to scratch; they would like a bit of a boost. In this section of the book, I'm going to focus on the three most asked-about areas of work-related problems: improving productivity; dealing with workplace negotiations; and expanding your creative powers.

I think we'd all agree that the modern workplace can be an incubator for stress. For those of us who commute, even the journey to and from work is bad enough. The push and shove of getting in and out of stations, buses or trains, continually surrounded by (or, more likely, crushed up against) other stressed people, is pretty unpleasant. After all this, it's no wonder we arrive at the office already frazzled.

Of course, some offices are nicer than others, but they all tend to generate stress in one way or another. Employees might have to deal with impossible deadlines, demanding workloads, discrimination, bad working conditions, unreasonable expectations or lack of support. Even if you're a happy freelancer who gets to choose when and where you work, or someone who isn't based in an office, the realities of modern working life make a certain amount of stress inevitable. Zero-hour contracts create a lot of strain, from slogging through eighty hours one week to worrying about having none the next, while many service roles are extremely high-pressured. On top of all that, we live in an increasingly competitive and connected world in which it's possible to be on call 24/7, so even when we stop working, we never really switch off.

People don't talk about the 'Sunday Blues' for no reason. After the joy of the weekend, letting our hair down and doing our best sloth impressions on the sofa, Sunday evening creeps around and doom descends. Then, if things have become really bad at work, on Monday morning we open our emails with a feeling of overwhelming dread and the growing conviction that this whole work business is really terribly unfair.

This feeling of being overwhelmed goes back to those premature cognitive commitments, or *samskaras*, that I mentioned in the section on mind and body, which we build up every time we have a difficult interaction with a person or in a particular place. Our body tends to hang on to bad memories (often in ways that are outside of our conscious awareness) because, evolutionarily, this helps us to avoid encountering the same danger more than once. Our nervous system remembers every instance of stress and unhappiness, building up a catalogue of information concerning each potential trigger.

This is why we feel anxiety at the prospect of doing something (or seeing someone) that previously caused us pain and distress. When you're miserably contemplating the week ahead each Sunday evening, it's a clear sign that your workplace has become a major source of stress.

The Cost of Workplace Stress

If you're reading this as someone who runs a business, you'll likely already understand the significant effects that workplace stress can have on both your workers and your profits. According to a recent UK government survey, poor mental health costs the economy between £74 and £99 billion a year; in the US it's thought to be $300 billion. This is just the economic impact; there are also profound social and societal implications.

On a human level, the consequences of this epidemic of stress are huge. In the UK, mental health issues like anxiety are the third main cause of UK sick leave (after colds/coughs and musculoskeletal problems). Stress suppresses the immune system (or causes it to go into imbalanced overdrive), which inevitably results in a large increase in sick days. With chronic stress, people also lack energy and inspiration, so they stay at home when they don't need to (absenteeism), or engage in avoidance behaviour while at work. If anxious or burned-out employees don't take time off, however, and decide to struggle on, it can lead to under-performance, low productivity and costly mistakes. If they decide to leave altogether, the resulting high staff turnover means that companies must bear the brunt of the money and resources involved in recruiting and training new staff. Stress can also lead to unethical behaviour, like taking shortcuts to get a job done in time or lying to customers to cover up our own errors. Businesses staffed by pressured employees might find that their reputation, as well as their bottom line, begins to suffer as a result.

If you work for yourself, or run a business, you need to take care not to put yourself under unbearable pressure. Many world-class business leaders have embraced corporate wellbeing, including Jeff Bezos (CEO of Amazon), Melinda Gates (co-chair of the Bill and Melinda Gates Foundation), media mogul James Packer, entertainment queen Oprah Winfrey, and Ray Dalio, CEO of the world's largest hedge fund. They all understand that it makes financial and human sense to ensure the mental wellbeing of both themselves and their workforce by reducing work-related stress.

HAPPINESS ⇒ SUCCESS

Happiness is a much more reliable formula for success than success is for happiness.

In 2014, I was invited to meet a group of scientists in Geneva whose job is to look after business leaders and elite sports people, especially Formula One drivers. They identified that one of the main factors in achieving high performance was whether people felt happy and settled.

These scientists help their clients find greater levels of happiness and connection to themselves, and their research has shown that meditation is one of the keys to that.

The Effortless Path to Success

So, how can meditation make you happier, more creative and more productive at work?

Biologically, what meditation does is switch on the CEO of your brain: your prefrontal cortex. Once this is activated, you'll have greater executive capabilities, while your concentration and focus will be broader and longer-lasting. You'll also get better at learning new skills and prioritising your workload. Meditation leads to a greater aptitude for innovative thinking and creative problem-solving, two skills that are also controlled by the prefrontal cortex. It also enhances your ability to empathise, which is vital for getting the best out of your team, as well as being important for anyone who wants to get along better with their colleagues.

Before they try it, many of my students in high-powered jobs are concerned that if they calm down they'll lose their 'edge'. I'm constantly intrigued by the amount of people who think that stress is necessary for success, although I can see how they may have come to that conclusion. In a stressed-out world, stress seems useful because it offers us the *illusion* of a competitive advantage – an edge that sets us above others. It's also true that when you're in fight or flight mode, you are innately competitive. After all, from an evolutionary perspective, when raw physical survival is at stake, those who win will live to fight another day.

Unfortunately, however, that's all it is – an illusion. We simply cannot sustain peak performance using stress or adrenaline because it's not biologically possible to continually switch on the stress response without wearing out the very faculties that give us our so-called competitive advantage. Under stress, our prefrontal cortex gets suppressed, and all sorts of vital functions like our capacity for decision-making, memory, concentration and focus begin to suffer. Not to mention the effect this has on the ability to achieve consensus, read people's body language and get others to co-operate.

We might be able to keep ourselves in alert mode for a little while and get things done, but before long the systems that keep us going will be crying out for rest. This is why, at some point, so many people who live a workaholic lifestyle (and the word 'work*aholic*' is no coincidence, it *is* an addiction) get burned out. They might end up having cardiovascular issues, high blood pressure or any of the other physical manifestations that we talked about in the mind/body section of this book. It also makes it much harder to be creative, for reasons I'll go into in a moment, so stress really does undermine your capacity to work at your best.

The form of meditation I teach can bring about success in a much calmer, gentler way, improving your ability to cope with stress, make decisions, and maintain concentration and focus, not to mention all the benefits from increased memory skills. Once that's happening, you'll realise that stress is not needed for success and that you can achieve your goals in much more effortless ways. As you become clearer and more capable, you'll still be able to be a high achiever – perhaps even more so – but you can do this within the context of a fuller, more relaxed and balanced life.

Let's look at some of these benefits in more detail.

Avoiding Burnout

'Burnout – and awareness about its dangers – is now a front-burner topic, both collectively and individually ... it's finally coming to be regarded as the public health issue it is.'

ARIANNA HUFFINGTON,

THRIVE GLOBAL

As we saw in Noel's story earlier, stress and extreme overwork will all too often lead to burnout. This isn't a desirable outcome for anyone. Extreme fatigue, endless physical illnesses (like colds and flu), anxiety and depression all come together in a perfect storm – often accompanied by other wearying symptoms. You feel horribly tired and generally under the weather, and are unable to see a way out of your situation. The worse you feel, the harder it is to force yourself to work, and in the end the sheer effort of it all can push you beyond the threshold of burnout into a full-blown breakdown.

Usually in cases of burnout, an overwhelming work routine has been in place for an unsustainably long period of time. This may be due to workplace culture, peer pressure or a lack of self-worth that makes you work yourself into the ground in order to gain approval. If this goes on for too long, it has a tendency to grow into an all-consuming, self-defeating cycle, skewing your perspectives and leading to social isolation. You may miss your child's birthday party because you need to work, for example, or repeatedly cancel on your friends because you're worried about a deadline. As well as a general sense of exhaustion, burnout brings increased risk of heart disease, cognitive impairment, memory problems, elevated levels of stress hormones and depression.

There was a time (back in the 1980s, perhaps) when, in some professions, burnout and very high levels of stress were seen as almost inevitable, even a badge of honour. We got into the habit of making a virtue of how hard we worked or how little we slept, to the point of seeing overwork as almost heroic. If someone said, 'I worked sixty hours last week,' the likely reply would be: 'Well, *I* worked seventy-five.' Those who pointed out poor working practices were branded as complainers, and when employees took well-earned time off they were suddenly accused of letting the team down. How much we actually got done was irrelevant – it was all about flagellating ourselves at the altar of work, where suffering on the job was commended and the simple act of being present conferred an odd sense of morality.

All this is intimately linked to the Protestant work ethic, which very much defines Western culture. The idea is that it's a person's duty and responsibility to achieve success through hard work and thrift. It's no coincidence that by and large it's in the Protestant-influenced cultures of the world that we find the most stressed-out people (with the possible exception of Tokyo). Although it's transcended its religious origins now, that concept of finding salvation through work has seeped into our society, and it's a hugely pernicious legacy. Everyone's trying to show each other how busy they are, rather than demonstrating how effective they are. Stress helps us feel busy, as if we're doing lots of work, but are we doing it well? Or are we pouring huge amounts of energy into a job while still not achieving much of importance, ignoring the long-term health of the business and ourselves?

Adapting to Change

The Vedic perspective sees change as an opportunity rather than as a threat. Meditation will strengthen your resilience, so you'll have plenty of adaptation energy to take with you in the morning to work. Then, if you get a little dip at 3 o'clock in the afternoon, listen to your body and take twenty minutes for a tactical afternoon 'zing' to get those energy levels back up. There are lots of ways to find the time and a place to do it, since it only takes about the same time as a smoking break or popping out for a coffee or snack. Some of my students lock themselves in the loo, or find a quiet meeting room, or a lobby; others have been known to go and sit in their car. If you feel self-conscious about sitting there with your eyes closed, stick some earphones in your ears and everyone will just think you're listening to music.

Making Good Decisions at the Point They Need to Be Made

'Making a small number of key decisions well is more important than making a large number of decisions. When you're talking about decisions and interactions, quality is more important than quantity.'

JEFF BEZOS,

AMAZON CEO

Have you ever made a really terrible decision when you've been tired, stressed out or just too plain busy? Being successful in business or work (as well as in life) is about making good decisions – but many of us find it hard to take decisive action. Instead, we avoid the issue. Sometimes we can even convince ourselves that we're waiting to see how a situation unfolds, when really, we're just procrastinating. Wait too long, however, and the cost can be significant. Windows of opportunity rarely stay open for long. If we forever remain in a holding pattern, repeating what we know, we stifle growth. This is especially true in business.

More often than not, it's worry that's holding us back. What if these decisions don't deliver spectacular results? The reality isn't usually as bad as we fear. Once we take the leap, we find that we're able to cope, regardless of the outcome. This knowledge gives us the strength and the courage to keep leaping into the unknown, helping us take worthwhile (and well-considered) risks. This isn't about being reckless or thrill-seeking, but having the self-confidence to make challenging decisions that drive us forward – a necessary part of personal and business life.

To me, one of the most interesting benefits of meditating daily is the sharpening of your intuition (I'll go into this more in our final section on 'finding greater purpose and meaning in life'), which allows you to develop more faith in yourself. You chip away at the deeply ingrained fears and anxieties that have been holding you back and you begin to truly believe in your ability to be decisive. The result is a confidence that enables you to avoid costly procrastination and take the leaps that will ultimately bring success.

Being in tune with your intuition also gives you strength to say no, even when desperation is calling you to say yes to a bad deal. As my dear dad once said to me when I was a kid: 'Some of the best decisions you'll ever make are the ones you say no to.' I agree with that, but I also believe that it's better to regret the things you've done than the things you haven't. Do you struggle to know which way to swing sometimes? Meditate!

Brain Power – Stay on the Peak

When you meditate, some pretty interesting things happen in your brain.

During meditation, brain activity mirrors what happens in moments of peak performance. Through repeated practice, you are able to cultivate this patterning, and if you do it long enough, one day it will start becoming semi-peak or peak all the time. Remember that UCLA study I mentioned at the beginning of the book, where they hooked up meditators to EEG skullcaps to measure their brainwaves? When they began to repeat their sound, their brainwave frequencies slowed down from a beta state into the alpha range in all areas of the brain. This alpha wave state is very beneficial to cognitive capability, and the fact that all areas were affected meant that the meditators approached 'peak performance' thinking. On top of that, meditators' brains are able to simultaneously process more information, because there's more activity in the corpus collosum, the band of nerve fibres that joins the two hemispheres of the brain. Your hippocampus will also grow, so you'll be much better at remembering key information.

PEAK PERFORMANCE BRAIN FUNCTION – WHAT YOU NEED TO KNOW

1. Regulating your negative emotions is critical to peak performance. When you try to inhibit negative emotions that you feel – anger, frustration, or disappointment – in the workplace, the rational and emotional parts of you compete with each other. When your brain is busy trying to stamp down negative feelings, you become too distracted to perform well. 'Two systems in your brain are competing,' according to Dr Hans

Hagemann, from the Munich Leadership Group. 'That leads to not being focused on anything any more.' To regain cognitive control, he suggests that you recognise and 'label' how you feel.

2. Peak performance is not about entering a stress state. 'Peak performance means that you find the environment that gets you in a position, and in a situation, where you can really perform at your best,' Hagemann says. The peak performer is someone whose emotions are under control, and as such they can think optimally. 'The best possible situation in this context is experiencing flow, where everything seems to go very smoothly and you are very creative and everything is coming to your mind easily' – which is the state that meditation will get you to.

3. Gender and age matter. Hagemann refers to the amount of intellectual arousal needed to help an individual achieve peak performance. That amount will be different between men and women, old and young. Some people need a lot of arousal to hit their peak. Others can hit their peak with fewer stresses placed on them, and this is certainly true of experienced meditators.

4. Lean towards rewards, not threats. Every company has a 'reward' circle and a 'threat' circle. In a 'threat' state, 'you get a rush of cortisol in your bloodstream. That makes your muscles stronger, but it can cut off your cognitive thinking if it is strong enough,' says Hagemann. In 'reward' circles, people feel good and perform better.

5. Create a psychologically safe workplace. 'In the end, there is one thing that determines the highest performance, and that is psychological safety ... if the team knows it is psychologically safe – which [includes] the reward cycle, the climate

of appreciation, being respected and accepted – there is a high predictability for high performance.' You'll have much more likelihood of creating that kind of workplace if you and your colleagues have increased your empathy through meditation.

Being More Productive

Iona is a very warm person who isn't afraid to laugh at herself or see the humour in a situation. When I first met her, though, she was extremely stressed. She was trying to support her partner, who was an alcoholic, while simultaneously working in a very high-pressure work environment. It was her desire to support him that first brought her to meditation, but she soon realised the benefits of it for herself. As time went on, she used meditation to get her through a very difficult time in her relationship, but also found that it had enormous benefits for her work, and for her overall sense of self.

Iona

'It allows me to take a step back.'

I had a long-term relationship with a guy called Andy who had a nervous breakdown.

He'd been struggling with depression and anxiety, but then he started to use vodka to self-medicate. Soon he became psychotic. Therapy didn't help, and neither did medication. It got worse, and he became an alcoholic. Eventually he was sectioned. During his six weeks in hospital, they taught him mindfulness and he started doing yoga. When he came out, he said he wanted to learn to meditate. So I said:

'Find somewhere, I'll support you. Just get yourself better, whatever you need to do – meditation, anything – just go for it. I'll come with you.'

We met to go to an introductory talk, and I realised he was drunk. We went in and sat there, and I was so angry, worrying that everyone would be able to smell the alcohol on him. He wasn't only drunk, but guilty, and nervous, which is why he'd been drinking in the first place. So, I'm sitting there, my arms crossed, really angry, and then Will starts talking through the benefits, of being able to focus on things and concentrate more, and I think: *Ooh, that would be good.* When he describes the kind of people who would benefit from meditating, he basically describes me. Andy and I both start laughing, and that breaks the stand-off between us.

So, we booked a course. All the way through I was thinking I was just doing it for him, to support him, but then I began to get really interested and thought to myself: *Oh my God, this is quite something.*

I got into meditation really easily, and did it straight away because I needed something to cling on to. My whole world was spiralling out of control. Andy was somebody I thought I was going to be with for the rest of my life, and then in a year he'd lost the plot, two jobs, and ended up in a psychiatric hospital. He just kept spiralling downwards. I'm a pragmatist, a realist, a problem-solver, but I couldn't solve his problem.

I needed something to still my brain and keep me calm, to stop me going bonkers. Meditation did that; it gave me a coping mechanism to get through the day.

It also made me much more productive at work, which I really needed. I'm the head of a department at a big organisation, and suddenly I couldn't keep up my fourteen-hour days in the office because I had to be thinking about where Andy was going to be and make sure I was home for dinner.

Because I'm quite time-poor, I taught myself very quickly to do my meditation on the Tube, on buses, on trains, and learned how to use it as a tool. I have two different types of meditation. The morning one is usually when my brain's solving all the problems I need to address that day, so I come out of it knowing all the actions I need to take to make things flow. And then there are the other meditations, when I have a clearer head, and these are very deep, restful times for me.

Meditating twice a day calms me down and makes me more effective. It makes me a better boss, too, because it stops my knee-jerk responses to stressful situations. I think it allows me to take a step back, and I think it also lets me see the other person's viewpoint. It makes me a more rational person. I think you also take more risks when you meditate – but not the dangerous kind. When you have the stability of meditation, you're able to push your boundaries a bit and get out of your comfort zone, too, which can be really useful in a work context.

My ability to negotiate or navigate committee meetings is much better, too. My company recently did this big tender and I had to speak at a meeting in front of a large group of people. I meditated before I went in and I was completely calm. When we did a practice run in front of our board, I hadn't meditated, and I could hear my heart pounding in my ears. The difference was huge.

A week ago, I'd been told that we'd almost got a deal, but I couldn't tell anyone until I'd finalised it, because if we did it would fall through. I worked through the night to get everything sorted. It was really stressful. When we finally told everyone, people reacted really badly because I hadn't told them before. I was so tired, so on edge, and so emotionally relieved, that I just got swept up into their world. That's when I knew I needed a deep meditation, to get myself into a chilled state again.

In the end, after Andy got thrown out of the second rehab, I realised he would die if he stayed in London with me, so I sent him to his parents. That was very, very hard. Meditation definitely helped with making that decision, ending a ten-year relationship that I didn't want to finish. I still loved him. He is now very much of the opinion that if I hadn't ended things, he would be dead by now.

Meditation has helped me a lot, both personally and professionally, and I'm careful to keep it up. When I haven't meditated, I know it. I'm scratchy and stressed, a bit grumpy and anxious, because I've got lots going on in my head and I'm trying to think it all through at once. Sometimes, if there's a day when something's happened in the morning and I've lost that moment to meditate, I just go to the loo and do it there, or find a chair to sit in somewhere. It works really, really well for me – I'm so glad I learned how to do it.

Calming Yourself on Your Commute

It's a great idea to meditate – like Iona – on your daily commute. For one thing, it can be a convenient time to fit those twenty minutes in. It also has the benefit of helping you deal with what can often be a stressful journey. The jostling to get on and off buses or trains sets off a low-level fight or flight response. Then, as that bus or train gets busier, some people tend to tip over the edge, and that has an effect on everyone else.

Why is that? Well, the answer involves electromagnetic fields, which are created whenever an electric current flows. The world is full of them, although they're invisible to the naked eye. Our bodies are full of electricity – every nerve impulse is an electrical signal sending coded information to our neurons to make our bodies do something, whether it be nodding our head, laughing or blinking. We're a veritable hotbed of electrical activity, and research has shown that we create electromagnetic fields around us. The strongest one of these comes from our heart, which has been shown to beat in a very different way when we're feeling positive emotions.

And if that wasn't incredible enough, the electromagnetic field emitted by our hearts affects the brain states of everyone within an 8 ft radius, so if you're feeling stressed, that's going to create disturbance in your train carriage or around you on the bus.

In addition, when levels of the stress hormone cortisol are raised, you start emitting a cloud of 'alarm pheromones' through the pores of your skin. The people around you subconsciously detect this through their sense of smell, which then activates *their* stress response, and generates a further release of alarm pheromones, creating a vicious cycle and resulting in more stressed-out strangers. During peak commuting times, trains, tubes and buses become hotbeds of stress chemistry and electromagnetic disturbance.

So, besides quitting the office altogether, what can you do about what seems like an unavoidably stressful journey to work? Reading those free newspapers, listening to music or playing video games on your phone might distract you psychologically, but they don't immunise you from the biological stressors floating through the air. Meditation, on the other hand, will help you to partially, or even fully, transcend the unpleasant aspects of being on this moving stress wagon and put you in a space whereby you become physically and mentally *more* energised as you travel, not less.

It's really simple. Just close your eyes and go for it. And again, if you feel self-conscious, stick some earphones in your ears, or just pretend to be asleep.

Meditating for twenty minutes will calm your amygdala so that, by the end of your journey, you feel relaxed and ready for work rather than jumpy and on edge. Your brainwaves will go into a heightened state of synchronised coherence that's mostly immune to the electromagnetic craziness transmitted by your fellow passengers. And by putting you in a hypometabolic state, in which your metabolism is calmed right down, meditation will also mean that you ingest far fewer of those stress pheromones. (Humans, like many organisms, trigger a reduced metabolic state to help survive stressful circumstances and process the consequences of high stress levels.) So not only do you get to benefit from all these effects, your colleagues and your family and friends will benefit from a calmer, happier you when you arrive to and from work.

Finding Internal Stability

Protecting yourself from the stresses of life is a great skill to be able to tap into. Obviously, Iona was under a great deal of stress herself, coping with and trying to help her partner. She also had to deal with her colleagues and staff at the same time. I was interested in her story about them being angry about the recent deal that she couldn't tell them about. One of the problems with stressed people is that they want you to be a part of their drama, because it makes them feel validated. They'll use all sorts of means, conscious and unconscious, to draw you in and drag you down.

Instead, like Iona did, it's far more beneficial to find a place to meditate, put yourself in a nice space, and immunise yourself from being pulled into other people's drama. Instead of amplifying it, you'll have a cooling effect on it all.

Iona talks about how the stability of the meditation meant that she could push herself out of her comfort zone a bit more and take risks. That's a very big benefit. Being able to do things differently, to adapt, is so necessary these days. Just think of how your phone has changed over the past five years. What about your job? How many changes have you had to adapt to since you first started working? It's understandable that these changes can make us feel a little unstable. So many of us are looking for a sense of stability from owning a house, having a secure job, having a lifelong partner, but in most cases, the bank owns the house, we can be made redundant without warning, and partners can seek solace elsewhere. Rather than relying on external sources of security, therefore, it's much more preferable to find an anchor within yourself.

If you can find that internal stability through meditation, by being able to calm yourself and feel your real self no matter what's happening externally, then it doesn't matter about the uncertainty. You can turn up every day, give the best of yourself, and you will adapt to whatever circumstances present themselves. Instead of bringing neediness to your relationships, you'll bring fulfilment. You'll give your workplace, partner, friends and children the best version of you.

It really is possible for each and every one of us to find a place of peace and calm inside of ourselves. We just need the tools to help us discover the place where our essence resides – the place that feels like home. The more we connect to this part of ourselves, the more we bring it to the surface. It begins to imbue our everyday being, so we can meet the world from a place of fulfilment rather than from a place of need. And that will have a cascade effect on every single one of our relationships.

It's a much better idea to find stability within adaptability, rather than stability through rigidity, because stability through rigidity always leaves you weak. Take a piece of granite, for example. It's very rigid and very stable, but there will be a fault line there. As any mason will know, if you just tap that fault line with a chisel, the whole thing falls apart. Life, as we all know, has a tendency to exploit the cracks. It will find those weak spots and tap them – and if your approach to life is through rigidity, then you'll simply fall apart. If that happens as a result of something seemingly small or insignificant, what's going to happen to your sense of self? You'll start to wonder if you'll ever find stability, and this can cause major anxiety issues. Flexibility is key, and this form of meditation will help with that, by developing your prefrontal cortex. It will help you to fire on all cylinders, giving you a boost in the morning with your first meditation, then again in the afternoon or evening.

Letting Go and Becoming More Productive

Iona touches on something that I talked about in our last section of the book – knowing when to let go, when to say goodbye to a relationship that isn't working any more. Meditation gave her the clarity of mind to realise that she was making the right decision both for her and her partner.

It's tricky, because we are very emotionally invested in our relationships, not to mention attached to ideas about what our future is going to look like. The simple reality is that just as we can't control people, we can't control life. Attempting to do so only brings frustration and despair when things inevitably don't work out the way we wanted. When we're overly attached to an idea or person, it also means that we become blinkered to how things really are, and how they need to be changed in order for everyone involved to be able to truly thrive. In business, there is a term called the 'sunk cost effect', which means that if you've invested lots of time, energy and money into a business or a project, you're much more likely to persist with it to the bitter end, even if it's no longer optimal to do so.

When Iona came to that first intro talk, she had invested a

lot of time and energy into her relationship with her partner. Although she had come to support him, she became intrigued by the benefits of meditation herself – particularly the greater focus and concentration it could provide. Looking after her partner was taking up a lot of the time she usually spent at the office, and she was struggling with her workload. After she learned to meditate, however, her productivity at work shot up. Rather than needing to work overtime, she found that she was now able to get everything done in normal hours.

By helping all parts of your brain be more connected and synchronised, this form of meditation helps you to perceive things more clearly; it helps you to think more rationally (by activating your prefrontal cortex) and, as I mentioned before, it helps you to feel your way through things more intuitively, which, as Iona found, led to greater productivity at work. It gives you the self-confidence to realise that you can thrive no matter what the external circumstances. The combined effect of all this is a sense of peace at letting go of things that are no longer serving you, or others; of letting go of the need to be invested in a certain outcome in order to feel whole inside. It makes you more flexible, more adaptable, more willing and more able to understand the way forward – all key to a more productive life.

Navigating
Workplace Confrontation

We find confrontation in all parts of our lives, but dealing with it in the workplace requires particular skill and resilience. I first met Gary on one of my corporate courses. A lot of people are fairly sceptical when they first turn up to these, partly because they're not paying for it with their own money, so they may not be as immediately invested. I can see a whole raft of questions going through their minds. Is this really going to work? Is this guy going to try and get me into some cult through the back door? Am I even going to be able to do it? It's one of my greatest pleasures as a teacher to see how, when people are exposed to experiential knowledge like this, it doesn't take them long to realise they're on to a really good thing.

Gary was one of the sceptics – I could tell from his body language – but at least he was willing to give it a go, and later was able to use meditation as a way of completely redefining his approach to negotiation and navigating difficult work situations. Meditation doesn't take away conflict – that's part of life, and will always be there – but it will make you much more able to deal with it. I'll let Gary tell you how.

Gary

'I was able to have this brilliant negotiation.'

In 2015, I decided to do a year of personal development, and take advantage of courses that were available at work. I'd already done all the other ones, like how to work your computer, how to have a difficult conversation – the usual ones that everyone does. My company's great for training – they have a whole website dedicated to it, so you just go on it, pick one, tell your manager and that's it.

I noticed there was a meditation course on the website and I thought: *That fits into my personal development plan, so yeah, why not?*

There were about twenty of us – mostly lawyers (I work with a lot of them) – and while I was listening to what Will had to say, I'll admit my first thought was: *This is a load of bollocks, really.*

What clinched it for me was the challenge Will set: for us all to meditate twice a day for four months and see what happened. You know how in the *Back to the Future* films, if Marty McFly gets dared to do a thing, he has to do it? Well, more or less as soon as Will said that, I thought: *Oh, now I'll have to do it.*

And so, on the first day I went home and did it, and it was actually really powerful, and I thought, *Maybe this isn't complete bullshit.* I did it again on the second day and then, on the third day, we all meditated together. Then I wandered off back to work, and as I was walking down the street I just burst into tears. I'm not prone to doing that, so it was a bit strange, but it was quite cathartic at the same time, and so I thought: *There's definitely something interesting in this.*

After four months of meditating, I'd completed the

challenge, but thought I might as well carry on. I was liking the little changes I'd noticed, like the absence of anxiety, and not feeling the need to drink a load of coffee at work.

Then I started to notice even bigger changes. I work for a broadcaster, and my job is to support TV programme commissioning, so when someone commissions a show, I have a conversation with the production company and agree how much we're going to pay, who gets what out of it – all the financial and legal stuff, basically. So during the course of a normal day I'm negotiating with people and, quite often, disagreeing about the price of a show, so it can sometimes be quite a combative environment. (There are some pretty argumentative people in the TV industry . . .)

There's a particular company who make brilliant stuff, but they're complete and utter bastards to deal with. It was my turn to work with them, which I wasn't looking forward to. The man who runs it is notoriously difficult; he'll start negotiations by just coming in and shouting at you. It's really unpleasant; he's reduced lots of my colleagues to tears. He starts at a very aggressive level and then escalates. It's a nightmare.

It was a difficult, complicated project and we'd got to the point where I'd agreed the total price for it all. And then, just to clarify, I sent him a note saying: 'This is just to make sure this is the total amount of money we're going to pay you for this.' His response was: 'No, this is the episodic price, and you need to multiply that number by three.' At that point, I had to say, 'Come off it, I'm not giving you three times that – this is it, just take it or leave it.'

Every time I met them, they tried their normal tactics. The guy would be phoning me at 11 o'clock at night and would just start shouting at me. But I was just unflappable. I held my ground. I was able to have this brilliant negotiation with him, where it all just worked. For some reason, I didn't feel fazed, didn't have the pit-in-my-stomach feeling; I felt completely in control. I knew it was going to be okay, and it was. In the end we got what we wanted.

That was just a total game-changer: knowing that I could take on someone notoriously difficult, and for it to all be okay. Everyone at work noticed it – all wondering how on earth I'd managed it.

Since meditating, my approach to work has changed a lot. I think I can now say it's about building relationships and trying to have a sensible conversation, rather than an out-and-out ruck. I used to be quite combative – now I'm much more relaxed with people.

That includes my children, too. It's not very nice to be snappy with your kids, constantly telling them off, but that's how I was a lot of the time. Now I'm able to handle myself much better around them. This morning, for example, my four-and-a-half-year-old came and sat on me while I was meditating. He gave me a big hug, then tried to talk to me. I gently 'shh-ed' him with a smile, and it was fine. In the past, I would have found this hugely irritating, and I would have shouted at him. Now I thought it was lovely, really sweet – he just wanted to hang out with me while I was meditating. He was quiet, and we shared a really precious moment together.

I'd say this new, relaxed me is about two things. The first is immediate response. Before, if someone called me a prick, I'd rise to it immediately. Practising meditation builds in a delay. So, when I was doing that negotiation, the guy would come in and shout at me, 'I'm not having this, take it or leave it, we'll go somewhere else,' and I'd simply say: 'Okay.' Which was not what he was expecting. Normally people buckle under the pressure – 'Oh my God, we'll do anything you want. Please don't go somewhere else.' Having this delay time – it might be just two seconds – is incredibly powerful. I found that it got longer and longer over time, so you get more of a window to decide what to do. That feels like a bit of a victory because you're handling stuff that you never used to be able to.

The second thing is sleep. My sleep's changed, big time. I always found it difficult to get to sleep and to stay asleep, and I wasn't much of a morning person, so I really resented my children for waking me up every day. I had a bit of baggage about that, really. But now I'm able to get up before them, without really trying. It makes it much easier to cope.

It's also given me a greater appreciation of the things external to me, like the environment, nature, and other people. As a result, there's this increased sense of connectivity, which definitely makes life easier, because you're able to forgive people. Suppose I'm driving, and someone cuts me up. Now I can just let it go. Meditating calms down that 'aggro' part of me that I used to channel through fighting – physically fighting, like karate – in my younger days.

As I said before, I work with mostly lawyers, and it's difficult to win an argument with a lawyer, because they're very good at it. Soon after I'd started to meditate, I fell out with one of the lawyers that I work very closely with. We sit next to each other in the office, and it got to the point where we stopped speaking. It got so bad that we had to have a meeting about it, with her boss mediating between us. The pre-meditation me would have f***ed up that meeting, I know it. There would have been a big row. But now, if I've got a thing that I know is going to be particularly difficult, sometimes I save up my morning meditation and do it just before the moment of truth. I did that for this meeting. There were lots of opportunities to f*** it up, but I managed not to fall into any of them.

I'm definitely going through a transition at the moment. I've always felt quite confident and secure, but I know there's a few things underneath that undermine that. I feel like I've got a better understanding of myself. At the same time, I'm much more light-hearted now; I'm always walking around smiling at people, and laughing. There's a lot of spontaneous laughter about stuff that I might just observe or notice. My perception has widened in quite a big way.

I had no intention of this being the life-changing thing that it has been. It's been a really fun, interesting journey, one that I feel like I'm probably only at the beginning of. It's great.

Taking a Step Back

Like Iona, Gary talks about being able to take a step back, to not react immediately. He's doing it at work, and also with his children. And that's something really important. The 'aggro' side of him that he talks about comes from an over-taxed nervous system, which allows the survival instinct of aggression to come out, just as it did with Arjun.

If you've got a nervous system that's already overloaded, it's always going to be on red alert, which means that even very minor triggers can push you over the edge. And once that aggression is let out of the cage, it's incredibly hard to put it back. One of the reasons a lot of men play sport (whether they know it or not) is to get rid of that accumulated build-up of energy and aggression, so they don't take it with them into the rest of their lives, back to their relationships or the office.

Meditation is a great way of calming down your nervous system so that the triggers that would have pushed you over the edge don't get the chance to any more. Instead of being on red alert, you're on amber alert. Instead of your bucket of stress being full, ready to spill over the moment it's disturbed, you're siphoning off a large part of the contents, making it harder for the little things to have such an impact. If you're not constantly on the brink, you're going to be able to handle stressful situations much more easily.

Back to the Future

I think it's very funny that Gary thought of Marty McFly when he rose to my four-month challenge. The reason I specified four months is because that's towards the upper limit of time it takes for some people to see significant results. The majority see results much more quickly than this, and, scientifically, brain changes have been shown to kick in within eight weeks, so the four-month target gives you time to bed in these changes and start to enjoy the results of your meditation practice.

How Meditation Helps Companies Boost Productivity

The reason Gary's company had meditation on offer was that they understood the need for stress management and staff wellbeing. Even in the coolest companies, with nice working environments, people are still stressed, or overwhelmed.

Meditation helps because efficiency goes up and there's greater harmony within teams. The people who are grumps (and Gary would happily admit to having been one of them!) become easier to approach and work with; there's better morale and more of a buzz around the office. All of this increases employees' engagement at work and therefore boosts productivity.

If you're an organisation that's going through change, getting your employees to meditate is particularly useful. If people are locked in stress mode, they can't help but be fearful, and when people are fearful, they don't like change. If people meditate, they'll be enthusiastic about change as a source of possibility, of creativity, even excitement. You don't even need everyone in a company to start meditating – that would be pretty dreamy, but is probably not realistic! – because when just a few people start, others will tend to follow, because they'll hear how good it is. Gary the arch-sceptic has inspired lots of people to come and find out how they can make the most of meditation, so they can live a fuller, richer life.

Enhancing
Your Creativity

S o that's productivity taken care of. What about that most valuable – often most elusive – of resources: creativity?

Creativity is something much admired. We look at the brilliant, inspired ideas of others and wish we had their originality and boldness. There's an air of glamour and romance in the popular imagination that surrounds those who dedicate themselves to the creative life (think of the seductive image of the penniless artist toiling away in a Paris attic, or the solitary writer tapping away at their typewriter).

Creativity doesn't just have to be about art, however. Ultimately, creativity is about turning ideas and imagination into reality. There are two parts to that: firstly, seeing things in new and interesting ways and coming up with innovative ideas; and secondly, bringing those ideas into the world. Both of those can be hard if you're feeling stuck or overwhelmed.

Meditation can help creativity flow by dealing with the barriers to that process, which could include any or all of the following:

Lack of Inspiration

Inspiration is a very powerful thing, but you need space to get it. You can't force it, either; it's something that comes *to* you and *through* you. When every idea you have feels like a cliché or you've drawn a blank and can't think of any new ideas at all, sometimes taking time out to meditate will allow your subconscious to kick-start your creativity. My students often report that they have fantastic ideas while they're meditating – some of them even keep a notepad close so that they can write them down just after they've finished.

Time-Wasting

Sometimes it's not the first part of the creative process – the imaginative, daydreamy bit – that's the problem, but the sitting down and actually making something out of it. For some, this is when distraction and procrastination kick in, especially when the entirety of the internet is at your disposal. Through developing the prefrontal cortex, meditation will lead to improved concentration and productivity, so you can stop time-wasting and turn that initial spark of an idea into something real.

Fear

As well as distraction and procrastination, fear has disastrous effects on creativity. The stress that deadlines bring tends to strangle the flow of new ideas and the best expression of them. Meditation will deal with the anxiety brought on by stress. It will also, by increasing your belief in your own decisions and intuition, help you trust your own creative process, bringing an end to the paralysis that sometimes comes with caring too much about being judged. Fear of what other people think is a terrible barrier to creativity – be bold!

Overcoming Unhelpful Stereotypes

One of the romantic images of a creative's life is that of bohemianism, hard whisky-drinking and staying up all night with just a typewriter and an overflowing ashtray. As irresistible as this idea can be, the majority of famously wild artists, musicians and writers created great work *despite* their lifestyle, not *because* of it. I may be wrong, but I believe Hunter S. Thompson is the exception, rather than the rule, as far as the creative's life goes. Jack Kerouac, one of my personal favourites, and a notorious boozer, described bohemian hedonism in *On the Road*. The unsustainability of that lifestyle and the breakdown that it led to (which he describes in *Big Sur*) meant he never got to enjoy his dotage. He died aged forty-seven from long-term alcohol abuse.

It's probably not realistic to expect yourself to eliminate all of your less-than-healthy habits, and you might not even want to. Even so, this form of meditation will certainly make you healthier and help you stay fresh and well rested. Stress and exhaustion aren't at all conducive to creativity, so it's really vital to let your brain slow down and get good-quality sleep.

Despite the other popular idea, shared by a fair few artists, that you have to 'suffer for your art', you'll also generate your best work when you're happy. The myth that great work is only produced by 'tortured souls' is just that – a myth. I know of plenty of people who don't fit that model, like the moviemaker David Lynch, who is positively evangelical about meditation and its benefits, and continues to make his dark, thrilling – and very successful – films.

SOCIAL MEDIA – CONNECTION OR ADDICTION?

'In my attempt not to miss out on anything – by being continually plugged in – I was in fact missing out on something very important: the art of being.'

NORMAN ROSENTHAL,

THE DOCTOR WHO DISCOVERED

SEASONAL AFFECTIVE DISORDER (SAD)

Speaking of focus, and its enemy procrastination, let's talk about technology and social media. Our relationship with both is complex. On the one hand, technology gives us the opportunity to do more, achieve more, wherever we are and whatever time it might be. On the other, it means we're always available. As the pace of life accelerates, we find ourselves in a continual state of heightened stress. We believe we're saving time when we deal with emails on the way to work – and yes, you may have sent out those responses – but your stress levels have started to rise and you've failed to notice that the sun is shining.

Likewise, social media keeps you up to date with what's going on and connected to people in your networks, but we all know how much time is frittered away on browsing. It will make very little difference to your life, and is sometimes just an outlet for distraction from pain, stress or loneliness.

Recent research suggests that the average person spends 135 minutes a day on social media. Meditation wouldn't be a bad way of using some of those minutes. And, apart from all the benefits we've talked about elsewhere, meditation will enhance your ability to connect with other people, not on a screen, but live and in real-time.

When you're in this state of calm and balance, social media

can be used as an occasional tool, rather than a closet addiction. You also might not feel the need to look at your phone all the time, because if you're meditating regularly, and giving yourself a regular hit of endorphins, you won't be looking for a dopamine rush. Double benefit!

Freddie

'I'm able to think more expansively.'

I really took to Freddie as soon as I met him. He's a very warm, charismatic guy with great energy and a fantastic smile. He was a lovely example of the type of person who comes along to see me when they're already successful and simply wants to get a bit more out of life. He'd been a director at one of the most creative advertising agencies in the world and had just set up his own company dealing with some of the biggest names in the corporate and creative media space. He wasn't having problems accessing his creativity; he wasn't stuck. He was already super switched on – he just wanted to enhance things further.

> I know there are legions of people for whom meditation is part of a spiritual quest, but that's not my experience. I have no prejudice against that, but I see meditation instead as an unbelievably useful practical everyday tool for life and work.
>
> When I went along to learn how to meditate with Will, and I was listening to the stories of the other people in the room, and their reasons for coming, I felt a bit out of place, because I could see there were people there who seemed to have much clearer and bigger problems than I did.
>
> What I could also immediately see, especially when he was

talking about the neuroscience aspect of it, were the sort of benefits that might appeal to a creative individual. The more I listened, the more I could see that this could be incredibly useful for people whose job it is to think expansively.

That was very exciting to me because I'm the co-founder of a company that works in the intersection between arts, culture, entertainment and the world of brands. There's a lot of creativity involved.

When we did the first meditation, all together, I immediately got into a really relaxed state. It was very physical – it was a big deal. I really went under. It was like when you see those free-divers going down and down and down, and it gets darker towards the bottom. It felt like I was doing the same, and the further down I got, the more peaceful and ethereal it got.

I've been meditating ever since, and what I've really noticed is that, very often, really good-quality creative ideas pop into my head while I'm practising. They really come from somewhere deep inside of me. Now, I can't work out whether that's just being able to shut out the noise of running a busy business when I meditate or whether there's something more fundamental going on, but either way, it doesn't really matter, because it's there.

I think unconsciously we're trying to solve problems the entire time. Every time somebody presents you with a problem, it gets logged, along with the ninety-nine other problems you're trying to solve – some of them professional, some of them personal. Meditation allows you to self-select which problem is the most pressing or is closest to reaching a solution. That makes it unbelievably useful and powerful as an alternative to banging your head against the wall or engaging in the normal kind of chaotic brainstorm searching.

Everything is a creative endeavour, whether that's coming

up with an advertising campaign or managing people, and so what I find incredibly helpful about meditation is that whatever problem I'm trying to solve, whether that's a personnel problem; a growth problem; finding a new office in a city I don't know – I'm able to use the meditation to have better access to my creative capacity to solve that problem.

What meditation also seems to allow you to do is to think more expansively. I was already pretty good at it, but now it's really taken off. The opposite of expansive thinking is reductive thinking, and it's fear that drives that. I've read research that says most human beings experience a fight or flight response in a professional or social situation once every seven to eighteen minutes. It could be at a very basic level: fear of saying something out loud and people not thinking it's a very good idea, for example. Meditation helps you break out of that reductive thinking, which can often be something we rely on in all areas of our life because we think it's going to get us through difficult situations.

I think now I'm also less reactive, or less quick to go, 'Oh no, we need to do X, Y or Z to get through this situation.' I take a moment to process. I think meditation helps with that because you become used to pausing, to putting in a moment of contemplation. It's not a case of 'There's a big crisis, so now I'll go and meditate'), it's not like that, it's simply part of my daily routine.

Being a bit less reactive also means you can be more expansive, and if you're being expansive it means that you're probably being a bit more creative about how to solve the problem. That's really rewarding, and I'd really like to see more people in my industry adopting this as a practice.

Something else I've noticed is that my public speaking has massively improved. In my younger years, I was crippled with fear about addressing large audiences, but now I massively enjoy it. Of course, over the years I've practised a lot, but since I started meditating it's gone from something that I can do to something that I can do really well, and even look forward to.

Meditating beforehand is a pretty good way to learn your lines, to focus and bring your heart rate down etc. I not only feel calmer, but when I'm standing up there, there is this sense of openness and genuine connection with the audience which is definitely new. Even though previously I'd do a good job, it now feels more like a dynamic performance – where I'm giving some energy out and then getting it back from the audience.

I'm sure that's connected, because I used to enjoy the buzz of it but not necessarily doing it. Now I really do, and when people see that, it becomes a virtuous circle.

I think part of it is about allowing yourself to be vulnerable, and that's another thing that meditation does, in a sideways way: it helps you sit and look inside when it's way easier just to ignore what's going on below the surface.

For me, learning to meditate was a transformative experience, and it has to a degree changed my life. I haven't shaved my head and left my job to be a lumberjack or anything. I think that actually you only have to change a tiny part of your everyday routine in order to facilitate something that offers you lifelong change. I think for many of us it does change our lives, and that doesn't have to be in a fundamental way, just improving it.

Finding Your Flow

Freddie talks about having lots of ideas when he meditates. I'm not surprised. As all great artists know, meaningful and resonant creativity doesn't come from the intellect. It is something that comes through them, from a very subtle plane of existence.

Meditation helps you find that place of flow, where your brain is connected to something deeper, and it's very compelling to go there and access that, and then express what's coming through in daily life.

However, when life begins to take over – when the deadlines come in and you've *got* to produce, you've *got* to create – the stress response can cause a shutdown of our prefrontal cortex, and we begin to lose our access to that much-needed creative flow.

Unconscious Creativity

Often artists are asked about the inspiration for their work, and usually reply with something seemingly vague along the lines of 'It just came to me' or 'I dreamt it'. This might sound a little too good to be true, but there is real truth behind those statements.

Noel Gallagher of Oasis explains his writing of 'Don't Look Back in Anger' like this: 'I don't ever sit there and think that I wrote that, you know. I think it came from somewhere else. I think it was a song that was there somewhere, and if I hadn't have written it, you know, Bono would have written it. You know, it's like those great songs … you know, they're there. If they fall out the sky and land on your lap, then lucky you.'

Likewise, Paul McCartney dreamt the melody to 'Yesterday', woke up and just started playing it on the piano next to his bed. It has since become the most played (and covered) song of all time!

This kind of unconscious creativity doesn't just happen to artists, either. Roger Penrose, who discovered many of the features of black holes, found the key to his understanding of these complex scientific phenomena on a leisurely walk. Legend has it that Archimedes had his Eureka moment while getting in the bath.

The common denominator of all these examples of 'aha' moments through history is the relaxed, de-focalised state that preceded them, which allows the subconscious brain to formulate ideas into something coherent. Whilst we can't claim that those songs, or those moments of inspiration, happened because of a meditation practice, we do know that if you practise this form of meditation, you will experience huge boosts in creativity and inspiration. When your nervous system is less stimulated, and the prefrontal cortex area of your brain is firing on all cylinders, the sky's the limit.

To help get your brain into a more creative state, we've come up with an audio track, available on www.theeffortlessmind.com. Lie down with your headphones on and listen to the alpha brainwave-inducing sounds we've created for you. It's a great way of getting your creative juices flowing!

ON THE OTHER HAND: AN EXERCISE FOR STIMULATING RIGHT BRAIN ACTIVATION

Getting lost in an activity is usually an excellent way to get your creative mojo flowing, and if you haven't got time to tune into the creative audio exercise on our website that I mentioned just above, then use your non-dominant hand to write or draw for five minutes. It's an excellent way to activate your right brain, and with it your creativity. By using your 'wrong' hand, and doing this in a focused way, you will find yourself more creatively and emotionally attuned. You'll also be more intuitive.

Performing Under Pressure

When you meditate, your prefrontal cortex will become more active and grow thicker, which will make you more rational (and able to take that all-important step back), and be more creative, as well as being calmer.

And, as Freddie says, that calm is incredibly helpful if you have to perform. If you've got an interview or a presentation to do, it takes away the nerves and the anxiety and allows you to be at your best. You're able to present yourself clearly and articulately; your manner and delivery relaxed, which is a very powerful thing to be able to carry off in front of lots of people. What's also really lovely is that, if people challenge you with a question at a presentation, or if you're at an interview and they try to test how well you can think on your feet, you're completely switched on. You won't get flustered – instead, you'll come out with something great, something that makes people go 'Wow!' It's well known that many interviewers make a conclusion about you in the first five seconds – so if you go in there calm and confident, and at ease, you're much more likely to get the job.

Thinking in New Ways

All human beings are, by their nature, creative. We've had to be, to survive. Working out how to create fire, how to make weapons to fight off those predators back on the savannah, how to cope with floods and drought – all these situations required vast amounts of creativity and the ability to adapt to new circumstances. Although we're no longer having to come up with new solutions to stay alive (although fight or flight might make it *feel* as if you are when you're trying to figure out a way to deal with an overbearing boss or even a jammed photocopier), we still have those ingrained powers of creativity and adaptation.

Not being afraid to think in new ways will really pay off, something that is commonly remarked upon by people I've taught. Once your neural pathways start to change, you'll be able to come up with creative solutions to problems – to truly 'think outside the box' – because you won't always revert to learned (and sometimes negative) behaviours.

Freddie's right – there were people on the course that he attended who had much bigger problems than him. But, like him, there are always plenty of folks who learn proactively. Not all of them are feeling stressed. They might be feeling fine and really enjoying life, but they'd like to see what else is possible. And as Freddie said, changing your life in what seem like small yet sustainable ways, like learning to meditate, can affect you in much larger ways than you'd previously imagined. It's like a glorious butterfly effect of positive changes. I'd never have thought that sitting down and closing my eyes and repeating a sound in my head just twice a day for twenty minutes would lead to the changes I've seen in myself, but I'm very glad that they have.

Freddie is right about something else, too: *everybody* is responsible for creativity, because we are all solving problems, all the time. If you can manage to get yourself in a calm, balanced state, then that will have a massive impact on those around you. Indeed, of all the cognitive functions that become most enhanced with this practice, creativity demonstrates the biggest improvement of all. And the very happy by-product of this is that people find that their ability to solve problems goes up remarkably. You're also calmer to be around, which will have a knock-on effect and make others calmer too. We can all make the world a better place, we can all be a part of solving the problem – you need only start with the little world around you.

What's Your Measure of Success?

*'To do more for the world than the world
does for you - that is success.'*
**HENRY FORD,
AMERICAN INDUSTRIALIST AND FOUNDER OF
THE FORD MOTOR COMPANY**

So, you might have started meditating and, as a result, you've upped your productivity, hit a big deadline, smashed your targets or had a record year of profits. And those would generally be seen as good things. Culturally, we tend to view success as the achievement of a specified goal, or reaching a certain status. We even measure our country's success in terms of Gross Domestic Product.

But is this really what success means? Think of all the things you've tried to achieve in your life and think about the ultimate, underlying reasons for striving to achieve them. In almost all cases, I'd say it's in pursuit of happiness or fulfilment.

So why aren't happiness and fulfilment our benchmarks for success? Admittedly, they're not as easy to measure as the size of your house or your salary or bank balance. In a study by Princeton economist Angus Deaton and eminent psychologist Daniel Kahneman (both of them Nobel Prize-winners), they found $75,000 or £48,000 to be the thresholds beyond which any further increase does very little, if anything, to our levels of everyday contentment or happiness. So why bother giving it such major credence?

The problem is, because we've been culturally conditioned into caring so much about our status in relation to others, it's hard not to feel as if we're in competition with each other. That approach will always lead to putting off the potential for happiness into the future, when you've achieved your goals, rather than being able to be happy right now. If you look at the etymology of the word success, it originates from the Latin *successus* and the verb *succedere*, which means 'to come close after'. The word itself implies succession, continual evolution, rather than an absolute state. So don't kid yourself that success can be achieved and then that box can be ticked as done. The pursuit of it will continue throughout your life and is unique to every individual. What it means to you will evolve and change.

> 'The gross national product does not allow for the health
> of our children, the quality of their education or the joy
> of their play. It does not include the beauty of our poetry
> or the strength of our marriages, the intelligence of our
> public debate or the integrity of our public officials. It
> measures neither our wit nor our courage, neither our
> wisdom nor our learning, neither our compassion nor
> our devotion to our country. It measures everything,
> in short, except that which makes life worthwhile.'
>
> **JOHN F. KENNEDY,**
> **FORMER US PRESIDENT**

Perhaps it's time to review. Stop, take a breath, and really see what's around you. Feel your body. Feel deeply into the centre of your being. Tune into who you really are, and what really is important to you. Pay attention to what you find, to what you require in order to feel fulfilled. Be sure to discern if it feels like something that helps you to feel genuinely fulfilled, rather than merely fleetingly happy. And likewise, is it something you genuinely believe is important to you, or is your motivation for wanting it because it is something that you think other people will be impressed by? Try to be as honest with yourself as possible.

Now recalibrate your notion of success to reflect what will

help you experience true fulfilment, and make adjustments to help usher in those new soul-satisfying goals. It will be a deeply rewarding exercise because it will reflect who you really are, which is absolutely worth finding, exploring, celebrating and embodying.

I'll talk about this more in our next section on 'Finding Greater Purpose and Meaning in Life'.

FINDING GREATER PURPOSE AND MEANING IN LIFE

So far, we've been focusing mostly on the practical side to meditation and how you can use it as a tool to help you cope with the stresses and strains of 21st-century life – physically, mentally and emotionally. But there is another side to it, just as there is another side to each of us – something more than our minds and our bodies that can be described in many different ways – our spirit, our essence, our soul. In the Western world, this isn't given half as much recognition or attention as our mind and body. Yet, isn't our spiritual wellbeing at the *heart* of our mental and physical wellbeing?

So here I want to talk about spirituality, and how meditation can help us develop that side of ourselves, so that we can find greater purpose and meaning in life.

What is Spirituality?

Spirituality is a word that means different things to different people, and comes with a lot of assumptions and pre-conceptions, so to start with, here's how I understand it.

Because it's something that's so hard to define, or truly comprehend, many people reject spirituality as a concept out of hand. Some assume it's always linked to religion; others associate it with hippies, self-indulgence, or going off somewhere exotic to 'find yourself'. The language associated with it can be difficult, with terms like 'transcendence' or 'consciousness' muddying the waters even further. Yet go into any bookshop and you'll find shelves and shelves dedicated to this very subject, because it's something that continues to attract us – that sense that there is something else out there, something *more* that will add meaning to our lives.

This sense of 'something else' has been discussed, debated and written about for thousands of years. Around 380BC, Plato, one of the great founding fathers of Western culture, wrote in

The Republic about men who had all their lives been chained deep within a dark cave. The prisoners see shadows cast upon a wall by a fire that is burning behind them and they think this is reality. One of them frees himself and leaves the cave, where-upon he discovers sunlight and the wider world. He realises that the shadows he saw in the cave were not reality at all. At first, because he's so unaccustomed to the light, it stuns and confuses him. Eventually he sees things clearly, and, vastly excited, returns to the others to tell them what he has discovered. The prisoners reject his report as being barely credible, having not experienced the truth for themselves, and do not even attempt to break their chains – their world is all they know.

The eminent physicist Carlo Rovelli uses Plato's *The Allegory of the Cave* in his book *Reality Is Not What It Seems* as a metaphor to describe science: 'We are all in the depths of a cave, chained by our ignorance, by our prejudices, and our weak senses to reveal to us only shadows. If we try to see further, we are confused: we are unaccustomed. But we try. This is science.' He goes on to say that

scientific thinking explores and redraws the world, gradually offering us better and better images of it, teaching us to think in ever more effective ways. Science is a continual exploration of ways of thinking. Its strength is its visionary capacity to demolish preconceived ideas, to reveal new regions of reality, and to construct novel and more effective images of the world. This adventure rests upon the entirety of past knowledge, but at its heart is change. The world is boundless and iridescent; we want to go and see it. We are immersed in its mystery and in its beauty, and over the horizon there is unexplored territory. The incompleteness and the uncertainty of our knowledge, our precariousness, suspended over the abyss of the immensity of what we don't know, does not render life meaningless; it makes it interesting and precious.

These may be the words of a physicist, but his thoughts on science are very closely aligned to my approach to spirituality, which is all about making it possible to see the world differently, to explore the things you couldn't see before. Following this definition, I too am a scientist – a spiritual scientist who, rather than exploring ways of thinking, explores ways of *being*.

Presence and Connection

For me, spirituality is all about connection. Firstly, it's about self-connection, about finding your true self and feeling grounded through that. Then it's about recognising and celebrating the fact that we're all connected to each other by virtue of our common humanity and shared experience. Because we're all in this thing called life together, and because we share the same biological and emotional make-up, we can connect through love, compassion and empathy.

Once we have grown in our connection to each other, we can start to widen that to all of life on earth and beyond. Have you ever looked up at the stars and felt an innate sense of connection? Imagine experiencing that 24/7. Pretty good, right? Now amplify that by a hundred and imagine *that* being your 24/7 experience. That's what being spiritual feels like. And that's why, once people experience that level of connection, they make it a big part of their life.

It's almost like being a child again – being fascinated by everything you see, feeling very sensitive to your surroundings and having a sense of wonder about the world. You're filled with love and purpose, and that makes you feel great from the moment you wake up every morning to the moment you drift off to sleep. There's a sense of knowing, of being really alive, of finally having come home. And that's a very precious feeling.

It's also about presence – about really being in the moment, with our whole selves. And that's important in all parts of our lives. When we're more present at work we get our tasks done more easily, more productively and ultimately more successfully. When we're more present in our relationships, they feel fulfilling, and we come away from our interactions with people feeling that something really positive happened there. When we're more present in nature, then our soul is uplifted by that. When we're more present with our children, they feel genuinely nourished and grow up to be better-adjusted human beings as a result.

What robs us of presence is our fight or flight function, our hypervigilance, making us worry about the future, investing our hopes and dreams in it. And then there are all the painful memories we haven't yet fully processed, giving us a tendency to review the past. All that noise, all that stimulation, all those memories, all those distortions mean that we have a lot of thoughts and a lot of emotions that take up significant chunks of bandwidth and mean we can't be fully present. It is for this reason that you can't just simply *think* yourself present – those physiological barriers that I've just mentioned need to be tackled first. The good news is that the form of Vedic-inspired meditation I teach, by working at a physiological and unconscious level, will do exactly that, bringing all the many benefits of enhanced connection and presence.

Transcendence

This is another term that needs definition, I feel, because it conjures up all sorts of notions and images, many of them stuck in 1960s and '70s hippy counterculture.

Put simply, transcendence means 'to go beyond' – beyond your mind, your ego, your stresses, your storylines – to a place inside where your deepest essence resides. It's a place of bliss, and vast expansive experience. If you practise meditation properly, and for long enough, you will get to this place, and when you do, it is deeply fulfilling, but you don't *need* to experience transcendence for the meditation to work. Even if you simply move closer to it, you'll find yourself letting go of unnecessary mind clutter, emotions and stored-up baggage.

More generally, transcendence is to move beyond whatever situation you are in. There's a wonderful expression in Sanskrit, *niwartadhvam*, which connotatively means 'to transcend where you are'. This is a perfect encapsulation of what I'm hoping to teach people to do. I'm giving them a tool that helps them transcend wherever they are spatially, but it also means they can transcend any limitations and blockages they feel so that they can be a freer human being, be more themselves and fulfil their greatest potential.

Consciousness

'A scientific world-view which does not profoundly come to terms with the problem of conscious minds can have no serious pretensions of completeness. Consciousness is part of our universe so any physical theory which makes no proper place for it falls fundamentally short of providing a genuine description of the world.'

SIR ROGER PENROSE,
OXFORD UNIVERSITY PHYSICIST,
SHADOWS OF THE MIND, 1996

What do I mean when I talk of consciousness? Well, at the deepest level, at the universal level, it's the awareness and the intelligence that governs everything.

All those thousands of years ago in the Himalayas, what was happening was an explosion of consciousness, an awareness that there were things in life that were not yet understood, but which were awaiting our discovery. People began to develop some masterful capabilities, then taught others to help them to move towards their level. More and more people became highly conscious and started uncovering the mysteries of life, contributing to this growing body of knowledge. That bred a whole culture of people who came up with many innovations – amazing understandings of the science of life, of the body, of the gut, of the brain, of mathematics, of yoga.

When the notion of consciousness first came up in Western texts, in Latin, around five hundred years ago, it seemed to be quite well aligned with the ancient Eastern understanding that there is basically one indivisible whole awareness or conscious-ness throughout the world and throughout the universe, and we are all unique aspects of a wider field of consciousness. But then, later on, in the 18th century, consciousness began to be talked about in the West as a very individualised, mind-borne phe-nomenon, and that changed our view of what it was all about.

From an ancient Eastern perspective, your nervous system is the conduit through which your consciousness expresses itself. So, if your nervous system is cluttered up with rubbish, then your consciousness is also going to end up being filtered through that lens of noise, pain and negativity. It's like having some beautiful, pure water straight from the glaciers of the Himalayas and putting it in a cup that's dirty and scratched. If you try to look at that crystal-clear water through the dark, frosted glass, what you're going to see is murk. So even though what's inside is pure, all the world will perceive is something muddy and clouded.

Probably the best single word we have for it is awareness. My only slight concern with the use of that term is that it's poten-tially limiting, because we can only be aware of what we think we know. It describes only the conscious, not the unconscious.

Whereas for me, consciousness is everywhere – it extends beyond what we are consciously aware of. It's simply a case of how much of it you have access to, because it transcends every single model, every single paradigm and every single limitation that you have.

By expanding your consciousness, what you're really doing is expanding your present limitations. And there are some very good reasons for doing that. Firstly, and very importantly, it will help you feel like you're experiencing your full potential. Vedic-inspired meditation will allow you to feel less stressed, be more aware of yourself and of other people, have more energy, more love and more attention to give. You will feel more connected, you will be more spontaneous, more joyous. You will have more trust in yourself, and you will intuitively know where you need to go and what you need to do. Your life will feel more punctuated with a sense of clarity, and of flow. You will be operating with more empathy and compassion, and you will ultimately feel more at peace.

This will have an inevitable knock-on effect on others, whether that's people who are close to you, like partners, children, colleagues and friends, or the wider world.

Returning once again to good old Einstein's observation that 'problems cannot be solved from the same state of consciousness that created them': if you only have a very limited understanding of what's going on in the world, and your solutions are coming from the same limited place that caused the problems to arise in the first place, then how are you going to solve them? Without higher levels of conscious awareness, we will find it difficult to truly fix our own problems, let alone the problems of the world. We'll only give issues like climate change or the destruction of the rainforests ten minutes of our attention, and then go back to living our everyday lives, because we're in survival mode and we've got a mortgage to pay. It's very easy to get sucked into our own small dramas because that's what we're faced with right here and now, and because often it's easier to zero in on them rather than take in the bigger picture.

I feel that it's time for us to take (meaningful) responsibility. In the old days, we wanted God to fix it. Now we want our politicians to fix it. They're not going to. Some of them might have good intentions but there are too many other interests at play. The responsibility for fixing it lies with us, the people, the collective body of humanity. More powerful consciousness can conceive of the unforeseen consequences of our actions – which is important. Let's make those positive, rather than negative.

Enlightenment

Now we come to the final term in our list of definitions: enlightenment. From the Vedic perspective, it's what we're driven to search for (often unwittingly) throughout our lives, hence our continual pursuit of sustained happiness. The Vedic perspective would also suggest that enlightenment can only come from within, from really connecting to yourself.

Contrary to popular opinion, enlightenment isn't a state we suddenly find ourselves waking up to overnight, rather, it's something we evolve into over time. And it is not a binary state of being, where you either are or you aren't; it's far richer and more nuanced than that.

Enlightenment is simply an overarching term for all the more integrated 'higher' states of consciousness that we humans are capable of, but rarely reach. And the reason we rarely reach it is because so few of us are actively seeking it as our main priority in life. If you were to survey a hundred people at random, how many of them would say their number one goal in life was enlightenment? I suspect it would be zero. You would probably need to get into the tens of thousands before you even got a single hit, so no wonder it's such a rarity. But it needn't be. That's not to say that enlightenment *should* be your goal in life (and, indeed, it works better as a process rather than a goal), but opening yourself up to the idea of what enlightenment represents and having that as a direction in life is no bad thing. Consciousness itself is a continuum of infinite gradations, much like a rainbow – which is made of seven broad colours, but in reality has innumerable shades of colours within it. Just think about the Pantone colour chart. It contains 1,867 colours, and there still may not be an identical match to the colour of the walls of your house, or the shoes you're wearing! As the horizons of our expanded awareness grow, so too does our experience of life.

The key to getting there is to not strive too hard to achieve it. Simply lead a full and purposeful life and take a twice-daily twenty-minute dip into transcendence. Relax and enjoy the ride, and remember it's a process, not something you should aim to achieve fully overnight. Simply follow your intuition about where to go and what to do, and enjoy every moment you can.

How Meditation Helps You Reach Your Deepest Essence and Find Greater Meaning and Purpose in Life

All those thousands of years ago, the forefathers of the Vedic tradition left a legacy of really useful techniques. From master to student, they passed on the knowledge of how to bring about change in ourselves, providing us with the power and capability to transform ourselves in the most meaningful ways possible.

Connecting to Yourself

By systematically putting yourself in a restful place, you allow your nervous system to start repairing itself and clearing out all the noise, clutter and negative associations you've picked up in your life.

One of the first things that my students report noticing is their heightened sensory capabilities. Things seem brighter and more vivid; tastes are stronger; life is larger. This greater recognition and enjoyment is the enlivened connection between the 'functioning' you and the inner, richer you. It's the first budding of awareness, which then begins to spread to other areas of your life.

As I discussed in Anna's story, meditation is an extraordinary tool for dissolving the unconscious programming that has previously held you back. As time goes on, and your practice develops, you'll become far more aware of your emotional reactions, recognising patterns of negative behaviour and thought processes. The negative neural pathways that result in reactive and emotive responses begin to loosen and dissolve, and this continues to unfold the more and more you meditate. You'll feel more balanced, aware and conscious of yourself on an emotional level, so you're able to be more connected and move towards more positive actions and reactions.

With greater awareness of yourself comes the ability to connect with and understand other people. As your inner connectivity grows, you'll start to feel more at one with the world around you. That benefits your relationships, as we've looked at earlier, but people also often report a sense of connection to something that's beyond the mind, body or ego – something that's all-embracing and pervading.

Intuition

As I've mentioned before, one of the best outcomes of this form of meditation is that you'll feel yourself navigating life with a strong sense of intuition, by which I mean being able to easily make decisions and acquire knowledge, guided by something that isn't intellect or reason. It's an ability that transcends the logic of our Western mindsets but it's an innate quality of humans everywhere.

The problem is that our ability to feel connected to our intuition is compromised by our sense of internal disconnection, by our defence mechanisms and coping strategies, by our over-stimulated nervous systems. There's so much noise and clutter there – we're subject to so many internal signals – that it's hard to make sense of what's coming through.

Sometimes, of course, we simply don't want to listen to what's coming through; we don't want to follow our intuition. This is because deep down we feel vulnerable, and our instinctive reaction when this is playing out is to want certainty. Until your intuition is very strong, it doesn't feel certain, and our intellectual projections of what *will* happen give us a greater sense of stability, so we cling to the security of apparent knowingness, and ignore what we know we should do deep down.

But when you're feeling more connected within, there is a greater internal certainty, and the greatest internal certainty of all is that you can cope, survive and even thrive in the face of any demand. When you have that level of inner certainty, brought about by lots of deep meditative experience, an openness to learning important life lessons, and a willingness to embrace progressive change, then instead of needing certainty, you have what I call flow. You have the skill and the mastery to adapt and thrive, regardless of what else is going on outside, and because of that, following your intuition becomes the easiest thing in the world.

INTUITION – THE RESEARCH

Steve Jobs called intuition 'more powerful than intellect'. Albert Einstein called it the sacred gift. Some of the most important partnerships, products and theories have been born from our subtle sense of intuition. But because science is yet to understand it (although there is more and more research being done on unconscious cognitive processing, non-analytical problem-solving and other processes similar to intuition), it's all too easily dismissed as chance or magical thinking. However, in randomised controlled experiments, the predictive power of intuition has been shown to be greater than that of intellect. This strongly suggests that intuition is a far more powerful force than many of us may realise.

There's no denying we have a tendency to dismiss anything we don't understand, and I believe that's what's happened with regard to intuition. But there's so much smoke as far as intuition is concerned, however, that there has to be fire, and the experiences of my students in reporting much better intuition definitely make me want to fan those flames!

Inner Peace

'A bird sitting on a tree is never afraid of
the branch breaking, because its trust is not
on the branch but on its own wings.'
ANON.

As well as finding a sense of effortless flow, meditation is very helpful indeed when it comes to finding something perhaps even more elusive: inner peace.

Inner peace will never come from your external circumstances, because external factors are ephemeral. This state, which is beyond the normal, relative experience we're used to, can only be found through systematic experience of transcendence.

As I've discussed before, you can't rely on any person or any situation to always stay the same. You'll always need to adapt to changing fortunes, and the only thing that can remain permanent is your ability to maintain balance and equanimity through all of life's twists and turns. That's what will give you peace.

That's partly what I was talking about just above, when I looked at intuition and the great security that comes with knowing that you can cope with any eventuality. The other part to it is that, by using the special sounds of this form of meditation in a way that connects you to your deepest essence and expands your consciousness, you begin to realise that you are part of something greater than your mind and body. You are something much more essential – an aspect of universal consciousness that can't be broken by any of life's dramas. And that is a very strong position to be in.

I should point out that this isn't experienced as an abstract, intellectual concept – it's something you will really feel, as it permeates mind, body and soul.

All this means that you can become fearless. Secure in your inner peace, the ever-changing nature of life is something that you can embrace, rather than constantly fear. You can dance with the flow of life, adapting to its rhythms, rather than rejecting or fighting them. When you're in this state, all sorts of positive attributes flow outwards, such as your ability to love, to be kind, patient, compassionate and generous of heart.

Religion and Spirituality

I get lots of people asking me if this form of meditation really is non-religious before they embark on learning it, either because they don't want it to clash with their own religious beliefs, or because they don't want anything 'spiritual' from the practice at all, because that feels too New Age-y or like something from a cult.

There is a difference, however, between spirituality and religion, and it's worth looking at.

Some people feel empowered by their religions, and there is no doubt that they provide great comfort for many. Lots of us look for meaning in our lives, to help us understand why certain things have happened, or why the world is the way it is, and by subscribing to one school or another, you can find some level of that. But for many others, religious doctrine can be very limiting and disempowering. Although the great founding fathers of religion all seem to have been enlightened masters who attempted to teach people tools and principles that have great merit, their followers, who built up religions in their name, have not always been so enlightened. If you look at most world religions, you'll see they each encompass varying degrees of doctrine, articles of faith and beliefs about the right and wrong way to behave. Some of these tenets, many would agree, are wholly sensible ('Do unto others as you would have done to you,' for example), others perhaps not so much. What all religions have in common, however, is a basis in *belief* – in a God, or in a particular view of the world.

I consider spirituality to be materially different to religion; its essence is something that's universal, and so involves no specific beliefs or articles of faith. There are no rules to follow – just your conscience. Because of that, it promotes self-sufficiency; you're not dependent on a particular divine presence or an external set of rules. To me, personally, this feels much more empowering. In a world that doesn't seem to know what to believe, I would suggest, as an alternative, tuning in deeply to yourself, to those around you, to the universe, to a place that is beyond boundaries and hard-and-fast rules.

From my perspective, any spiritual school should seek to teach you techniques that will open your mind beyond your present, limiting beliefs and enable you to feel more balance and perceive more in life. Truly spiritual schools are happy for you to use their techniques regardless of whether you see the world as their founding fathers did.

If you want these tools for purely practical reasons, then that's perfectly valid and in keeping with being a better you. It's very much like yoga in that sense, which has its own very rich and comprehensive philosophy. You don't need to buy into that in any way to get the practical benefits of stretching and strengthening your body and opening up your physiological pathways. As such, it's a practice than can be both practical and spiritual – atheists and believers alike can enjoy it. It's the same with meditation.

The beauty of this form of meditation is that, if you're a rationalist, it will make you sharper, clearer and less stressed. If you practise religion, then it will give you greater access to that ineffable being that you worship, and it will help you better understand the teachings of your founding master or prophet – you'll begin to have access to an expanded state of consciousness that's closer to what they themselves were perhaps experiencing. And if you're someone who is of a more universally spiritual nature, then meditation will make you more universal still.

VIOLET FLAME CLEANSING EXERCISE

Here's an exercise that comes from outside of the Vedic tradition, but which is great for cleansing not only mind and body, but your spirit too.

1. Sit comfortably and focus your attention on the centre of your chest, right in the middle of your breastbone (sternum), just above the solar plexus (between the nipples). Now move that attention about four inches inside your body, to the very centre of your chest. This is known as your heart centre.

2. Maintaining that awareness of your heart centre, simultaneously focus your attention on the area inside your brain, where your pineal gland is. To locate this, place two fingers above the tops of your ears and imagine the midpoint between these two fingers, in the middle of your skull.

3. Now imagine a line of energy, or violet light, that connects the heart centre and the pineal gland, and focus your attention on mind, heart, and the connection between the two.

4. Keeping your attention on these three things, close your eyes, take a deep breath through your nose and exhale out of your mouth.

5. Now, repeat the following phrase inside your mind, for five to ten minutes: 'May the violet flame burn brightly throughout my mind, body, spirit and aura, to cleanse and heal me. And so it is.'

For a guided version of this exercise, go to my website: www.theeffortlessmind.com.

Reconnecting to Yourself

As I've said before, if you've undergone trauma, or if you've experienced or are experiencing a lot of stress, it can be very difficult to feel connected to yourself or to the world. All that noise – all that emotional charge related to memories we haven't yet processed, all that reviewing of the past – takes up a lot of space in our minds, and it means we can't be present, we can't connect.

When I first received an email from Hattie, after her husband had died following a long illness, I could tell she was incredibly fragile. It was like she didn't know who to trust any more and I knew she was struggling to put her faith in me. Even though her sister-in-law had had an amazing recovery from an awful facial nerve condition called trigeminal neuralgia after learning to meditate, and her niece and nephew had also had great results with it, it was almost as if she couldn't bring herself to believe that there might be a solution to her grief, to her fragility and to her loss of trust.

We had several email conversations back and forth and, bit by bit, I could see her warming to the idea. And then, when I met her, I found myself feeling incredibly fond of her. Underneath the pain was this very classy lady with a lovely mixture of strength and softness, and as the weekend progressed the brittle exterior started to melt away and the real Hattie started to emerge.

Hattie

'It brought me back home.'

I've always had an enquiring mind. As a child, I grew up in the countryside and I was free to roam, and to wander, and get lost in my imagination. There was that element of connection to something that I couldn't quite describe. As a child, you're quite sensitive to your surroundings, and I just loved experiencing that freedom, that nurturing feeling I found in nature. Then, when I got a bit older, school and other people took over. I began to lose that connection and I became focused on my studies instead. I still explored my creativeness, through storytelling and art, and I think art gave me that sense of dropping into a meditative place, which I suppose I couldn't label at the time.

That sense of connection really came back to me in my twenties. I was curious, open-minded, and I was always trying to find something that seemed to be missing. Again, however, that search closed down a little bit when I married my husband, Andrew. Then, when I had my two daughters, the whole experience of motherhood opened up other questions. Everyday responsibilities took me away from pursuing that spiritual route.

Everything changed for us when Andrew was suddenly diagnosed with a brain tumour. Our daughters were three and seven, and it was a terrible, terrible shock. We didn't know what was going to happen, whether he was going to die within six months, or recover, or what. Those first few months were awful – yet I don't really remember much of it. All of my focus was on looking after my family.

Andrew was very strong, and he got through the treatment, and went back to work. We decided to move out of

London to the countryside, to a beautiful little house in
the woods.

We had three or four years there, and things were really
good, but then Andrew started to deteriorate again. It was a
very sad time. I had my family nearby – that was one of the
reasons we'd moved there – and we'd made some friends, but
we hadn't been there long enough to get really close to them.

It was hard; I felt as if I was managing everything on my
own. I found solace in my art and set up a little studio in the
garage – that was my way of escaping, looking really deeply
into a painting, creating. I read a lot, too – lots of spiritual
books – but the whole time I felt like I was in an egg timer,
with very thin glass that was about to crack, and that I had
to put on this façade. For a while, I began to close off.

Nature was important, having that peace. We'd go walking, Andrew and I, and just being able to experience that
with him was very important, because we connected then
in a very different way. Once he'd accepted that he was
going to die, he became much more open and less angry. He
was a bit of a control freak, but once he let go, things were
quite extraordinary. When he eventually passed away, it was
at home. We played music; we had candles and prayer. I'd
describe it as feeling very sacred.

Then, after the first few weeks, came the adjustment back
into reality, because we couldn't stay in that space – we had
to get back into the real world. And that terrified me, because
I'd realised I'd gone into a bit of a cocoon in order to manage
everything.

I was feeling pretty numb; it was almost like a paralysis.
I think my grief was operating on so many levels, and there
was also an element of letting go. Somebody dying takes on
a life of its own, as it were, and when it ends you wonder
what to do, because your life has been organised around

this person dying, managing it and making sure they were okay. I'd lost touch of my own needs. I had no plans; I lived, literally, hour to hour.

I would just wake up, and nothing made sense – being alive didn't make sense. The one thing that got me through was having the girls. No matter how I felt, I'd have to get up, make breakfast, get them to school. But all the time I had this nauseous feeling in me, this sickening fear about how I would cope. Grief made me feel not capable, and I lost all my confidence in everything I did. I found small tasks really hard. I hated going into a supermarket, being surrounded by too many people. It was a very distrustful stage, too; I wasn't sure of people's intentions. I was very reactive, finding that the smallest things would cause me to fly off the handle.

It was at this point that meditation came knocking at my door. My sister-in-law had learned with Will, with amazing results, and so I went to see him. After I'd got my sound, I said to him: 'What do I have to do next?' Will said, 'Well, nothing,' and I found that really hard to get to grips with because I thought: *Surely it's not just going to happen without me trying*. Once I got into that space, however, where you just say your sound, and just be, I found it hugely calming. I felt an immediate release of something, and a little flicker of light was reignited. There was a little element of happiness in that first instant and I had a feeling of being me.

The girls could sense that it was something important, and whenever I said, 'I'm going to meditate,' they immediately gave me my space. One of the things I liked about it was that I was giving myself twenty minutes of time for myself. I could close the door, and that was like saying: 'Please don't disturb me.' So, for the first time I suppose, I began to get my voice back, to articulate what I needed. Before that it had been so blocked.

The girls came along with me a month later and did a shortened version of the meditation. They took to it immediately. I felt that it was something new we could share and that we could do in our new little family set-up, which we needed, because we'd begun to drift apart. This was something we could talk about; and, crucially, it was unrelated to everything that had gone on before.

When my husband died, Izzy, my eldest, was about to do her GCSE mocks that summer, and she managed to hold it together. Meditation kept her strong and focused, and it gave her something to do. Molly, the younger one, needed to calm her mind – she's very imaginative, and for her to get an inkling of what it's like to be not thinking is a big deal. They both use it in different ways; they keep their tools in their little toolboxes and take them out as they need.

For me, it immediately helped with the grief I was dealing with, but I found it useful on so many other levels too. Once I gave it the space, I felt that the meditation was healing all sorts of other traumas that I hadn't even been aware of. I just let it sort it all out, on the very unconscious level. What I liked was the simplicity, the fact that I didn't have to think. And so, very slowly, one thing got sorted at a time. I found the whole process very gentle.

In a way, the meditation showed me how to acknowledge grief as an emotion, and then let it go. I think it allowed me to disentangle myself from the sadness, too, so it wouldn't cling to me. These emotions would come and then they would go. I felt myself as a person, not just made up of my emotions. And with that, I found that I could focus for longer stretches. Before, I'd always be thinking, *Oh my God, I've got to get up, I've got to do this*, because when Andrew was ill, all the time I was thinking: *Has he been fed? Has he had his medication? Have you done this? Have you done that?* That constant questioning gradually began to abate, and soon I began to feel I could actually just sit and *be*.

I found myself going off for longer walks. Everything became more meaningful, and I could actually enjoy things. I still found it quite traumatic to look ahead; everything had become very present, but actually, I think that was good. Instead of worrying about what was going to happen tomorrow, or next week, or next year, I just wanted to be. Before, I'd been terrified of facing reality, so I was always trying to escape.

I wasn't very grounded at that point – I was very much still up in the air. A part of me hadn't wanted to let go of that, because I thought that once I did, I would have to let go of Andrew. But really, letting go of Andrew made me free. I met a lecturer who's Native American, and his culture honours the spirits and death. We did this fire ritual, the three of us, and him, we had a photograph of Andrew there, and we honoured his life. I would say that doors started to open for me then. I was feeling clearer, more focused, a little bit more grounded – it was as if I was sort of coming back into my body.

In the summer after Andrew died, the girls and I went to Canada, where he was originally from. We went to the Rockies, and walked and camped. We meditated on mountain tops and by lakes, and when we came home, we were changed. The girls had found a place within them that is always there, that they can go to when they meditate. Izzy even tried to offer the idea of meditation to her school. She met with all the teachers, but they just imposed so many limits that it didn't work.

For me, I think I'm really starting to find my own spirit and trust again. Something that's coming up a lot is the need to release old patterns of behaviour that are no longer relevant in my life. I think that's due to the meditation – the freedom to say: 'Actually, I don't need those patterns any more, they're not going to serve me.' It's about harnessing everything that's happened, bringing it all together, and moving it into a calm state of being.

If I had to say, in one sentence, what meditation did for me, I'd say it brought me back home. It reconnected me with my humanity. There's a lovely tree near our house that got damaged in a storm; half of it had fallen to the ground. Over the past four years, I've watched it come back to life. It's absolutely there. It's healthy; it has survived. And so have I.

Celebrating Life and Death

Hattie went through a real spiritual journey around Andrew's death. I'm so glad that, through her rituals later on, she could celebrate and honour his life. There is a real need to celebrate life as well as mourning the passing of it. Of course, when someone dies, we feel a great sense of loss, but their departure is also an opportunity to celebrate everything that they were, everything that we shared with them, everything that they helped us see and gave us, and everything that we gave them.

When we live life from a place of celebration, we come to realise that we can all give or teach each other something, because we are all connected. If we open ourselves up to those lessons, and those shared experiences, then we're going to feel more whole, more complete. We're going to feel less of a sense of loss when our loved ones die, because we understand the true meaning of their being here in the first place.

That said, Hattie had a lot of healing to do. She had coped for so long, managing her family through a traumatic time, and had been under such chronic stress, that she had almost forgotten how to look after herself. She was vulnerable, and was afraid of that vulnerability, and so couldn't trust. In fact, vulnerability is the most amazing thing, if we can only embrace it. It's not weakness, it's strength. It's real, and it's who we are sometimes. If we shut down on who we are – if we fear the perceived lack of strength that comes from vulnerability, then the stress of it causes an inhibition of oxytocin, that lovely molecule that helps us trust. We might begin to feel confused, or irrational. By meditating, we can calm our nervous system and begin to trust again.

Gaining More by Doing Less

I remember Hattie asking me what she had to 'do' after I gave her the personalised sound, and how she could hardly believe me when I said 'nothing'. That's the beauty of this form of meditation – it's effortless. For once, you don't have to think, you don't have to try to achieve; you can just switch off and let your body and mind heal themselves. We're very caught up in 'doing', and the more we do the more we think we need to do. When she started to meditate, Hattie found time for herself, to say 'do not disturb'. Giving yourself time is so crucial. It's the only way to stay connected to who you are, and what you're really about.

There's a wonderful verse in an ancient Indian text that says, 'established in being, perform action', which essentially means that successful actions can only be taken when you are fully connected and in touch with your own sense of self. Once you are 'established in self', you are able to make all of your actions in life powerful and meaningful. It's also essential for you as a human being to establish yourself 'in being', so that you can express yourself, your gifts, your love, your insights and your ideas into life, and also have the time, space and bandwidth to allow life to express its gifts, its love and its ideas to you and through you.

Finding Your Voice

Hattie also said that the meditation helped her regain her voice, which is very important. We all have many feelings and ideas in life that we might want to express, but from a young age we're actively encouraged to simply conform rather than be an expression of our truest selves. There are cultural conventions that become ingrained, and there are various paradigms that we don't question. It's like a fish swimming in a goldfish bowl – it doesn't realise it's swimming in water, that's just the medium through which it travels. In the same way, we don't even see the paradigms that we're in – we just accept that they're there.

As a result, we keep our counsel, we hold it in, we don't say what we want, or feel, or mean. Sometimes, there's no need for action – we just need to be heard.

Meditation helps you find your voice, and in an incredibly gracious way. Because it helps you improve your self-esteem, as I discussed in Dylan's story, instead of bottling things up and waiting until they explode out of you, possibly in a very ungraceful way, you will find yourself speaking up when it feels right. You'll also do so in a more reasoned, rather than emotionally charged, way. Another great thing that meditation will do is dissipate or discharge any of the suppressed energy that comes from those emotions that we have little choice but to hold in, as we saw in Anna's case, so you can use it tactically to restore your emotional equilibrium.

As well as finding her voice, Hattie managed to release old patterns of behaviour that are no longer relevant to her life. This really is one of the biggest benefits that comes from this form of meditation. Once you manage to do that, through generating more coherent neural patterns within the meditation, as I've explained before, you can help create new pathways that then allow you to do things differently next time. That will give you an enormous amount of satisfaction. Rather than going round in circles, repeating the same patterns of behaviour throughout your life, and beating yourself up about it, you break the pattern at an unconscious level.

Meditation helps liberate you from your conditioned responses, enabling you to have more heartfelt, or soulful, reactions. It will also allow you to have the response that's appropriate to the moment, to your life situation at that point in time, rather than simply repeating the way you've habitually dealt with things in the past.

It also helps with denial, which is important, because for as long as we exhibit pride, we create dynamics of denial, and block ourselves from accepting the need for change. Real change – not just surface-level change. Without the willingness to admit that we're not always right, to admit that something isn't as good as it could be or that an area of our life would benefit from improvement, we're liable to cling on to the safety of the ever-repeating known. As we all know, however, if you keep doing the same thing over and over, you'll keep getting the same results. Whereas if you look into your heart and ask yourself if that's what you really want, beyond the layers of fear and doubt and complacency which make you afraid of trying another way ('better the devil you know'), you'll probably find that you do indeed hunger for a different way, it's just that it feels vulnerable and uncertain. You may not even realise you think like this until you start meditating, and then, bit by bit, it becomes obvious. Then it's down to you to try something new, which you'll be able to do because your unconscious has been freed from its habituated need to keep running around in circles.

Expanding a Child's Potential

I've spoken about children and meditation in this book before, in Tom's story, where it really helped each member of his family and their family dynamics. Here I want to expand on this.

It's such a shame that, when Hattie's daughter tried to bring meditation into her school, the teachers responded to her in the way that they did. Think about the way many children act at school. They have short attention spans, which causes distraction in class. They fight or bicker in the playground. Many of those children, for all the reasons we've gone into in this book before, are a bundle of stress and tension. A quarter of children in the US have clinically defined anxiety, and the number of anti-depressants prescribed to children there has increased by 400 per cent in the past ten years.

Socrates famously described education as 'the kindling of a flame, not the filling of a vessel'. Education should help children think differently and encourage their creativity, but this is increasingly difficult in a world where children's attention spans and creative potential are being steamrollered by waves of information and stress activation. Just like adults, children's brains need to switch off from time to time so that they can reboot. Instead, they rush from lessons to the playground, then back to lessons, then home, to screen-time, homework and yet more tasks. And that's not even mentioning the barrage of standardised tests they're expected to undertake.

Bringing meditation to schools would yield so many benefits, and some educators are beginning to realise this. Between 2008 and 2010, a school in San Francisco introduced a meditation programme. In that period, staff turnover went from being extremely high to zero. Children demonstrated a 40 per cent decrease in stress, anxiety and depression. Meditating students improved their exam scores by 10 per cent more than the non-meditating students, and demonstrated a 30 per cent increase in brain coherence and functioning. There was also a very significant closing of the achievement gap. Alongside this, they received 82 per cent fewer detentions over two years, a 65 per cent decrease in bullying and conflict and increased levels of resilience and self-confidence and sleep quality, along with reduced incidence of ADHD, and a 30 per cent decrease in sick days.

A simple ten-minute session timetabled within the school day can achieve all of this. It would give children the opportunity to find their own inner flow, their own essence, and keep it throughout their school years, into adolescence and adulthood, rather than losing that spark as they try to fit in with a world that has been created by adults, many of whom are in a place of shutdown.

As Hattie and her daughters found, meditation allows you to navigate your way through life. Sometimes life just feels open, like a big old prairie, and other times it feels like you're walking on a tightrope. When you're on the tightrope, the meditation is like having a stick that helps you balance as you make your way across the ravine. If you try to walk a tightrope without a stick, well, good luck to you – but when you've got the balancing stick, you can almost take joy in sauntering across the wire.

I'll let the girls have the final word:

'Things that irritated me about what other people did,
irritating things that you pick up, you don't let them
get to you, you just sort of move on and it doesn't
affect you as much. I don't get as worried about
things; I'm less anxious around big groups of people.
It's definitely helped socialising and going to a new
college. I've found it's really helped with that.'

IZZY,

AGED SIXTEEN

'I love meditating because whenever I repeat my
sound I suddenly feel I'm alert but I'm in another
consciousness and I feel really positive and safe
and it just generally makes me calmer and more
peaceful, so afterwards I have a lovely feeling.'

MOLLY,

AGED TWELVE

Reaching Your Spiritual Potential

I meet many people who've been looking for something, in a spiritual sense, for a long time. They tend to have tried a range of techniques, and have got to a point where they're feeling pretty good, but something is missing, or they simply want to go further. Vedic-inspired meditation is the next step on what might have already been a pretty long journey.

Jane and I first met at one of my introductory talks, and I could tell she had clearly done lots of work on herself – she was radiating a glow of happiness that was plain for all to see. As the talk progressed, it was clear that she had a lot of knowledge, and yet she came across as humble and willing to learn more, which elicited deep respect within me. Several weeks later, she showed up to get her sound and it was a true delight to see her. I hadn't been sure she'd come, and was so heartened when she did. As we chatted, my initially positive impression of her was further enhanced by her charming nature, and also by her willingness – and desire – to understand experientially the difference between this particular method and mindfulness. It was also evident that underneath her iridescent glow was an underbelly of anxiety, and I was keen to help her overcome that, so that she could grow spiritually in a more full-spectrum way, without fear and blocks preventing her.

Jane

'Wherever you go, there you are.'

It's almost exactly a year ago that I started this particular form of meditation, but I've been practising yoga and different types of meditation since the year 2000.

From childhood onwards, I think I was looking for something. Even though my parents weren't very religious, I liked going to Sunday school. I was also in the choir. I liked the feeling of singing together, that unity.

By the time I was nineteen, I had my dream job, working on a magazine. I'd been obsessed with magazines ever since I'd been a teenager, so I was pinching myself every day because I was doing what I really wanted to do, and it was very creative. In my thirties, I moved on to more glossy magazines, and I became the beauty and health director of one of them.

One day, I met a huge champion of Ayurvedic medicine and yoga, who'd been taught by one of the big Himalayan masters. He's a businessman as well, and I was doing a shoot at his headquarters. He did a healing treatment on me and I felt a huge awakening all through my body. Friends of mine always say that I was never the same after that. It was almost like it was what I had always been waiting to discover. I felt a massive recognition. From then on, I became much more conscious: I started following yoga, eating well. This man taught me the most important lesson, which I still think about now: he wasn't doing anything special in that treatment, he was simply facilitating. Everybody has that ability to heal themselves and each other, so he was just tuning into a natural energy that we all have.

He'd fired up my confidence and I got a new job as the

editor of a magazine that was focused on health and well-being, so I could really explore all these things. But then, after three years, the magazine folded, and so I decided to really throw myself into yoga. I went freelance and started to really practise. I did all the different styles – Bikram hot yoga, Kundalini, all of it – for about five or six years.

But I was still struggling in terms of exploring my 'self', asking those big questions like 'Why am I here?', 'What's my purpose?', 'Who are we?'

I got an offer of another great job at one of the big magazines. It was another level of glamour and fashion and meeting people and I really threw myself into it. But, part of the way through, I started to feel really empty. I started to question what it was all for. It was at a time when the magazine was going really 'bling', and it was basically hammering things down people's throats, endorsing £350 face cream and the like.

At this point, I was loving the yoga more and more. I was also trying out different types of meditation. I started to think about training as a yoga teacher. I'd always wanted to go to India and explore further, and so I decided to do just that. I quit my job and went to stay in an ashram. That was massive. It was there that I really felt it all come together and realised that the essence of it all was the meditation. All of this practising of postures was ultimately about dealing with the mind.

When I came back, I started teaching. I was also writing about these things, and as time went on a lot of people started asking me to write about yoga and meditation. I was still exploring all sorts of meditation at that point – Buddhist, Zen, Yogic – though I'd mainly focus on breath and use 'so hum' as a mantra; those were the two things I settled on.

More and more I was enjoying the fruits of the practice. I have a tendency to anxiety and stress, definitely, and that was still going on, but I was definitely a lot calmer. Freelancing means you never know where the next feature is coming from and yoga teaching is a good antidote, but the pressures there are also big. There's a saying, 'Wherever you go, there you are,' and it was true – I still felt those anxieties. I was still feeling pretty great about all these opportunities, though, and I started to travel a lot, reviewing wellness and yoga retreats, going to India, meeting teachers and gurus.

One day, I was asked to write a piece about the difference between mindfulness and meditation. I knew a little bit about Vedic meditation, and when I started researching, someone told me about Will. I thought: *Right, I'm going to go to this, but as me, not as a journalist.* So, I went to an intro talk and I was really impressed, both by the way he explained meditation, but also the context he put it in – modern life. I'd been given a mantra before by a swami in an orange robe, but it felt almost like religion, because it was so ritualistic. When Will explained it, it didn't feel ritualistic in any way, and so I could immediately relate to it.

I thought to myself: *I've literally spent my life savings on training as a yoga teacher, going to India, following all these different things, going on all these courses – I can't spend any more money. Am I going off on another tangent?* Even then, I knew I'd do it.

So I went and got my personalised sound, which was an amazing experience. It was so profound, and it was unlike any other mantra that I'd been given. Right from the get-go it completely turbocharged my practice. It was almost like the door had been pushed open so many times, yet this time I could really go through it.

I think I'd already gone a long way, without realising, getting little moments of transcendence, but this was a huge step. And a year later, I'm still getting light bulb moments and great highs.

I think people used to think I was calm, but I was one of those people who was really running on nervous energy. I can be calm, but my natural default is to be anxious. Before, I used to finish yoga, go outside and get on the Tube and then I was suddenly frazzled again. But now I've got this background of calm that's always there. The big thing with this was that I let go of the need to be in an idealised state, to think *I've got to get to this, it's over there somewhere*. It's more subtle than I ever thought. I'm no longer swinging from black to white; I can settle myself into the meditation so easily, and I'm also able to access this sense of calm more readily when I'm not meditating, so I feel much more stable as a result.

What the Vedic method also gives you is this massive clarity on what your priorities need to be. You just know what you need to do, and you start really following this path of what you know is right. Whereas before I would be dithering a lot, and procrastinating, I now know what I need to do, and I'm getting better and better at following that instinct and every time it works out really well.

What I've also realised is that spiritual knowledge is not knowledge that you learn intellectually. You have to experience these things and you have to be able to make sense of them in your life as you go about your day to day. That's what it's doing for me now – it's making me see that, and know that there's no rush. It's almost like: *Okay, so that doesn't resonate with me right now, but it's there*. The light bulb might come on later. I just have so many of these illuminations now, these moments of recognition, big and small.

All our lives we're taught that you have a linear trajectory – that if we do this, we get this – but it's not really like that. All those milestones like passing your exams, getting to university, all that stuff. Now I haven't got this kind of mentality of 'I need to do this to get there' any more. Instead, I can see it as an ongoing process of human development, which for me has been massively opening. It's more like: 'I'm going to enjoy the process' – and I do!

Taking a Spiritual Journey

As I said before, I see many people who've come a certain way along their spiritual journey, but are looking for more. One of the reasons I chose to teach this particular form of meditation is that it touches people very deeply, connecting them to themselves, other people, and the rest of the world, in a way that many other practices just don't achieve.

That's not to say that this form of meditation has the monopoly on the deepest experiences, but of all the things that are available out there it is the one that seems to consistently deliver the most exquisite level of experience and development for people, and it does that with the most ease. In fact, it almost certainly does so *because* of its easiness, not in spite of that.

That's why the practice works for people straight off the street who've never done it before, and also acts as a brilliant method of progression for all those who have been involved in meditation, yoga, or other spiritual practices, and who are looking to go further.

Initial courses are labelled for beginners, but they work for everybody – even if you're super-advanced, they build on all of the great work that you've done with all of your other practices up to that point. No matter where you start from, this meditation takes you a lot further.

This reminds me of one of my most satisfying early teaching experiences. I met an Australian man in India who'd been there for twenty years trying all these different techniques. He'd stayed in ashrams, up mountains, in mud huts by the River Ganges, studying with the masters, and he ended up becoming a Vipassana monk for seven years. We had a great conversation, and he was quite intrigued about what I was doing. It was only four weeks after I'd graduated that I taught him, and he was just blown away by it all. A year later, he came to the UK and went on one of my retreats. Because of his vast experience, I gave him a slightly stronger programme, and as he was leaving he came to me and said: 'When I was in India, we used to make a hole in the ground and sit there in the lotus position for two months of solid meditation, only coming out to eat and go to the bathroom. What I've just experienced in the past three days feels like the equivalent of what I used to get out of many weeks of sitting. It's incredible.'

We get lots of experienced people coming to check out what we're doing, and the ones who are humble, who are open to learning, try it and they thrive. Then there are others who walk away, who maybe feel their path lies elsewhere, but I always say to them that, if in a few years' time they still haven't found what they're looking for, then they should give me a call. Some of them do, and it's always a delight to help them find what they've been seeking for all those years.

Healing Yourself

I'm incredibly interested and inspired by Jane's observation that we all have the ability to heal ourselves.

All ancient cultures were convinced that we have a natural energy running through us and that this energy had the power to heal and transform. So much so that there are even forty-nine different names for this energy from forty-nine different cultures. In India, they call it *kundalini*; in China, it's called *chi*. It seems to me that when so many cultures independently arrive at the same conclusion, it's always worth the rest of us keeping an open mind about it.

It hasn't necessarily been an area that we in the West have been hugely interested in, and nor has there been much investment into research, at least that I'm aware of, to explore the subtle nuances of the energetic workings of the human mind, body and nervous system. In my experience, both personally and observationally as a teacher, there is most certainly a healing energy there. It's as if this energy is getting trapped in all of these places around our body, and when it gets stuck, it can cause strong sensations such as pain, weakness and feelings of tightness. But once you start unknotting your body, whether that's through complementary therapies like massage or reflexology, or physical exercises like yoga or Pilates, you achieve greater flow of that energy. You can feel it – it's an experiential knowledge.

When you get somebody else, like a masseur or a reflexology practitioner, to unknot those tensions, they're working from the outside in, and that's a bit like a gardener trying to nourish the tree by watering the branches and the leaves. By tending to the roots, however, you allow the effects to ripple throughout the tree, all the way to the fruits. That's what meditation does – it waters your roots, however, it nourishes you at a deep level, which echoes out into every fibre of your being, releasing all of the knots along the way. It's a beautifully empowering way to heal and transform yourself and to bring yourself into your fullest potential.

Connecting With Your Inner Truth

All of us have an inner truth, and connecting with that is at the core of feeling spiritually at peace. I remember very well my first phone conversation with Marie. She was so enthusiastic about wanting to explore her relationship with herself and with life. Back in those days, we didn't have an international reputation, and so most of the people who came to see us were within a hundred-mile radius of London. But here was Marie, willing to travel over from Belgium for a weekend to come and learn with us. Since then, we've had people coming from all over the world, but she was the first, and so I was really excited to meet and teach her.

When she and her husband turned up, they were just the most beautiful couple I'd ever seen – inside and out. Marie was evidently much more spiritually open than her husband, who was more of a practically minded entrepreneur, but it was really interesting to see the contrast between the two because, although he was there to gain a stress management tool and she was there to connect with her inner light, they both walked away from that first session really happy, just in very different ways. By the end of the course, you could see that they had a real spring in their step, and an even greater bond of love between the two of them.

I wished them well and wasn't sure if I'd ever see them again, but really hoped I would, because they were both such shining lights. And then, wonderfully, a year later, they both came back over from Belgium for a weekend retreat and we continued their meditation education. By that point, Marie had very obviously really connected with her deep inner truth. There was so much awareness, clarity and consciousness in the questions that she was asking – it was a real joy to behold.

Marie

'It's not something I think, it's something that is.'

To say that this kind of meditation changed my life is an understatement. I'd say it blew me off my feet.

When I was very young, I always had the urge to look for something I couldn't comprehend – aware that there was something more in life, that there was this mystical thing. My brother died when I was thirteen and I think for me that was the starting point. When I got into my early twenties, I really got into spirituality, but the easy way in – with the New Age-y stuff. I was reading books about life after death, obviously because it related to what I had experienced, and that was enough at that time. Then, as I got into my thirties, something was calling me to go deeper. You find a lot of contradictions in all these books, and I was kind of confused.

That call was very important, however, and it said: 'I want to know the truth, I want to know the truth about everything. Tell me the truth.' And I thought: *Okay, who can give me that?* First I looked outwardly, and then I said to myself: *No, I think I have to have kind of a practice where I can go inwards, where I can see what's happening.* Nobody seemed to be able to give me a good solution, so I thought: *Right, I'll do it myself.*

I'd been meditating on and off, online mostly with YouTube, following some guided meditations. I did some yoga classes, but not much, as inside I had another slight resistance, because there were all those people claiming that they had the highest truth and I just couldn't grasp that. I was like, 'Act normal! Act normal!'

Then I found out about Will. I called him, and we talked for about half an hour. He said he was doing a course in two weeks, so I went with my husband. As soon as he gave me my sound, I thought: *Oh my God, I'm coming home.* It was such a gift. I was glowing. I said: 'This is a life-changer for sure. I'm going to do something with this.'

Three weeks later, I found out I was pregnant for the first time. It was a very strange time. I started the meditation and it was amazing, but then, after about five or six weeks, I went into this darkness. I called Will again. He was super-kind, and explained that it was a kind of purifying, that I was shedding layers of past pain. Though it might feel overwhelming, it would pass, and it would be good to clear this from my system, so the baby had a healthier home to grow in. After a couple of months, I felt a lot better in my pregnancy. I'd found a way through the darkness, and that felt like a huge achievement. I was so proud of myself!

As I approached the birth, I was meditating three times a day, and I felt like I was really connecting with the baby inside me. Internally, everything felt lighter, more relaxed. And then, one afternoon, my contractions started.

I'd decided to have my baby at home, with a doula. It got to midnight, and the doula was on her way. It was a difficult labour. I felt like I was dying – the pain of the contractions were so intense, and my cervix wasn't opening at all.

Will doesn't recommend that you meditate during labour, because meditation processes excess lactic acid from your muscles, and lactic acid build-up is actually helpful for the birthing process, so I didn't.

The pain became even worse. It got to 7 o'clock in the morning and I said: 'Okay, there needs to be a shift.' I went to have a bath upstairs, then came down to the place where I meditate every day, and it filled me with this feeling of confidence. I gave birth, and then we just got into bed. The doula went after an hour, and then it was just the three of us.

I tried to meditate while breastfeeding, but it was very tough because my daughter was really hungry, feeding 24/7. I didn't have time to wash my hair, let alone meditate, but I thought to myself: *Okay, I have to go with the flow. I'm not going to push myself.* So, for the first three months, I didn't meditate. It felt like the natural thing to do, because you have to give your attention to what needs it most.

I never stopped working on ambitious projects. Then, last summer, my best friend said to me: 'Marie, enough. You're putting all your energy into other people, and it stops you seeing what you are capable of.' I thought: *You're right, I do have something to share that's valuable.* After that, I started to study Vedic knowledge very intensively, and last year, for the first time, I went to India to study with a master Will had put me in touch with.

The teacher gave me a very intensive practice. I keep my original form of meditation as a base, and I build a lot around it. There's a lot of reading; it's a practice that I spend two hours a day on, so it's pretty intense, but I cannot imagine a day without it. I look forward to it – it's like a new romance.

If I look back to the person I was and how I perceived the world, it's like day and night. Now, I observe myself; I think *I am Marie* with my mind, and I identify myself with my thoughts and with my everyday life. My body is not my main identification at all, and it gives me glimpses, on some occasions, of things beyond perception, beyond what you can see with your eyes and with all your senses.

The most important thing is that I experience things now, instead of merely knowing or reading about them. I experience it, literally. It's not something I think, it's something that is. And that is transcendent.

I'm doing meditation teacher training now. And I'm writing a book, for children. I want them to know what I know now; I want them to discover it much earlier than I did.

I want to share what is coming through me to serve the world, and that's something that came with the meditation very strongly. You feel like you're not doing it for yourself, because your sense of isolation doesn't exist any more. You're part of this collective and the interconnectedness is just so strong that you cannot do otherwise.

We all have a responsibility, and by meditating you're doing a huge favour to the world because you lift up the collective consciousness. Everything around you rises, and the ripples of this are so huge. **'**

Connecting to the Rest of the World

Marie talks about collective consciousness, a phrase first coined by the French sociologist Emile Durkheim at the end of the nineteenth century to describe the shared beliefs, ideas and moral attitudes that bind a society together. So where do all those beliefs, ideas and attitudes come from?

Although much of Western psychology refers to the unconscious as something that is purely individual, in 1916 the Swiss psychiatrist and psychoanalyst Carl Jung introduced the notion of a *collective* unconscious, which he saw as a series of unconscious memories, symbols and impulses that are common to all humanity and which arise from a shared history. Rather than developing individually, they're inherited. Although we're not really aware of the contents of this collective unconscious, they're expressed through myths, symbols and archetypes that resonate with all of us, regardless of culture or individual experience (such as the Great Mother, Tree of Life, Wise Old Man, etc.). The collective *unconscious* is one explanation of how we are all connected to each other in some very important ways, and an explanation of what stands behind collective *consciousness*.

Another way of understanding the collective consciousness of humanity might be to think about the *zeitgeist* (literally, 'the spirit of the times'), used to describe a common feeling or mood between people in a certain culture at a certain time. No one quite knows where it comes from – who can explain why a particular song or a book or even a TV show just seems to capture people's imagination and seems exactly right for that particular moment (who knew a programme about baking would be one of the most popular things on British TV for the past five years?!).

There are, of course, many other unconscious forces, or subtle sensory signals – chemicals such as pheromones or complex social forces – that can influence groups of people, whether that's in a room, a building, a company, or a group of friends. And this effect provides the context within which we live and make important life choices.

If you want to really thrive, and find greater meaning and purpose in life, you need to understand the context of our wider humanity and engage with it in a healthy way. The beauty of this form of meditation is that it not only benefits you, in all the ways that we've seen in the real-life stories in this book, but it also benefits your friends, your family, and everyone you interact with.

When you meditate, two things unfold to make this happen. Firstly, it reduces your attachment to collective conditions or influences, so you can connect with your deeper, more uniquely expressed self. You can really be you. Secondly, by being much more conscious yourself, you can raise the bar of the consciousness of the people around you and help point things in a much more positive and progressive direction. A rising tide lifts all ships, as they say.

And, as Marie says, the world is very much in need of this, whether that's to cope with deforestation, declining fresh water supplies, climate change, unsustainable debt, inequality, the energy crisis, rising extremism or the demographic time bomb, to name just a few of the very urgent issues at stake.

It's up to us to be the change we wish to see in the world. The ripples of meditation are huge. Start now.

Afterword

'Your attitude, not your aptitude,
will determine your altitude.'
ZIG ZIGLAR,
AMERICAN AUTHOR AND MOTIVATIONAL SPEAKER

I really hope this book has enlightened you to the possibilities of what can be achieved through this form of meditation. The techniques that I teach are very easy to learn and simple to practise. And that – it may surprise some of you to know – is the reason they're so powerful, because it helps not to overcomplicate stuff if we want to reach our deepest essence and allow ourselves to heal and grow in the most profound ways.

The only way you'll ever know if this will work is if you open yourself up to giving it a go. That's why I've written this book, because I wanted to help people understand just how easy, and just how brilliant, meditation can be when you find a technique that's right for you. The question isn't: 'Why would you meditate?' The question is: 'Why wouldn't you?' It's a total no-brainer!

There may be some part of you that feels resistance. If that's the case, ask yourself: is it perhaps because some part of you is scared of change? We all are to some extent, because change is scary, but fears never dissipate unless you do something to move beyond them. As Martin Luther King once said: 'If you can't fly then run, if you can't run then walk, if you can't walk then crawl, but whatever you do you have to keep moving forward.'

I love and respect all of the people featured in this book, precisely because they tried the meditation in spite of any fears they may have had, they kept moving forward, and to me, they are all heroes. This is your chance to be your own hero in your own story – to take that first or next step, regardless of any concerns or fears.

All of us face adversity – it's part of the human story, the human condition. All of us sometimes feel dissatisfaction with ourselves, with others, with the world. Yet it doesn't have to be that way. Life is about finding a way through, about digging deep and finding a reservoir of courage, or even just a little trickle, to give us the strength to power through the challenges and seize the day in every conceivable way.

If you're not in a good place at the moment, this will help make life better. If you are in a good place, it will make life better still. Clarity, creativity, vitality, inspiration and a whole lot more besides will result. If you want to live a life extra-ordinary – as I suspect we all really do – then this is a great way to do exactly that. It will allow you to access your fullest potential and be the best possible you at all times. There's an amazing journey that lies ahead of you – if you wish to take it.

Unless you're someone who's in a complete state of fulfil-ment (and if you are, congratulations, I salute you!), then all I can do is encourage you to try out this particular form of meditation. If you want to come and learn with us, we're here for you, anytime. You don't need any special talent. You don't need to have a quiet mind, or even be able to sit still – all you need is a willingness to give it a go.

As our old friend Einstein once said: 'I have no special talents. I am only passionately curious.'

Be curious. Explore the possibilities.

ACKNOWLEDGEMENTS

My heartfelt thanks go out to:

Laura, without whom this project would have been very difficult if you hadn't helped out when various publishers came knocking at my door. You are an absolute trooper, and massive kudos to you for meditating twice a day EVERY SINGLE DAY for the past eighteen months!

Claire, for helping me find the right home for me to express myself through the book, and for guiding me through the ins and outs of publishing.

Claudia, for taking a chance on me and my idea for telling the story of meditation through other people's journeys. You are a superstar!

Melissa Bond, Gemma Conley-Smith and everyone else at Simon & Schuster.

Catherine, for helping me to make this book a reality.

Holly, for coming to the rescue when I couldn't see the wood for the trees.

Liam, Anna and Lucia, for throwing all of your creative and emotional energy into helping us take meditation to the world. I will be forever thankful for the incredible contributions you have made. You are truly meditation musketeers!

Helen, Catherine, Bill and Steve, for all of your help in supporting our meditation community in having the best possible chance to change their lives for the better.

Andy, Andy, Brian, Toby, Lee, Megan, Tom, Harriet, Nick, Holly and Smiles, for doing all the spadework behind the scenes; without you guys, I wouldn't have a life!

Eyal, Yoyo, Bill and Helen, for reviewing the book and helping me avoid any rookie errors!

Charlie and Liddy, for putting integrity first.

Shelley and Nick, for supporting us in the early years and doing the heavy lifting when we couldn't afford to employ people. You deserve a very happy retirement!

The Williams Massive, for helping to support and inspire me to be my best, even when I was trying to be Keith Richards!

The Majorca Six, for being the greatest tribe any man could hope to have grown up with.

Jess, for being you.

FURTHER RESOURCES

For more information on Vedic meditation and the courses I run:
www.willwilliamsmeditation.com
www.theeffortlessmind.com

Download our app:
Search Will Williams Meditation on the App Store or go to
willwilliamsmeditation.com/app

Check out our podcasts:
Search for Will Williams Meditation or go to
www.willwilliamsmeditation.com/podcasts

Further Reading

Ayurveda

Deepak Chopra, *Perfect Health* (London: Bantam, 2001)
Jasmine Hemsley, *East by West* (London: Bluebird Books, 2017)
Hari Sharma and Christopher Clark, *Contemporary Ayurveda* (London: Churchill Livingstone, 1997)
Thomas Yarema, Daniel Rhoda and Johnny Brannigan, *Eat Taste Heal* (Whitefish, MT: Five Elements Press, 2006, 2010, 2015)

Neuroscience

Deepak Chopra and Rudolph E. Tanzi, *Super Brain: Unleashing the Explosive Power of Your Mind to Maximize Health, Happiness and Spiritual Well-being* (London: Rider, 2013)

Norman Doidge, *The Brain's Way of Healing: Remarkable Discoveries and Recoveries from the Frontiers of Neuroplasticity* (London: Penguin, 2016)

Norman Doidge, *The Brain That Changes Itself: Stories of Personal Triumph from the Frontiers of Brain Science* (London: Penguin, 2008)

Epigenetics

Nessa Carey, *The Epigenetics Revolution: How Modern Biology is Rewriting Our Understanding of Genetics, Disease and Inheritance* (London: Icon Books, 2012)

Deepak Chopra and Rudolph E. Tanzi, *Super Genes: The Hidden Key to Total Well-Being* (London: Rider, 2015)

Richard C. Francis, *Epigenetics: How Environment Shapes our Genes* (New York: W. W. Norton & Co., 2012)

Microbiome

Dr Michael Mosley, *The Clever Guts Diet: How to Revolutionise Your Body From the Inside Out* (London: Short Books, 2017)

Gerard E. Mullin, *The Gut Balance Revolution: Boost Your Metabolism, Restore Your Inner Ecology and Lose Weight for Good* (Emmaus, PA: Rodale, 2014)

Biology

Robert Sapolsky, *Why Zebras Don't Get Ulcers* (3rd edition) (New York: Henry Holt, 2004)

Physics

Brian Greene, *The Elegant Universe: Superstrings, Hidden Dimensions and the Quest for the Ultimate Theory* (London: Vintage, 2000)

Carlo Rovelli, *Reality Is Not What It Seems: The Journey to Quantum Gravity* (London: Penguin, 2017)

Anthropology

Yuval Noah Harari, *Sapiens: A Brief History of Mankind* (London: Harvill Secker, 2014)

Current Affairs and Complexity Science

Thomas Homer-Dixon, *The Upside of Down: Catastrophe, Creativity and the Renewal of Civilisation* (London: Souvenir Press Ltd, 2007
See also www.homerdixon.com

Emotional Intelligence

Brené Brown, *The Gifts of Imperfection: Let Go of Who You Think You're Supposed to Be and Embrace Who You Are* (London: Hazelden Publishing, Simon & Schuster, 2010)

ENDNOTES

PREFACE

4   In this book I also want to share with you, in their own words, the stories of some of the people I've taught: All names have been changed.

WHAT FORM OF MEDITATION DO I TEACH?

13   The World Health Organization has called stress 'the health epidemic of the twenty-first century': See BBC, 'The Truth About Stress', www.bbc.co.uk/mediacentre/proginfo/2017/18/the-truth-about-stress.

14   Researchers at UCLA invited subjects into a lab and hooked them up to every possible monitoring device: R. K. Wallace, *Science*, 5/167: 1751.

15   The left side of the brain processes information in a very analytical way; it's focused on detail, and is very task-oriented. The right side of the brain processes information in a big-picture way; it's much more contextual, and tends to be more emotionally intelligent and collaborative in its approach. Better connections between the two leads to greater focus and heightened capability: See Iain McGilchrist, *The Divided Brain and the Search for Meaning: Why Are We So Unhappy?* (New Haven, CT: Yale University Press, 2012).

15–16   The engine of your stress response, the amygdala, becomes functionally less active. Instead of firing at any old trigger, perpetuating a need to firefight your way through life as if in constant survival mode, it begins to become more discerning as to what actually deserves a response: See Gaëlle Desbordes, Lobsang T. Negi, Thaddeus W. W. Pace, B. Alan Wallace,

Charles L. Raison and Eric Schwartz, 'Effects of Mindful-attention and Compassion Meditation Training on Amygdala Response to Emotional Stimuli in an Ordinary, Non-meditative State', *Frontiers in Human Neuroscience*, 1 November 2012, https://www.ncbi.nlm.nih.gov/pmc/articles/PMC3485650/.

16 **the hippocampus, part of the limbic system in your brain and responsible for consolidating information from short-memory to long-term memory, begins to grow, which gives you greater recall capabilities:** In 2014, Harvard neuroscientist Dr Sara Lazar compared the MRI brain scans of those attending a meditation course versus a control group who didn't. After eight weeks of meditation, those who attended the meditation course had thicker grey matter in several parts of the brain. These included the left hippocampus, a small horseshoe-shaped structure in the central brain involved in memory, learning and emotional regulation. Other areas of the brain that showed signs of development were the posterior cingulate cortex – again important for memory and emotions; the temporo-parietal junction, involved in empathising; and the cerebellum, which helps co-ordinate movement. Those who did not attend the course experienced no such structural brain changes.

16 **The prefrontal cortex becomes much more active, so that your ability to learn new skills, prioritise tasks, organise information, engage in lateral thinking, solve complex problems and express yourself creatively all become heightened:** See Rebecca Gladding, *You Are Not Your Brain: The 4-Step Solution for Changing Bad Habits, Ending Unhealthy Thinking, and Taking Control of Your Life* (New York: Avery, 2012). For a summary of the relevant effects listed in this book, see https://www.psychologytoday.com/blog/use-your-mind-change-your-brain/201305/is-your-brain-meditation.

16 **Both right and left frontal lobes become more balanced, leaving you feeling more able to make rational, healthy choices for yourself in a calm state of mind:** See previous note, op. cit.

16 **And, perhaps most significant of all, the ability to feel more connected to yourself and to others is improved. By enjoying a balanced flow of endorphins, and greater activation of your prefrontal cortex, you find that love, compassion and empathy begin to replace unnecessary aggression, anxiety or sadness:** This comes from a combination of the effects as mentioned by the previous six notes and also its effects on serotonin; for a further explanation see the IOC Institute website, 'How Meditation Boosts

Melatonin, Serotonin, GABA, DHEA, Endorphins, Growth
Hormone, and More', https://eocinstitute.org/meditation/dhea_
gaba_cortisol_hgh_melatonin_serotonin_endorphins/. There's also
a study highlighting the impacts on a key neurochemical called
DHEA-S, low levels of which are associated with cardiovascular
disease, obesity and breast cancer, and are also considered to have
anti-depressive qualities. Our DHEA-S levels decline significantly
as we age, and in the study, 423 practitioners of this technique were
compared with 1,252 non-meditators. The results demonstrated
that the meditators DHEA-S levels were comparable with control
subjects five to ten years younger. See J. L. Glaser et al., *Journal of
Behavioral Medicine*, August 1992, 15 (4): 327–41.

MIND AND BODY

39   **What's your understanding of the links between your mind
and your body?:** My thanks in this section of the book to experts
Eyal Pavell, Dr J. Dunn and Yolanda Smith.

40   **Maintaining a stable internal environment is a very dynamic
process, and our bodies are constantly monitoring and
adjusting as conditions change to achieve what scientists
call 'homeostasis':** Although here we discuss the energy your
body expends trying to maintain homeostatic balance, there is
increasingly strong evidence that what the body actually strives
for is an 'allostatic balance', which it does by adjusting according
to the situation at hand, rather than trying to maintain a specific
set-point. This means the process is much more dynamic, and helps
us to understand why we have such strong *anticipatory* responses.
For further insights into allostasis, please see the works of Peter
Sterling, Joseph Eyer and Bruce McEwen.

45   **In the ancient East they called these formative experiences
samskaras, from which we get the English word 'scar'. In the
West, we call them *premature cognitive commitments*:** Read more
about premature cognitive commitments in B. Chanowitz and E. J.
Langer, 'Premature Cognitive Commitment', *J Pers Soc Psychol*,
December 1981, 41(6): 1051-63, https://www.ncbi.nlm.nih.gov/
pubmed/6975812. The link between samskaras and premature
cognitive commitments is my own hypothesis.

46   **As Suzanne O'Sullivan very compassionately explained in
her 2016 book on psychosomatic illness, *It's All In Your Head*:**
Although this may innately feel like a controversial premise for a book,
it really is worth readers reviewing the work before jumping to any

prejudicial conclusions about whether this assertion is fair or not – the only way we as a society will improve our lot is if we challenge our assumptions and test these expert hypotheses instead of burying our heads in the sand every time an insight from the front lines makes us uncomfortable. As reviewers of the book said, it 'offer[s] a remarkable insight into the suffering of these patients, as well as the power of the mind over the body … it should be on the reading list of every medical student' (*The Guardian*) and it is 'an important study of psychosomatic illness, which shows it to be a serious disease of modern society: misunderstood, misdiagnosed and surrounded by fear' (*Telegraph*).

47 **Cells degenerate more quickly, and that puts the body as well as the mind under even more stress. That is when you get sick:** Stress has been linked to various degenerative disorders such as dementia. See Hongxin Dong and John. G. Csernansky, 'Effects of Stress and Stress Hormones on Amyloid β Protein and Plaque Deposition', *J Alzheimers Dis*, Oct 2009, 18(2): 459–69, https://www. ncbi.nlm.nih.gov/pmc/articles/PMC2905685/. See also Fei-Fei Wang, Qian Wang, Yong Chen, Qiang Lin, Hui-Bao Gao, and Ping Zhang, 'Chronic Stress Induces Ageing-associated Degeneration in Rat Leydig Cells', *Asian Journal of Andrology*, July 2012, 14(4): 643–8, https://www.ncbi.nlm.nih.gov/pmc/articles/PMC3720085/.

48 **In the 1970s, neuroscientists discovered that the human brain is neuroplastic:** See Christopher Bergland, 'How Do Neuroplasticity and Neurogenesis Rewire Your Brain?', *Psychology Today*, 6 February 2017, https://www.psychologytoday. com/blog/the-athletes-way/201702/how-do-neuroplasticity-and-neurogenesis-rewire-your-brain; Jon Bardin, 'Neurodevelopment: Unlocking the brain', *Nature: International Journal of Science*, 4 July 2012, https://www.nature.com/news/neurodevelopment-unlocking-the-brain-1.10925; Simon Makin, 'Blind Mice Cured by Running', *Scientific American*, 29 June 2014, https:// www.scientificamerican.com/article/blind-mice-cured-by-running/; Tom Valeo, 'Dyslexia Studies Catch Neuroplasticity at Work', The Dana Foundation, November 2008, http://www. dana.org/Publications/Brainwork/Details.aspx?id=43755.

48 **Although we all have our own genetic make-up, we also have something called the epigenome:** See 'We Are More Than Our DNA: Discovering a New Mechanism of Epigenetic Inheritance', *Science Daily* (27/04/17), source: CRNS, https://www.sciencedaily. com/releases/2017/04/170427111206.htm; 'How Epigenetics Regulate Vital Functions From Bacteria to Humans', *Science Daily*, (04/08/16), source: Boston University Medical Center, https:// www.sciencedaily.com/releases/2016/08/160804141246.htm.

49   **Then there's the microbiome:** See Chris S. Smillie,
     Mark B. Smith, Jonathan Friedman, Otto X. Cordero,
     Lawrence A. David and Eric J. Alm, 'Ecology Drives a
     Global Network of Gene Exchange Connecting the Human
     Microbiome', *Research Letter* 280, 8 December 2011: 241,
     http://akka.genetics.wisc.edu/sandbox/groups/genetics677/
     wiki/8bdf0/attachments/75e6c/Smillie_Nature_2010.
     pdf?sessionID=5f75701130c4ff048efd57eb029ee2ef6101de25;
     Earth Microbiome Project, http://www.earthmicrobiome.
     org/; Elizabeth Pennisi, 'The Right Gut Microbes Help
     Infants Grow', *Science*, 18 February 2016, http://www.
     sciencemag.org/news/2016/02/right-gut-microbes-help-
     infants-grow; Katherine Harman Courage, 'Your Poor
     Diet Might Hurt Your Grandchildren's Guts', *Science*, 13
     January 2016, http://www.sciencemag.org/news/2016/01/
     your-poor-diet-might-hurt-your-grandchildren-s-guts.

49   **We can recover from brain injuries and strokes. The sting
     in the tail, however, is that just as the brain can retain
     good information, it can also retain information that is
     less than healthy:** See Norman Doidge, *The Brain's Way of
     Healing: Stories of Remarkable Recoveries and Discoveries* (London:
     Penguin, 2016). Find out more from Jill Bolte Taylor's TED
     talk, 'My Stroke of Insight', https://www.ted.com/talks/
     jill_bolte_taylor_s_powerful_stroke_of_insight.

50   **Your brain will gradually loosen the neural pathways
     that trap you into habitual and restrictive thinking
     and form new ones that can make you feel much more
     positive and connected to the world:** See this very useful
     list of five studies on meditation and physical changes in the
     brain on the Meditation Research: Psychological Science of
     Meditation website: http://meditation-research.org.uk/2014/03/
     meditation-and-neuroplasticity-five-key-articles/.

50–51 **When you find new ways of being, and new ways of living,
     through meditation – perhaps changing some of your less than
     helpful habits – you are changing the way that your genes
     express themselves. And if you look after your microbiome
     (I'll explain how to do that later), you can go a long way to
     improving your mental and physical health:** See references above
     to microbiome and epigenetics.

51   **Stress is a particular disruptor of hormones. The fight or flight
     response causes our neurochemistry to react by** *over-secreting*
     the hormones that will allow our bodies to either flee from

or do battle with what it sees as an imminent threat (like the steroid cortisol), while *under-secreting* those that aren't essential to survival (such as sex hormones): See Salam Ranabir and K. Reetu, 'Stress and Hormones', *Indian Journal of Endocrinology and Metabolism*, Jan-Mar 2011, 15(1): 18–22, https://www.ncbi.nlm. nih.gov/pmc/articles/PMC3079864/; Robert Sapolsky, *Why Zebras Don't Get Ulcers* (3rd edition) (New York: Henry Holt, 2004), p. 69; F. Curtin and T. Steimer, 'Lower Sex Hormones in Men during Anticipatory Stress', *NeuroReport* 7 (1996).

51–52   This mechanism, combined with the extra cortisol that you'll also secrete (up to five times more than usual), will usually provoke weight gain, typically around your middle, because that's where cortisol particularly likes to deposit it: See Marilyn Grenville, *Fat Around The Middle* (London: Kyle Cathie Ltd, 2006), Chapter 1.

52   You can really help yourself by lowering your cortisol production and absorption by meditating to soothe your nervous system and reduce your tendency to fight or flight. See C. N. Alexander, P. Robinson and M. Rainforth, 'Treating and Preventing Alcohol, Nicotine and Drug Abuse through Transcendental Meditation: A review and statistical meta-analysis', in *Self-Recovery – Treating Addictions using Transcendental Meditation and Maharishi Ayur-Veda*, eds David F. O'Connell and Charles N. Alexander (New York, London: Harrington Park Press); Christopher R. K. MacLean, Kenneth G. Walton, Stig R. Wenneberg and Robert H. Schneider, 'Effects of the Transcendental Meditation Program on Adaptive Mechanisms: Changes in Hormone Levels and Responses to Stress After 4 Months of Practice', *ResearchGate*, June 1997, https://www.researchgate.net/ publication/223019612_Effects_of_the_Transcendental_Meditation_ program_on_adaptive_mechanisms_changes_in_hormone_levels_ and_responses_to_stress_after_4_months_of_practice.

52   Even if your weight issues are genetic in origin, these are all malleable and can be managed if you keep your stress levels low and your microbiome healthy: See Marilyn Grenville, *Fat Around The Middle* (London: Kyle Cathie Ltd, 2006), Chapter 8.

52   the suppression of hormones linked to reproduction can lead to disruption of the menstrual cycle: Harvard Health Publishing says 'FHA, or stress-induced anovulation, is one of the most common causes of secondary amenorrhea (1), and it accounts for the reproductive dysfunction seen in undernutrition, excessive exercise, severe emotional stress, and chronic disease', https:// www.health.harvard.edu/womens-health/amenorrhea. See also Lindsay T. Fourman and Pouneh K. Fazeli, 'Neuroendocrine

Causes of Amenorrhea – An Update', *The Journal of Clinical Endocrinology and Metabolism*, Volume 100, Issue 3, 1 March 2015, 812–82, https://academic.oup.com/jcem/article/100/3/812/2838996.

52 **Prolonged exposure to stress can even result in infertility:** See A. Negro-Vilar, 'Stress and Other Environmental Factors Affecting Fertility in Men and Women: Overview', *Environmental Health Perspectives* 101/2 (1993): 59.

52 **most guys know that getting in the mood is infinitely less likely if they feel under pressure or stressed out, and chronic stress can play havoc with both sexual function and fertility:** For the effects of stress on sperm quality and quantity, see Teresa Janevic, Linda G. Kahn, Paul Landsbergis, Piera M. Cirillo, Barbara A. Cohn, Xinhua Liu and Pam Factor-Litvak, 'Effects of Work and Life Stress on Semen Quality', *Fertil Steril.* August 2014, 102(2): 530–8, https://www.ncbi.nlm.nih.gov/pmc/articles/PMC4382866/; Honor Whiteman, 'Stress Linked to Male Fertility', *Medical News Today*, 30 May 2014, https://www.medicalnewstoday.com/articles/277543.php. For causes of problems in male sexual function, see the Cleveland Clinic website on sexual dysfunction in males, https://my.clevelandclinic.org/health/diseases/9122-sexual-dysfunction-in-males; Kingston Rajiah, Sajesh K. Veettil, Suresh Kumar and Elizabeth M. Mathew, 'Psychological Impotence: Psychological Erectile Dysfunction and Erectile Dysfunction Causes, Diagnostic Methods and Management Options', *Scientific Research and Essays* Vol. 7(4), 30 January 2012, 446–52, http://citeseerx.ist.psu.edu/viewdoc/download?doi=10.1.1.401.8776&rep=rep1&type=pdf.

53 **those who experience high levels of life stress are more likely to succumb to major depression. Stress is also implicated in triggering genetic predispositions towards depression. Sustained stress also depletes dopamine in our pleasure pathways, and noradrenaline from signalling the locus ceruleus of the brain. It also effects the synthesis, secretion, efficacy and breakdown of serotonin. An imbalanced profile of these three key neurotransmitters are intimately linked to most forms of depression (and anxiety):** For an overview of the links between stress and depression, see P. Gold, F. Goodwin, F. and G. Chrousos, 'Clinical and Biochemical Manifestations of Depression: Relation to the Neurobiology of Stress', *New England Journal of Medicine*, 319 (1988): 348; A. Zis and F. Goodwin, 'Major Affective Disorders as a Recurrent Illness: A Critical Review', *Archives of General Psychiatry*, 36 (1979), 385; H. Anisman and R. Zacharko,

'Depression: the Predisposing Influence of Stress', *Behavioral and Brain Science*, 5 (1982): 89; R. Turner and M. Beiser, 'Major Depression and Depressive Symptomatology Among the Physically Disabled: Assessing the Role of Chronic Stress', *Journal of Nervous and Mental Disease*, 178 (1990): 343; J. Roberts and J. Ciesla, 'Stress Generation in the Context of Depressive Disorders', in G. Fink, ed., *Encyclopedia of Stress*, 3, 512.

On major stressors preceding first major depression, see G. Brown and T. Harris, *Social Origins of Depression* (New York: Free Press, 1978); G. Brown, T. Harris and C. Hepworth, 'Loss, Humiliation and Entrapment Among Women Developing Depression: A Patient and Non-patient Comparison', *Psychological Medicine*, 25 (1995): 7. For some studies examining factors that predict who becomes depressed in response to major stressors, see: P. Maciejewiski, H. Prigerson and C. Mazure, 'Self-efficacy as a Mediator Between Stressful Life Events and Depressive Symptoms: Differences Based on History of Prior Depression', *British Journal of Psychiatry*, 176 (2000): 373; P. Mitchell, G. Parker, G. Gladstone, K. Wilhelm and V. Austin, 'Severity of Stressful Life Events in First and Subsequent Episodes of Depression: The Relevance of Depression Subtype', *Journal of Affective Disorders*, 73 (2003): 245.

On a predisposing gene, see A. Caspi, K. Sugden, T. Moffitt, A. Taylor, I. Craig, H. Harrington, J. McClay, J. Mill, J. Martin, A. Braithwait and R. Poulton, 'Influence of Life Stress on Depression: Moderation by a Polymorphism in the 5-HTT gene', *Science* 301 (2003): 386. For a similar finding in nonhuman primates: A. Bennett, K. Lesch, A. Heils, J. Long, J. Lorenz, S. Shoaf, M. Champoux, S. Suomi, M. Linnoila and J. Higley, 'Early Experience and Serotonin Transporter Gene Variation Interact to Influence Primate CNS Function', *Biological Psychiatry*, 7 (2002): 118.

On how stress alters neurochemistry relevant to depression, see G. Tafet and R. Bernardini, 'Psychoneuroendocrinological Links Between Chronic Stress and Depression', *Progress in Neuro-Psychopharmacology and Biological Psychiatry*, 27 (2003): 893; E. Sabban and R. Kvetnansky, 'Stress-triggered Activation of Gene Expression in Catecholaminergic Systems: Dynamics of Transcriptional Events', *Trends in Neurosciences*, 24 (2001): 91. For an immensely interesting link between glucocorticoids and the neurochemistry of serotonin, see K. Glatz, R. Mossner, A. Heils and K. Lesch, 'Glucocorticoid-regulated Human Seratonin Transporter (5-HTT) Expression is Modulated by the 5-HTT Gene-promoter-linked Polymorphic Region', *Journal of Neurochemistry*, 86 (2003): 1072; E. van Riel, O. Meijer, P. Steenbergen, and M. Joels, 'Chronic Unpredictable Stress Causes Attenuation of Serotonin Responses in Cornu

Ammonis 1 Pyramidal Neurons', *Neuroscience*, 120 (2003): 649. For a demonstration that uncontrollable, but not controllable, stress alters serotonin neurochemistry, see S. Bland, C. Twining, L. Watkins and S. Maier, 'Stressor Controllability Modulates Stressinduced Serotonin but not Dopamine Efflux in the Nucleus Accumbens Shell', *Synapse*, 49 (2003): 206.

53–54   calcium is another vitally important element in the body. After the menopause, many women suffer from osteoporosis, a weakening of the bones, which is linked to a lack of calcium. However, as well as bone strength, this mineral also has an impact on the thyroid, insulin secretion, energy production, nerve and muscle relaxation, the absorption of toxic metals and the digestion of fat. Stress siphons calcium out of your body by excreting it in your urine. If you're regularly in fight or flight mode, much of your calcium will be going down the toilet. And if you're in the exhaustion stage of stress, which comes after you've been exposed to it for too long, calcium will build up in your joints, arteries, kidneys and elsewhere, which has been shown to lead to premature ageing: See Anand Hollai, 'Stress Can Hurt Your Bones Too', *The Times of India*, 7 June 2013, https://timesofindia.indiatimes.com/life-style/health-fitness/health-news/Stress-can-hurt-your-bones-too/articleshow/19145909.cms. For the link between osteoporosis and stress, see H. Kumano, 'Osteoporosis and Stress', *Clin Calcium*, September 2005, 15(9): 1544–7, https://www.ncbi.nlm.nih.gov/pubmed/16137956. See also Robert Sapolsky, *Why Zebras Don't Get Ulcers* (3rd edition) (New York: Henry Holt, 2004), 158–9.

COPING WITH ANXIETY

55   one in four of us will suffer from mental health issues at some point in our lives: WHO Press Release, 'Mental disorders affect one in four people', http://www.who.int/whr/2001/media_centre/press_release/en/.

55   In the UK, the biggest single killer of men between the ages of twenty and forty-nine is suicide: Office for National Statistics, 2014, http://webarchive.nationalarchives.gov.uk/20160107060820/; http://www.ons.gov.uk/ons/dcp171778_351100.pdf. Depression accounts for 800,000 suicides per year: see 'Spirit of the Age', *The Economist*, 19 December 1998, 113.

55–56   If our brain continues to experience this level of hypervigilance, and neuroplastically wires it in, we may begin to experience what's known as 'trait anxiety': See Yori Gidron, 'Trait Anxiety', *Encyclopaedia of Behavioral Medicine*, https://link.springer.com/referenceworkentry/10.1007%2F978-1-4419-1005-9_1539 for an explanation of trait anxiety.

55   Feelings of anxiety and fear are caused by the activation of our fight or flight response by our hyper-stimulated amygdala – in particular, by a trait known as hypervigilance, which prepares us to run or fight even before we have definite confirmation that actual danger is upon us: Hypervigilance is a symptom of hyperarousal, common in PTSD, anxiety etc. See Lisa M. Shin and Israel Liberzon, 'The Neurocircuitry of Fear, Stress, and Anxiety Disorders', *Neuropsychopharmacology*, January 2010, 35(1): 169–91, https://www.ncbi.nlm.nih.gov/pmc/articles/PMC3055419/. For an explanation of hypervigilance from a counsellor/psychotherapist, see http://www.counselling-directory.org.uk/counsellor-articles/hair-trigger-stress-and-anxiety-hypervigilance.

56   The amygdala is so sensitive that if you subliminally flash a picture of something fear-inducing to someone with an anxious disposition, their amygdala immediately goes into overdrive: See Robert Sapolsky, *Why Zebras Don't Get Ulcers* (3rd edition) (New York: Henry Holt, 2004), 513.

56   The most likely cause would be a traumatic event that's been stored within the nervous system, often from when they were younger, or even in the womb: See Suzanne Babbel, 'The Connections Between Emotional Stress, Trauma and Physical Pain', *Psychology Today*, 8 April 2010, https://www.psychologytoday.com/blog/somatic-psychology/201004/the-connections-between-emotional-stress-trauma-and-physical-pain; Michael T. Kinsella and Catherine Monk, 'Impact of Maternal Stress, Depression and Anxiety on Fetal Neurobehavioral Development', *PMC*, 15 July 2014, US National Library of Medicine, National Institutes of Health, https://www.ncbi.nlm.nih.gov/pmc/articles/PMC3710585/; Robert C. Scaer, *The Body Bears the Burden: Trauma, Dissociation, and Disease* (Philadelphia, Pennsylvania: The Haworth Medical Press, 2001).

57   Biologically, we're programmed to go to sleep very early, so there are lots of functions that take place inside the brain from around the 9.30–10 p.m. mark: See Arianna Huffington, *Thrive: The Third Metric to Redefining Success and Creating a Life of Well-Being, Wisdom, and Wonder* (London: W. H. Allen, 2015); The National Sleep Foundation, 'Melatonin and Sleep', https://sleepfoundation.org/sleep-topics/melatonin-and-sleep.

65   Vedic-inspired meditation has been shown to be at least twice
     as effective as other relaxation or meditative techniques in
     reducing the symptoms of anxiety: *Journal of Counseling and
     Development* 64, 1985: 212–15.

65–66 Panic attacks are the result of a massive activation of the
       sympathetic nervous system, sending the mind, body and
       emotions into crisis mode. They also arise from elevated
       anxiety levels, usually brought about by psychological stress
       and adrenal exhaustion: See Gerald Klerman, L. Hirschfeld,
       M. A. Robert and Myrna M. Weissman, *Panic Anxiety and Its
       Treatments: Report of the World Psychiatric Association Presidential
       Educational Program Task Force*, American Psychiatric Association
       (1993), 44; Rick Nauert, 'How Panic Can Build Gradually
       from Chronic Stress', *PsychCentral*, https://psychcentral.com/
       news/2011/06/21/panic-can-build-gradually-from-chronic-
       stress/27102.html; David Orenstein, 'Panic Symptoms Increase
       Steadily, Not Acutely, After Stressful Events', Brown University
       website, https://news.brown.edu/articles/2011/06/panic.

66   When the stress response is engaged, you take short, sharp
     breaths in preparation for danger. And when that stress
     activation becomes chronic, you tend to only ever use
     the top third of your lungs, creating a permanent state of
     hyperventilation. This results in a poor exchange of oxygen
     and carbon dioxide in the bloodstream. A deficiency of carbon
     dioxide can lead to panic attacks, insomnia and extreme
     fatigue; and a lack of oxygen will deprive your organs
     and muscles of resources that are vital for their effective
     functioning. This low-level hyperventilation will lead to
     increased heart rate, palpitations, and a sense of anxiety
     combined with a feeling of being out of control: For links
     between anxiety and stress, hyperventilation and gas exchange,
     see *Hyperventilation Overview*, on Web MD, https://www.webmd.
     com/a-to-z-guides/tc/hyperventilation-topic-overview#1.

DEALING WITH DEPRESSION

71   Depression is a global epidemic. A recent World Health
     Organization estimate put it as the leading cause of ill health
     and disability worldwide, with an 18 per cent increase in
     rates of depression between 2005 and 2015: WHO Fact Sheet,
     February 2017, http://www.who.int/mediacentre/factsheets/
     fs369/en/.

76   Depression is linked to the unhealthy production of (or
     compromised receptivity to) certain neurotransmitters
     and hormones which are vital to psychological wellbeing,
     and which become destabilised by the chain reaction of
     physiological responses we experience when the stress response
     is regularly activated: See Rashmi Nemade (ed. Kathryn
     Patricelli), 'Biology of Depression – Neurotransmitters', Southwest
     Alabama Behavioural Health Care Systems website, https://www.
     swamh.com/poc/view_doc.php?type=doc&id=12999&cn=5; D. J.
     Nutt, 'Relationship of Neurotransmitters to the Symptoms of
     Major Depressive Disorder', *J Clin Psychiatry*. 2008, 69, Suppl E1:4–
     7, https://www.ncbi.nlm.nih.gov/pubmed/18494537.

76   Most people with depression have high levels of
     glucocorticoids, the stress-induced steroid hormones that
     go to your brain and inhibit anything not deemed useful
     for raw physical survival. Under threat, feeling joyful is
     completely superfluous – you can worry about getting
     happy later: Christoph Anacker, Patricia A. Zunszain, Livia
     A. Carvalho, and Carmine M. Pariante, 'The Glucocorticoid
     Receptor: Pivot of Depression and of Antidepressant Treatment?',
     Psychoneuroendocrinology, April 2011, 36(3): 415–25, https://www.
     ncbi.nlm.nih.gov/pmc/articles/PMC3513407/.

77   The chronic release of glucocorticoids also results in a
     shrinking of the hippocampus, the area of the brain that
     processes memory, so your ability to remember information
     is compromised. And the cortex, responsible for motor
     skills and abstract thinking, tends to be considerably less
     activated, resulting in apathy: See L. Cahill and J. L. McGaugh,
     'Mechanisms of Emotional Arousal and Lasting Declarative
     Memory', *Trends in Neurosciences*, July 1998, 21(7): 294–9; N. R.
     Carlson, *Physiology of Behavior* (11th ed.) (New York: Allyn
     & Bacon), 605; J. K. Belanoff, K. Gross, A. Yager and A. F.
     Schatzberg, 'Corticosteroids and Cognition', *Journal of Psychiatric
     Research*, 2001, 35(3): 127–45; R. M. Sapolsky, 'Glucocorticoids,
     Stress and Exacerbation of Excitotoxic Neuron Death', *Seminars in
     Neuroscience*, October 1994, 6(5): 323–31.

77   patients with depression have been shown to have higher
     levels of histamine/inflammation: See James Gallagher,
     Rachael Buchanan and Andrew Luck-Baker, 'Depression:
     A Revolution in Treatment?' BBC News, 24 August 2016,
     http://www.bbc.co.uk/news/health-37166293; Berk et al., 'So
     Depression is an Inflammatory Disease, But Where Does the
     Inflammation Come From?', *BMC Medicine*, 12 September 2013,

https://bmcmedicine.biomedcentral.com/articles/10.1186/1741-7015-11-200; Jeffrey H. Meyer et al., 'Role of Translocator Protein Density: A Marker of Neuroinflammation in the Brain During Major Depressive Episodes', *JAMA Psych*, 28 January 2015, https://www.medicalnewstoday.com/news/severe-depression-linked-inflammation-brain-288715.

77   **The growing body of evidence highlighting the interaction between mind and body suggests it's not enough to simply tell people with depression to 'cheer up' or that 'it's not that bad':** Depression is now recognised as a mood disorder and illness, not simply a fleeting emotion. Sufferers can't just cheer up, because of physical factors that have been previously discussed regarding neurotransmitters. See the Mental Health America website for more details, http://www.mentalhealthamerica.net/conditions/mood-disorders.

78–79 **When you experience that level of crisis, it's both physiological and neurological. Your body has effectively gone into trauma, and that can change the dynamics of lots of bodily processes. Now that we understand neuroscience, and the effect of stress on our epigenetic profile and the microbiome, as I briefly mentioned in the introduction to this section, we know that big switches can occur very quickly once trauma has set in. That trauma – a combination of conflicting wishes, messages from the surrounding environment, imagined consequences or the pressures of coping – can lead to psychosomatic disorders and outcomes:** See Stellenbosch University, 'Role of Gut Microbiome in Posttraumatic Stress Disorder: More Than a Gut Feeling', 25 October 2017, https://www.sciencedaily.com/releases/2017/10/171025103140.htm; Sophie Leclercq, Paul Forsythe and John Bienenstock, 'Posttraumatic Stress Disorder: Does the Gut Microbiome Hold the Key?', *Can J. Psychiatry*, April 2016, 61(4): 204–13, https://www.ncbi.nlm.nih.gov/pmc/articles/PMC4794957/; Jennifer S. Labus, Emily B. Hollister, Jonathan Jacobs, Kyleigh Kirbach, Numan Oezguen, Arpana Gupta, Jonathan Acosta, Ruth Ann Luna, Kjersti Aagaard, James Versalovic, Tor Savidge, Elaine Hsiao, Kirsten Tillisch and Emeran A. Mayer, 'Differences in Gut Microbial Composition Correlate with Regional Brain Volumes in Irritable Bowel Syndrome', 1 May 2017, https://microbiomejournal.biomedcentral.com/articles/10.1186/s40168-017-0260-z; Torsten Klengel, Divya Mehta, Christoph Anacker, Monika Rex-Haffner, Jens C. Pruessner, Carmine M. Pariante, Thaddeus W. W. Pace, Kristina B. Mercer, Helen S. Mayberg, Bekh Bradley, Charles B. Nemeroff,

Florian Holsboer, Christine M. Heim, Kerry J. Ressler, Theo Rein and Elisabeth B. Binder, 'Allele-specific FKBP5 DNA Demethylation Mediates Gene–childhood Trauma Interactions', *Nat Neurosci.*, January 2013; 16(1): 33–41, https://www.ncbi.nlm. nih.gov/pmc/articles/PMC4136922/.

81   As I mentioned before, those who are experiencing depression usually have an amygdala that is functioning abnormally. Through the power of sound, this form of meditation has been shown to normalise the activity of the amygdala, so that for Estrella it stopped becoming hyper-aroused every time she saw something sad. Her cerebral cortex and left prefrontal cortex were more activated, bringing her a greater sense of positivity. And there would have been far fewer of those pesky glucocorticoids inhibiting the function of her hippocampus, reducing her energy levels and generally wreaking havoc throughout her body. In their place would have come a more balanced production, uptake and disposal of neurotransmitters, especially noradrenaline, serotonin and dopamine, meaning she had a balanced complement of happy hormones lifting her mood: See Russell Hebert, Dietrich Lehmann, Gabriel Tan, Fred Travis and Alarik Arenander, 'Enhanced EEG Alpha Time-domain Phase Synchrony During Transcendental Meditation: Implications for Cortical Integration Theory', *Signal Processing*, November 2005, vol. 85, issue 11, November 2005, 2213-32, http://www.sciencedirect.com/science/article/ pii/S0165168405002100; Robert Keith Wallace, 'Physiological Effects of Transcendental Meditation', *Science*, 27 March 1970, New Series, vol. 167, no. 3926, 1751-4, http://www.jstor.org/ stable/1728295?seq=1#page_scan_tab_contents.

MANAGING ANGER

87   Once angry and frustrated, the ego can either retreat or seek revenge. When this happens, it changes our brain chemistry and creates neural pathways that are counter to our sense of wellbeing. We are effectively locking ourselves in a prison of our own making, and the more disenfranchised we become from a person or a group, the more we start to filter 'their' actions in a way that proves they are being unfair to 'us'. It's an incredibly toxic dynamic: For an understanding of how the ego causes physiological reactions, see Anna Freud, *The Ego and the Mechanisms of Defence* (London: Karnac, 1992 [1937]). Anger itself is the body's fundamental physiological response to

a perceived threat to you, your loved ones, your property, your self-image, your emotional safety or some part of your identity. As the following article from the University of Nottingham, https://www.nottingham.ac.uk/counselling/documents/podacst-fight-or-flight-response.pdf, suggests, 'To understand the Fight or Flight response it helps to think about the role of emotions in our lives. Many of us would prefer to focus on our logical, thinking nature and ignore our sometimes troublesome emotions, but emotions have a purpose. Our most basic emotions like fear, anger or disgust are vital messengers: they evolved as signals to help us meet our basic needs for self-preservation and safety. It would be dangerous to be indecisive about a threat to our survival so the brain runs information from our senses through the most primitive, reactive parts of our brain first. These areas of the brain control instinctive responses and they don't do too much thinking. This more primitive part of our brain communicates with the rest of our brain and our body to create signals we can't ignore easily: powerful emotions and symptoms.'

87   **Anger is also extremely bad for our physical health. There's a direct correlation between anger and unsustainably elevated heart rates, as well as high blood pressure, both of which compromise our cardiovascular health. It can also affect our immune system and leave us wide open to all sorts of diseases:** See Robert Sapolsky, *Why Zebras Don't Get Ulcers* (3rd edition) (New York: Henry Holt, 2004), 87, 'A strong, adverse emotion like anger doubles the risk of a heart attack during the subsequent two hours'; Karina W. Davidson and Elizabeth Mostofsky, 'Anger Expression and Risk of Coronary Heart Disease: Evidence From the Nova Scotia Health Survey', *Am Heart J.*, February 2010, 159(2): 199–206.

93   **Research has shown that 'venting' – going off on rants, slamming doors, or … swearing at people – actually perpetuates your anger:** See Jeffrey Lohr, 'The Pseudopsychology of Venting in the Treatment of Anger: Implications and Alternatives for Mental Health Practice', *Scientific Review of Mental Health Practice*, 2007; Ryan C. Martin, PhD, Kelsey Ryan Cooyier, BS, Leah M. VanSistine, BS, and Kelly L. Schroeder, BS, 'Anger on the Internet: The Perceived Value of Rant-Sites', *Cyberpsychology Behavior and Social Networking*, 16/2, 2013, http://online.liebertpub.com/doi/pdf/10.1089/cyber.2012.0130.

93   **Natural selection determined that those with the most instinctive response – within one hundredth of a second – had the greatest chance of survival:** The fight or flight response is a survival

mechanism for ensuring the longevity of the species. It follows that those who had the most powerful survival response would be the ones who had the greatest chances of survival. Over the long arc of human history, the human gene pool would become heavily skewed towards those who had the most acute survival response.

94   **The overactivation of the amygdala that many angry people suffer from leads to an inhibition of the prefrontal cortex (the part of the brain that's responsible for rational choices and control) and the activation of the limbic system, which is far more emotional and instinctive:** See Ruth Buczynski, 'How Anger Affects the Brain and Body [Infographic]', National Institute for the Clinical Application of Behavioural Medicine website, https://www.nicabm.com/how-anger-affects-the-brain-and-body-infographic/.

98   **As the very wise Jewish theologian and philosopher Abraham Joshua Heschel famously said: 'The opposite of good is not evil, the opposite of good is indifference':** See https://onbeing.org/programs/arnold-eisen-the-opposite-of-good-is-indifference-sep2017/.

99   **We know of 100–300 neurochemicals within our brain, and we're discovering more all the time:** There are three main categories of neurotransmitters, see https://en.wikipedia.org/wiki/Neurotransmitter; Robert Sapolsky, *Why Zebras Don't Get Ulcers* (3rd edition) (New York: Henry Holt, 2004), 278.

100   **Cannabis is a particular favourite of many people because THC (tetrahydrocannabinol, its main psychoactive constituent) has a molecular structure very similar to the cannabinoids we naturally produce:** Federation of American Societies for Experimental Biology, 'Human Brains Make Their Own Marijuana', 20 April 2009, Science Daily website, https://www.sciencedaily.com/releases/2009/04/090420151240.htm.

100   **The problem is that these *exogenous* chemicals (that come from outside, as opposed to the *endogenous* ones that we produce ourselves) aren't flawlessly structured molecules, and they affect us in a different way to the ones we naturally produce. We take them in arbitrary quantities; they go to arbitrary places in the body; and quite often they get stuck in the receptor site because they don't perfectly fit. When this happens, your brain either turns down its production of that chemical or turns down its sensitivity to it:** Addictive substances artificially interfere with neurotransmitter production in an unnatural way. This physical effect is why addiction is so hard to beat, and the

side effects of a number of drugs create many of the issues we see
in long-term substance abuse cases. For example, the breakdown
chemicals in cocaine are extremely damaging to the liver, while
the addictive effects of heroin are so profound that people will
forgo food, hygiene and basic self-care in pursuit of the drug. See
Scripps Research Institute, 'The Effects of Alcohol on the Brain',
https://www.scripps.edu/newsandviews/e_20020225/koob2.html;
Clinical and Research Information on Drug-Induced Liver Injury,
'Cocaine', https://livertox.nih.gov/Cocaine.htm.

BEATING INSOMNIA

108   According to the NHS, most of us need around eight hours
       of sleep a night to function properly – but it's the quality
       that matters most. The NHS also warns that regular poor-
       quality sleep can put you at risk of developing serious
       medical conditions: See https://www.nhs.uk/oneyou/
       sleep#XqEczHpWCPDdiQwy.97.

108   And if your amygdala's been activated by any other stresses,
       you'll have lots of anxiety-inducing neurotransmitters flooding
       your system – particularly between 2 and 6 a.m. – leading
       to those fretful early mornings: This is based on observation.
       Most people report anxiety peaking between these hours, which
       is fascinating because the ancient science of Ayurveda held that
       a quality known as 'vata' was prominent between these hours,
       and when someone has too much of this quality, they will have a
       propensity towards anxiety.

109   a typical ninety-minute 'sleep cycle': It should be noted
       that sometimes sleep cycles last up to 110 minutes. For more
       information, see: 'What is Sleep?', American Sleep Association
       website, https://www.sleepassociation.org/patients-general-
       public/what-is-sleep; Amie M. Gordon, 'Your Sleep Cycle
       Revealed', https://www.psychologytoday.com/blog/
       between-you-and-me/201307/your-sleep-cycle-revealed.

110   Good-quality sleep has a significant effect on your brain's
       prefrontal cortex, which is responsible for processes such as
       judgement, planning, decision-making and problem-solving.
       The brain is incredibly energy-intensive, using approximately
       20 per cent of your daily energy supplies: For an excellent
       article on the energy consumption of the brain, see Ferris Jabr,
       'Does Thinking Really Hard Burn More Calories', 18 July 2012,
       Scientific American, https://www.scientificamerican.com/article/

thinking-hard-calories/; for a good entry level article on the links
between sleep and the frontal cortex, see Joseph A. Buckhalt, 'The
Prefrontal Cortex During Sleep', 7 February 2013, https://www.
psychologytoday.com/blog/child-sleep-zzzs/201302/the-prefrontal-
cortex-during-sleep or http://www.independent.co.uk/life-style/
health-and-families/sleep-deprivation-how-affects-your-brain-
tiredness-insomnia-a7809756.html.

TACKLING ADDICTION

115   When something new triggers a pleasure sensation, we get
a nice big hit of dopamine. After that, however, it's not so
much the reward itself that triggers the dopamine release,
but the *anticipation of reward* that gets the brain eagerly firing
with expectation: See P. Jędras, A. Jones and M. Field, 'The Role
of Anticipation in Drug Addiction and Reward', *Dove Press*, 16
December 2013, vol 2014: 3, 1-10, https://www.dovepress.com/
the-role-of-anticipation-in-drug-addiction-and-reward-peer-
reviewed-article-NAN; Robert Sapolsky, *Why Zebras Don't Get
Ulcers* (3rd edition) (New York: Henry Holt, 2004), 451.

115–116 If, due to the stresses and strains of life, we find ourselves with
low levels of dopamine release, we're much more vulnerable to
finding something dangerously delicious and falling into the
cycle of dependency.
          This cycle exists because, if we keep taking the substance
that makes us feel good, triggering dopamine release, our
dopamine receptors will turn down the volume on their
sensitivity, otherwise the signals bombarding them would
become overwhelming. At the same time, the brain will be
tricked into responding to the overabundance of supply by
turning down its own production of dopamine: See Dr Kenneth
Blum, 'The Addictive Brain: All Roads Lead to Dopamine',
Colliers Magazine, April 2012, http://colliersmagazine.com/article/
addictive-brain-all-roads-lead-dopamine; Nora D. Volkow,
Gene-Jack Wang, Joanna S. Fowler, Dardo Tomasi, Frank Telang
and Ruben Baler, 'Addiction: Decreased Reward Sensitivity and
Increased Expectation Sensitivity Conspire to Overwhelm the
Brain's Control Circuit', *Bioessays*, September 2010, 32(9): 748–55,
https://www.ncbi.nlm.nih.gov/pmc/articles/PMC2948245/; N. D.
Volkow, J. S. Fowler, G. J. Wang, R. Baler and F. Telang, 'Imaging
Dopamine's Role in Drug Abuse and Addiction', *Neuropharmacology*,
2009: 56 (Suppl 1), 3–8, https://www.ncbi.nlm.nih.gov/pmc/
articles/PMC2696819/.

For more information, see: A. Kelley and K. Berridge, 'The Neuroscience of Natural Rewards: Relevance to Addictive Drugs', *Journal of Neuroscience*, 22 (2002): 3306–11; G. F. Koob, 'Allostatic View of Motivation: Implications for Psychopathology', in R. Bevins and M. T. Bardo, eds, *Motivational Factors in the Etiology of Drug Abuse*, Nebraska Symposium on Motivation, vol. 50 (Lincoln, Neb.: University of Nebraska Press); W. Schultz, L. Tremblay and J. Holerman, 'Reward Processing in Primate Orbitofrontal Cortex and Basal Ganglia', *Cerebral Cortex*, 10 (2000): 272; P. Waelti, A. Dickinson and W. Schultz, 'Dopamine Responses Comply with Basic Assumptions of Formal Learning Theory', *Nature*, 412 (2001): 43; P. Phillips, G. Stuber, M. Heien, R. Wightman and R. Carelli, 'Subsecond Dopamine Release Promotes Cocaine Seeking', *Nature*, 422 (2003): 614; C. Fiorillo, P. Tobler and W. Schultz, 'Discrete Coding of Reward Probability and Uncertainty by Dopamine Neurons', *Science*, 299 (2003): 1998; this and the previous study are discussed in R. Sapolsky, 'The pleasures (and pain) of "maybe"', *Natural History* (September 2003): 22.

On glucocorticoids and dopamine, see P. Piazza and M. Le Moal, 'Glucocorticoids as a Biological Substrate of Reward: Physiological and Pathophysiological Implications', *Brain Research Reviews*, 25 (1997): 359; F. Rouge-Pont, D. Abrous, M. Le Moal and P. Piazza, 'Release of Endogenous Dopamine in Cultured Mesencephalic Neurons: Influence of Dopaminergic Agonists and Glucocorticoid Antagonists', *European Journal of Neuroscience*, 1, 848 (999): 2343; P. Piazza and M. Le Moal, 'The Role of Stress in Drug Self-Administration', *Trends in Pharmacological Sciences*, 19 (1998): 6; V. Deroche-Gamonet, I. Sillaber, B. Aouizerate, R. Izawa, M. Jaber, S. Ghozland, C. Kellendonk, M. Le Moal, R. Spanagel, G. Schutz, F. Tronche and P. V. Piazza, 'The Glucocorticoid Receptor as a Potential Target to Reduce Cocaine Abuse', *Journal of Neuroscience*, 23 (2003): 4785.

On stress and dopamine depletion, see C. Gambarana, F. Masi, A. Tagliamonte, S. Scherggi, O. Ghiglieri and M. De Monti, 'A Chronic Stress that Impairs Reactivity in Rats also Decreases Dopaminergic Transmission in the Nucleus Accumbens: A Microdialysis Study', *Journal of Neurochemistry*, 72 (1999): 2039.

On stress and amygdala release of dopamine, see M. Wolak, P. Gold and G. Chrousos, 'Stress System: Emphasis on CRF in Physiologic Stress Responses and the Endocrinopathies of Melancholic and Atypical Depression', *Endocrine Reviews*, 11 (2002).

On neurons that are unresponsive to dopamine signals: Y. Ding, H. Chi, D. Grady, A. Morishima, J. Kidd, K. Kidd, P. Flodman, M. Spence, S. Schuck, J. Swanson, Y. Zhang and M. Moyzis, 'Evidence of Positive Selection Acting at the Human Dopamine Receptor D4 Gene Locus', *Proceedings of the National Academy of Sciences*, 99 (2002): 309.

116   **Interestingly, a history of stress (in the womb, or as a child) will make us much more susceptible to developing a dependency later in life:** In the womb, stress is linked to later mood disorders and mental health issues. People with mental health issues are more likely to become addicts. See Lamya Khoury, Yilang L. Tang, Bekh Bradley, Joe F. Cubells and Kerry J. Ressler, 'Substance Use, Childhood Traumatic Experience, and Posttraumatic Stress Disorder in an Urban Civilian Population', *Wiley: Depression and Anxiety*, December 2010, 27(12): 1077–86, accessed at https://www.ncbi.nlm.nih.gov/ pmc/articles/PMC3051362/; British Neuroscience Association, 'Fetal Exposure to Excessive Stress Hormones in the Womb Linked to Adult Mood Disorders', *Science Daily*, 7 April 2013, https://www.sciencedaily.com/releases/2013/04/130407090835. htm; Centre for Addiction and Mental Health, 'Mental Illness and Addictions: Facts and Statistics', http://www.camh.ca/ en/hospital/about_camh/newsroom/for_reporters/Pages/ addictionmentalhealthstatistics.aspx.

116   **stress will inhibit the production of many important neurochemicals, which will lead us to seek replacements from recreational substances and prescription medicines.** Second, it makes us much more vulnerable to developing addiction by creating a greater contrast between how we felt before we took the drug/had the drink/played the video game and the lushness of the subsequent high. It also makes us more likely to keep administering until we've crossed the threshold of addiction. That's why, if you're going to treat addiction, you need to reduce stress: See Rajita Sinha, 'The Role of Stress in Addiction Relapse', *Current Psychiatry Reports*, October 2007, Volume 9, Issue 5, 388–95, https://link.springer.com/ article/10.1007%2Fs11920-007-0050-6?LI=true.

122   **The Vedic-inspired meditation I teach will deliver much enhanced present-moment awareness – in fact it's been shown to deliver greater present-moment awareness than any other technique:** See C. N. Alexander et al., 'Transcendental Meditation, Self-Actualisation, and Psychological Health: A Conceptual Overview and Statistical Meta-Analysis', *Journal of Social Behaviour and Personality*, 6/5, 1991: 189–97. This comparative analysis of forty-two studies including TM®, Zen, Relaxation Response and other relaxation techniques found that TM® was around four times

as effective at delivering greater present-moment awareness than the other meditation and relaxation techniques.

126   On the physical level, one of the causal factors of substance abuse is a super-agitated nervous system, caused by high levels of anxiety and a hugely overactive mind. Sometimes these stem from trauma; other times, it appears to be the result of an accumulation of factors: See Joseph Troncale, 'Anxiety and Addiction: The Limbic System and the Cycle of Self-Medication', *Psychology Today*, 14 August 2014, https://www.psychologytoday. com/blog/where-addiction-meets-your-brain/201408/anxiety-and-addiction; Rajita Sinha, 'Chronic Stress, Drug Use, and Vulnerability to Addiction', *Ann N Y Acad Sci.*, October 2008, 1141: 105–30, https://www.ncbi.nlm.nih.gov/pmc/articles/ PMC2732004/.

126   I remember reading an interview with the musician Moby, who put it very well: 'One reason I drank was that my brain would get to a level of agitation, and one thing that was incredibly effective at diminishing the agitation was alcohol ... meditation is an effective tool at diminishing agitation and because it was agitation that often led me to drink, its lack – the lack of restlessness – makes me less inclined to do so': See Norman Rosenthal, *Transcendence: Healing and Transformation Through Transcendental Meditation* (London: Tarcher, 2001), 155.

129   Harvard-trained psychologist Charles Alexander reviewed nineteen studies of meditation over a 22-year period. In seventeen of those studies there were significant reductions in the use of cigarettes, alcohol and recreational drugs when people practised meditation: See Charles N. Alexander, PhD, Pat Robinson, PhD, OTR, and Maxwell Rainforth, MS, MA, 'Treating and Preventing Alcohol, Nicotine, and Drug Abuse Through Transcendental Meditation: A Review and Statistical Meta-Analysis', *Alcoholism Treatment Quarterly*, 11/1–2, 1994: 13–87, http://www.tandfonline.com/doi/abs/10.1300/ J020v11n01_02?journalCode=watq20.

129   An eighteen-month study of alcoholics showed that those who meditated had an abstinence rate of 65 per cent, which was far superior to standard counselling (25 per cent): See E. Taub, S. S. Steiner, R. B. Smith, E. Weingarten and K. G. Walton, 'Effectiveness of Broad Spectrum Approaches to Relapse Prevention: A Long-term, Randomised, Controlled Trial Comparing Transcendental Meditation, Muscle Relaxation

and Electronic Neurotherapy in Severe Alcoholism', *Alcoholism Treatment Quarterly*, 11/1–2, 1994: 187–220.

129 **meditation using personalised sounds has been shown to be 250 per cent more effective at reducing anxiety than any other methodology:** See James S. Brooks and Thomas Scarano, 'Transcendental Meditation in the Treatment of Post-Vietnam Adjustment', *Journal of Counselling and Development*, 64, 1985: 212–15.

GETTING YOUR DIGESTION INTO SHAPE

131 **When we're stressed, we don't produce as much saliva:** See Robert Sapolsky, *Why Zebras Don't Get Ulcers* (New York: Henry Holt & Co., 1994), 80.

133 **The largest ever study carried out on meditation measured the medical records of 2,000 people using this technique versus a control group. The meditators demonstrated a 51 per cent reduction in incidence of gastrointestinal disorders:** D. Orme-Johnson, 'Medical care utilization and the Transcendental Meditation program', *Psychosomatic Medicine*, 49/5, Sept–Oct 1987: 493–507.

137 **Let me explain what starting to meditate will have done to Mia's body and mind to restore balance:** See Sue McGreevey, 'Meditation may relieve IBS and IBD', *Harvard Gazette*, 5 May 2015, https://news.harvard.edu/gazette/story/2015/05/meditation-may-relieve-ibs-and-ibd/.

140 **did you know that 90–95 per cent of your happy hormone serotonin is produced in your gut?:** Caltech, 'Microbes Help Produce Serotonin in Gut', 2015.

140 **We now know that because the microbiome has so much DNA within its 100 trillion bacteria, it may well have a significant impact on how you're operating epigenetically (how your inherited genes can express themselves differently). So, all of a sudden, digestion isn't about just extracting kilojoules from carbs – it's the engine of our entire experience!:** On the microbiome having knock-on genetic effects influencing cancer risk, see Meredith A. J. Hullar and Benjamin C. Fu, 'Diet, the Gut Microbiome, and Epigenetics', *Cancer J.*, May–June 2014, 20(3): 170–5, https://www.ncbi.nlm.nih.gov/pmc/articles/PMC4267719/; Bidisha Paul, Stephen Barnes, Wendy Demark-Wahnefried, Casey Morrow, Carolina

Salvador, Christine Skibola and Trygve O. Tollefsbol, 'Influences
of Diet and the Gut Microbiome on Epigenetic Modulation
in Cancer and Other Diseases', *Clin Epigenetics*, 2015, 7: 112,
https://www.ncbi.nlm.nih.gov/pmc/articles/PMC4609101/.
On the relationship between diet, microbiome and genetics,
see Ben Locwin, 'How Epigenetics, Our Gut Microbiome
and the Environment Interact to Change Our Lives', *Genetic
Literacy Project*, 17 October 2016, https://geneticliteracyproject.
org/2016/10/17/how-epigenetics-our-gut-microbiome-and-the-
environment-interact-to-change-our-lives/.

140   As the Vedic civilisation understood thousands of years ago,
we now know that we actually have loads of neurons in the
intestinal tract (400–600 million). That's where having a
'gut feeling' comes from. And it's also one of the reasons
eating a greasy burger makes you feel rubbish – because it's
basically like shovelling rubbish into your (second) brain:
See Adam Hadhazy, 'Think Twice: How the Gut's "Second
Brain" Influences Mood and Well-Being', *Scientific American*, 12
February 2010, https://www.scientificamerican.com/article/gut-
second-brain/; Emma Young, 'Gut Instincts: The Secrets of Your
Second Brain', *New Scientist*, 12 December 2012, https://www.
newscientist.com/article/mg21628951.900-gut-instincts-the-
secrets-of-your-second-brain/.

RELATIONSHIPS

148   EEG scans show that Vedic-inspired meditation increases
the connectivity of your brain, allowing you to be more in
touch with everything you're thinking and feeling: See K.
Badawi, R. K. Wallace, D. Orme-Johnson and A. M. Rouzere,
'Electrophysiologic Characteristics of Respiratory Suspension
Periods Occurring During the Practice of the Transcendental
Meditation Programme', *Psychosomatic Medicine*, 46/3, May–June
1984: 267–76; F. Travis and A. Arenander, 'Cross-Sectional and
Longitudinal Study of Effects of Transcendental Meditation
Practice on Interhemispheric Frontal Asymmetry and Frontal
Coherence', *International Journal of Neuroscience* 116/12,
December 2006: 1519–38, https://www.ncbi.nlm.nih.gov/
pubmed/17145686.

150   recent polling suggests we are sleeping together less now
than we have been in decades: See 2014 *Observer* poll,
https://www.theguardian.com/lifeandstyle/2014/sep/28/
british-sex-survey-2014-nation-lost-sexual-swagger.

150 As we've already seen, stress has an impact at the hormonal
      level, too. When you're in fight or flight mode, your body will
      make stress hormones, not sex hormones. As a consequence,
      we produce less oestrogen, androgens and testosterone and
      so it's no surprise that our sex drive becomes inhibited. To
      highlight how strong this effect can be, it has been found that
      social stress can suppress oestrogen levels in female monkeys
      as effectively as removing her ovaries: For a discussion of the
      effects of stress on female libido, see two chapters by Sue Carter,
      'Neuroendocrinology of Sexual Behavior in the Female' and
      'Hormonal Influences on Human Sexual Behavior', in J. Becker, S.
      Breedlove and D. Crews, eds, *Behavioral Endocrinology* (Cambridge,
      Mass.: MIT Press, 1992); R. Rose, 'Psychoendocrinology', in
      J. Wilson and D. Foster, eds, *Williams Textbook of Endocrinology*,
      7th ed. (Philadelphia: Saunders, 1985); F. Curtin and T. Steimer,
      'Lower Sex Hormones in Men During Anticipatory Stress',
      NeuroReport, 7 (1996): 3, 101. On the suppressive effects of Officer
      Candidate School on testosterone levels, see L. Kreuz, R. Rose
      and J. Jennings, 'Suppression of Plasma Testosterone Levels and
      Psychological Stress', *Archives of General Psychiatry*, 26 (1972): 479.
      For the study on primates and eostrogen levels, see J. Kaplan,
      S. Manuck, M. Anthony and T. Clarkson, 'Premenopausal
      Social Status and Hormone Exposure Predict Postmenopausal
      Atherosclerosis in Female Monkeys', *Obstetrics and Gynecology*, 99
      (2002): 381–8.

151–152 As one of my favourite writers on this topic, Dr House,
          puts it: 'If we want the hormonal orchestra of our bodies
          to not sound like a brigade of six-year-old tuba players
          on LSD, we have to do everything in our power to live
          in a more parasympathetic state': See Dr House, 'Is the
          Pregnenolone Steal a Lie?', *Functional Medicine Costa Rica*, http://
          functionalmedicinecostarica.com/is-the-pregnenolone-steal-a-lie/;
          Andrew Goliszek, PhD, 'The Stress-Sex Connection', *Psychology
          Today*, 22 December 2014, https://www.psychologytoday.com/
          blog/how-the-mind-heals-the-body/201412/
          the-stress-sex-connection.

LETTING GO OF PAST TRAUMA

157 with 31 per cent of young women aged 18–24 reporting
      experiences of sexual abuse during childhood (according to the
      NSPCC in 2011): See https://rapecrisis.org.uk/statistics.php.

167 Despite living in the first half of the twentieth century,

American psychologist Abraham Maslow had a theory that I believe is very relevant to many people's problems today. He identified the importance of whether we have an external or internal locus of control, i.e. whether our sense of self is dictated by what other people think of us, or by what we think of ourselves: See Julian Barling and Frank Fincham, 'Maslow's Need Hierarchy and Dimensions of Perceived Locus of Control', *Journal of Genetic Psychology, Research and Theory on Human Development,* 4 September 2012, Volume 134, Issue 2, 313-14, http://www.tandfonline.com/doi/abs/10.1080/00221325.1979.10534064?journalCode=vgnt20; Saul McLeod, 'Maslow's Hierarchy of Needs', *Simply Psychology*, 2017, https://www.simplypsychology.org/maslow.html.

171 Meditation appears to stimulate the prefrontal cortex, even to the extent that just eight weeks of the practice is associated with increased cortical thickness: See Jeanne Ball, 'Keeping Your Prefrontal Cortex Online: Neuroplasticity, Stress and Meditation', *Huffington Post*, 17 November 2011, https://www.huffingtonpost.com/jeanne-ball/keeping-your-prefrontal-c_b_679290.html.

174 One very sad example of this is in children of pregnant mothers who witnessed 9/11, who have been shown to have a much higher predisposition towards anxiety and depression: See Mo Costandi, 'Pregnant 9/11 Survivors Transmitted Trauma to Their Children', *The Guardian*, 11 September 2011, https://www.theguardian.com/science/neurophilosophy/2011/sep/09/pregnant-911-survivors-transmitted-trauma.

BEING YOUR BEST

199 According to a recent UK government survey, poor mental health costs the economy between £74 and £99 billion a year; in the US it's thought to be $300 billion: See Paul Farmer and Dennis Stevenson, 'Thriving at Work: A Review of Mental Health and Employers', October 2017, 5, https://www.gov.uk/government/uploads/system/uploads/attachment_data/file/658145/thriving-at-work-stevenson-farmer-review.pdf; Paul J. Rosch, ISMA-USA Newsletter, https://workplacepsychology.files.wordpress.com/2016/07/isma-usa_spring2001.pdf.

199 In the UK, mental health issues are the third main cause of UK sick leave (after colds/coughs and musculoskeletal problems): See Phillip Inman, 'UK Workers Record Lowest Rate

of Sick Days Since Records Began', *The Guardian*, 9 March 2017, https://www.theguardian.com/uk/office-for-national-statistics.

203 **As well as a general sense of exhaustion, burnout brings increased risk of heart disease, cognitive impairment, memory problems, elevated levels of stress hormones and depression:** On increased risk of heart disease, see A. Appels and E. Schouten, 'Burnout as a Risk Factor for Coronary Heart Disease', *Behav Med.*, Summer 1991, 17(2): 53–9, https://www.ncbi.nlm.nih.gov/pubmed/1878609. For cognitive impairment, see Agneta Sandström, Rhodin Nyström, Mattias Lundberg and Tommy Olsson, 'Impaired Cognitive Performance in Patients with Chronic Burnout Syndrome', *Biological Psychology*, 2005, 69, 3, 271–9, http://www.diva-portal.org/smash/record.jsf?pid=diva2%3A358761&dswid=mainwindow. For elevated stress levels, see Ursula Ugarten, Arie Shirom, Luna Kahana, Yehuda Lerman and Paul Froom, 'Chronic Burnout, Somatic Arousal and Elevated Salivary Cortisol Levels', *Journal of Psychosomatic Research*, June 1999, Volume 46, Issue 6, 591–8, http://www.sciencedirect.com/science/article/pii/S0022399999000070.

203 **It's no coincidence that by and large it's in the Protestant-influenced cultures of the world that we find the most stressed-out people:** See University of Warwick, 'Research suggests suicide rates higher in Protestant areas than Catholic', https://medicalxpress.com/news/2012-03-suicide-higher-protestant-areas-catholic.html.

206–208 **Peak Performance Brain Function:** See Hans Hagemann and Friederike Fabritius, *The Leading Brain: Powerful Science-Based Strategies for Achieving Peak Performance* (New York: Penguin Random House, 2017).

BEING MORE PRODUCTIVE

213 **research has shown that we create electromagnetic fields around us. The strongest one of these comes from our hearts, which has been shown to beat in a very different way when we're feeling positive emotions:** See Rollin McCraty, Mike Atkinson, Dana Tomasino and William A. Tiller, 'The Electricity of Touch: Detection and Measurement of Cardiac Energy Exchange Between People', in Karl H. Pribram (ed.), *Brain and Values: Is a Biological Science of Values Possible?* (Mahwah, NJ: Lawrence Erlbaum Associates, Publishers, 1998), 359–79; Rollin McCraty and Dana Tomasino, 'Emotional Stress, Positive

Emotions and Psychophysiological Coherence', in B. B. Arnetz and R. Ekman (eds), *Stress in Health and Disease* (Weinheim, Germany: Wiley-VCH, 2006), 342–65.

213   **when levels of the stress hormone cortisol are raised, you start emitting a cloud of 'alarm pheromones' through the pores of your skin. The people around you subconsciously detect this through their sense of smell, which then activates *their* stress response, and generates a further release of alarm pheromones, creating a vicious cycle and resulting in more stressed-out strangers:** James R. Anderson, 'You Really Can Smell Fear, Say Scientists', *The Guardian*, 4 December 2008, https://www.theguardian.com/science/2008/dec/04/smell-fear-research-pheromone.

214   **Meditating for twenty minutes will calm your amygdala so that, by the end of your journey, you feel relaxed and ready for work rather than jumpy and on edge. Your brainwaves will go into a heightened state of synchronised coherence that's mostly immune to the electromagnetic craziness transmitted by your fellow passengers. And by putting you in a hypometabolic state, in which your metabolism is calmed right down, meditation will also mean that you ingest far fewer of those stress pheromones. (Like humans, many organisms trigger a reduced metabolic state to help survive stressful circumstances and process the consequences of high stress levels.):** See Norman Rosenthal, *Transcendence: Healing and Transformation Through Transcendental Meditation* (London: Tarcher, 2001), 151. On brain coherence, see Iain McGilchrist, *The Divided Brain and the Search for Meaning: Why Are We So Unhappy?* (New Haven, CT: Yale University Press, 2012). On calming the amygdala, see Gaëlle Desbordes, Lobsang T. Negi, Thaddeus W. W. Pace, B. Alan Wallace, Charles L. Raison and Eric Schwartz, 'Effects of Mindful-attention and Compassion Meditation Training on Amygdala Response to Emotional Stimuli in an Ordinary, Non-meditative State', *Frontiers in Human Neuroscience*, 1 November 2012, https://www.ncbi.nlm.nih.gov/pmc/articles/PMC3485650/.

ENHANCING YOUR CREATIVITY

230   **Recent research suggests that the average person spends 135 minutes a day on social media:** See Statista, The Statistics Portal, https://www.statista.com/statistics/433871/daily-social-media-usage-worldwide/; http://www.adweek.com/digital/mediakix-time-spent-social-media-infographic/.

235   Noel Gallagher of Oasis explains his writing of 'Don't Look
      Back in Anger' like this: 'I don't ever sit there and think that
      I wrote that, you know. I think it came from somewhere else.
      I think it was a song that was there somewhere, and if I hadn't
      have written it, you know, Bono would have written it. You
      know, it's like those great songs ... you know, they're there.
      If they fall out the sky and land on your lap, then lucky you.'
      See Robin Murray, 'Noel Gallagher Talks "Don't Look Back In
      Anger"', *Clash,* 26 May 2017, http://www.clashmusic.com/news/
      noel-gallagher-talks-dont-look-back-in-anger.

238   Indeed, of all the cognitive functions that become most
      enhanced with this practice, creativity demonstrates the biggest
      improvement of all: See K-T. So and D. Orme-Johnson, 'Three
      Randomized Experiments on the Longitudinal Effects of the
      Transcendental Meditation Technique on Cognition', *Intelligence,*
      29: 419–40, 2001, effect sizes versus controls ranged in magnitude
      from 0.77 to 0.34, with the order of effect size being from highest
      to lowest: creativity (0.77); practical intelligence (0.62); field
      independence (0.58); state anxiety (0.53); trait anxiety (0.52);
      inspection time (0.39); and fluid intelligence (0.34). In behavioural
      sciences, an effect size is considered to be large at 0.8 units or more,
      medium at 0.5 units, and small at 0.2 units.

239   A study by Princeton economist Angus Deaton and eminent
      psychologist Daniel Kahneman (both of them Nobel Prize-
      winners) has shown that, in fact, in the Western world, once a
      certain level of income is reached ($75,000, or £48,000), any
      increase after that does very little, if anything, to our levels of
      everyday contentment or happiness: See Daniel Kahneman and
      Angus Deaton, 'High income improves evaluation of life but not
      emotional well-being', *Proceedings of the National Academy of Sciences
      of the United States of America,* 4 August 2010, http://www.pnas.org/
      content/107/38/16489.full. NB: Kahneman and Deaton did say that
      life assessment, i.e. the way you think about your life, tended to
      improve if you kept on earning past that limit. My comment would
      be that you can either gain increased 'life assessment' fulfilment
      from increasing your income *or* from improving the way you
      engage with life. Meditation, through increasing your performance
      potential, will enhance your earning capability, but will also help
      you engage with life, so it's a double bonus!

FINDING GREATER PURPOSE AND MEANING IN LIFE

246 **The eminent physicist Carlo Rovelli uses Plato's *The Allegory of the Cave* in his book *Reality Is Not What It Seems* as a metaphor to describe science:** Carlo Rovelli, *Reality Is Not What It Seems: The Journey to Quantum Gravity* (London: Penguin, 2016).

256 **Steve Jobs called intuition 'more powerful than intellect':** See Walter Isaacson, 'The Genius of Jobs', *New York Times*, 29 October 2011, http://www.nytimes.com/2011/10/30/opinion/sunday/steve-jobss-genius.html: 'Mr Jobs came to value experiential wisdom over empirical analysis. He didn't study data or crunch numbers but, like a pathfinder, he could sniff the winds and sense what lay ahead. He told me he began to appreciate the power of intuition, in contrast to what he called "Western rational thought", when he wandered around India after dropping out of college. "The people in the Indian countryside don't use their intellect like we do," he said. "They use their intuition instead ... Intuition is a very powerful thing, more powerful than intellect, in my opinion. That's had a big impact on my work."' Mr Jobs' intuition was based not on conventional learning but on experiential wisdom. He also had a lot of imagination and knew how to apply it.

256 **Albert Einstein called it the sacred gift:** There are many quotes attributed to Einstein on the value of intuition and imagination, the most famous one being: 'The intuitive mind is a sacred gift and the rational mind is a faithful servant. We have created a society that honours the servant and has forgotten the gift.'

However, this appears to be a paraphrasing of his various comments over time. The specific word 'gift' can be found in a comment remembered by Einstein's friend and doctor, János Plesch, who invented the first device for measuring blood pressure. He reports Einstein as saying: 'When I examine myself and my methods of thought I come to the conclusion that the gift of fantasy has meant more to me than my talent for absorbing positive knowledge.'

Likewise, Einstein had a number of quotes about the intellect being secondary to intuition, and the language of the intellect 'serving' can be found in a quote from his book *Out of My Later Years*: 'And certainly we should take care not to make the intellect our god; it has, of course, powerful muscles, but no personality. It cannot lead, it can only serve; and it is not fastidious in its choice of a leader.'

256 **However, in randomised controlled experiments, the predictive power of intuition has been shown to be greater than that**

of intellect. **This strongly suggests that intuition is a far more powerful force than many of us may realise:** As for experimental evidence, British biologist Rupert Sheldrake has conducted numerous studies suggesting intuition is a bona fide capability and skill, and in another study, subjects were monitored for stress responses while being shown random images, some of which were quite horrific, such as car accidents and bloody incidents of war. What the results showed was that people's stress responses started switching on even before the stressful image was shown to them, but they never switched on before being shown a benign image. This study is referenced in Rudolph Tanzi and Deepak Chopra's book *Super Brain*, which also states that there are 'hundreds of studies in cognitive psychology to prove that intuition is real, while our social attitude towards intuition is largely doubtful and even negative.' See also, Travis Bradberry, 'Your Intuition is More Powerful than Your Intellect, and Just as Easily Expanded,' *Quartz*, 10 January 2017, https://qz.com/880678/intuition-is-more-powerful-than-intellect/.

RECONNECTING TO YOURSELF

268   **if we fear the perceived lack of strength that comes from vulnerability, then the stress of it causes an inhibition of oxytocin, that lovely molecule that helps us trust:** See Paul J. Zak, *The Moral Molecule: The Source of Love and Prosperity* (New York: Penguin, 2016), 188.

271   **A quarter of children in the US have clinically defined anxiety, and the number of anti-depressants prescribed to children there has increased by 400 per cent in the past ten years:** See Laura A. Pratt, PhD, Debra J. Brody, MPH, and Qiuping Gu, MD, PhD, 'Antidepressant Use in Persons Aged 12 and Over: United States, 2005–2008', NCHS Data Brief, 76, October 2011, https://www.cdc.gov/nchs/data/databriefs/db76.htm.

271–272   **Between 2008 and 2010, a school in San Francisco introduced a meditation programme. In that period, staff turnover went from being extremely high to zero. Children demonstrated a 40 per cent decrease in stress, anxiety and depression. Meditating students improved their exam scores by 10 per cent more than the others and demonstrated a 30 per cent increase in brain coherence and functioning. There was also a very significant closing of the achievement gap. Alongside this, they received 82 per cent fewer detentions over two years, a 65 per cent decrease in bullying and conflict and** increased levels of resilience and self-confidence and sleep quality, along with reduced incidence of ADHD, and a 30 per cent decrease in sick days: See TM® Foundation Blog, http://www.tm.org/blog/video/tm-in-san-francisco-schools/.

REACHING YOUR SPIRITUAL POTENTIAL

278 There's a saying, 'wherever you go, there you are': This comes from Jon Kabat-Zinn, who wrote a book with this title: *Wherever You Go, There You Are: Mindfulness Meditation for Everyday Life* (New York: Hyperion, 1994).

CONNECTING WITH YOUR INNER TRUTH

287 Although much of Western psychology refers to the unconscious as something that is purely individual, in 1916 the Swiss psychiatrist and psychoanalyst Carl Jung introduced the notion of a *collective* unconscious, which he saw as a series of unconscious memories, symbols and impulses that are common to all humanity and which arise from a shared history: See Carl Jung, 'The Structure of the Unconscious', in *Collected Works*, vol 7. (1953 [1916]), 263–92.

288 (who knew a programme about baking would be one of the most popular things on British TV for the past five years?!): This is a reference to 'The Great British Bake Off'. See Georg Szalai, 'Great British Bake Off Ends BBC Run With Its Highest Ratings Ever', *Hollywood Reporter,* 27 October 2016; Aimée Grant Cumberbatch, 'The Great British Bake Off breaks records for Channel 4 after 1 Million Viewers Watch the Show on Catch-Up', *Evening Standard*, 6 September 2017.

291–292 As Martin Luther King once said: 'If you can't fly then run, if you can't run then walk, if you can't walk then crawl, but whatever you do you have to keep moving forward.' The exact origin of this phrase is the Bible, specifically the book of Isaiah. Later, however, Dr Martin Luther King, Jr, used this phrase in his speech at a college rally.